THE "NEW CHUM"
IN
AUSTRALIA
OR
THE SCENERY, LIFE, AND MANNERS OF AUSTRALIANS IN TOWN AND COUNTRY

BY

PERCY CLARKE, LL.B., F.R.C.I.

ILLUSTRATED BY
An Etching and over 40 original Sketches by the Author

An Up-Country Coach

SECOND EDITION

LONDON
J. S. VIRTUE & CO., LIMITED, 26, IVY LANE
PATERNOSTER ROW
1886

LONDON:
PRINTED BY J. S. VIRTUE AND CO., LIMITED,
CITY ROAD.

PREFACE.

IT appears to be the proper thing to write something by way of preface, whether one has anything to write about or no—at least, so my friends tell me. Friends of the present day, as those of the Patriarch Job in olden time, have an uncomfortable way of banding themselves together, and, by sheer force of superior numbers, if nothing else, of making their points good, thereby suggesting the words of the entertaining author of the "Ingoldsby Legends,"—

"Needs must where the Elderly Gentleman drives."

As one cannot afford in these hard times the luxury of having enemies, much less that of *making* them, these few introductory words are written.

What is a "new chum"? The question naturally suggests itself to any one as yet unaware if the article may be animal, vegetable, or mineral, and, if animal, bird, beast, or fish. I cannot conceive that this book will have altogether failed in its purpose if it shall have thrown some light on an expression significant, though somewhat colloquial, and fraught with so much serio-comic interest in the Australasian colonies. A new chum, then, is——what the reader may easily find out by perusal of this volume, and can no more expect me to divulge at this early point than a novelist can be expected to anticipate the doings and sayings of his hero and heroine.

Having disposed of the title, I come next to the contents, and with regard to them can only say that I have endeavoured, without garnishing, to relate such experiences and describe such scenes as any one may come across while travelling in " the land of the golden fleece " with his eyes open.

I must, however, at this stage warn those uncomfortable people who like to take their medicine without disguise, that this volume is not written for them, but for those more practical and comfortable human beings who prefer to lose the flavour of the powder in a spoonful of syrup, thus at one and the same time deriving benefit and pleasure—or, in other words, prefer to receive information and recreation together.

The illustrations I may dismiss in a few words. They are reproductions from my original sketches, and serve a manifold purpose, as I can promise the reader a unique effect, should he not be able to discover their " right way up ", for viewed either from the top, bottom, or sides, they *may* appear equally varied and puzzling.

Finally, I would say that it is not without some paternal anxiety that I commit my literary infant to the cares of its numerous nurses—my readers; but I shall deem my labours of pen and pencil well rewarded if I may have thrown any light upon Australian life and manners of the present day.

P. C.

CANNON HALL, HAMPSTEAD,
   June, 1886.

CONTENTS.

CHAPTER I.

Self-Introduction.—Leave-taking.—The Bay of Biscay.—The Fatal 29th.—Tea and Coffee.—Gibraltar.—Artists' Colours at a discount.— Char-à-bancs.— The Galleries.—Voyage to Malta.—Fortifications at Valetta.—St. John's Church.—Milk.—Interior of the Island.—A Big Draftboard.—Ride to the Catacombs.—The Traffic Returns.—The Catacombs.—A Maltese Cabman.—Voyage to Port Said 1

CHAPTER II.

Nearing Egypt.—No local Colour.—Port Said *versus* the Pyramids.—Local Companions.—Olive Wood from Jerusalem.—Through the Canal.—A Mirage.—French Gardens.—Suez Hills.—An Adventure with Boatmen.—The Red Sea.—Hot Weather.—Aden.—The Tanks. — Hotel Eggs.— Flying Fish.— Ceylon's Spicy Breezes.—Colombo.—The "Columbines."—Washing and Tailoring.—A Blind Guide.—Cinnamon Gardens.—Public Char-à-bancs.—Catamarans.—Singhalese have been libelled.—Voyage to Australia.—Our Passengers.—Quarantine Regulations.—Humour and Pathos.—At the Quarantine Station.—Trip to Melbourne.—Landing at the Quay.—Melbourne Shipping . . 12

CHAPTER III.

English Language at the Antipodes.—" New Chums" and Colonials. —" It's a 'New Chum's' Trick."—Taking the Train to the City.—Hangers-on.—"The City" and the Suburbs.—Mixed Nomenclature.— Broad Streets. — Sanitary Arrangements. — Cologne rivalled.—Novelties in Odours required.—Climate of Melbourne.—The North Wind.—Melbourne's End.—Architecture.—Hotels and Living.—The Blocks and the Blockheads.—Eight Hours Labour System.—Fashions in Melbourne.—Protection and Free Trade.—Books.—Newspapers.—Colonial Literature and Art.—National Gallery.—Museum and Library.—Buying Pictures by the Square Yard and Books by the Cartload.—Burke and Wills' Monument and History 24

CHAPTER IV.

Churches.—Bells *versus* Bed.—The Pro-Cathedral.—Not a Thing of Beauty nor a Joy for any Time.—" Why do you go to the Cathedral ?"—St. Patrick's Cathedral.—Ambition of the Children of the Emerald Isle.—Music.—The Hurdy-gurdy.—Salvation Salvoes.—The Drama.—Passes.—The Houses of Legislature.—The

Edifice.—A Debate.—The Upper Form set a Good Example.—
Is it Marble or Paint?—Lint at a Premium.—The Medical Fraternity.—"You've forgotten to call for your Brains!"—Fearful
Feud on the Franchise Question.—"Who shall say between the
Two?" 39

CHAPTER V.

Public Gardens.—The Era of Beauty.—Botanic Gardens.—The Mosquito and his Remarks.—Government House or Barracks.
Which?—Reserves.—Cricket and Football.—Bicycling *sans peur*
but not *sans reproche*.—Country round about Melbourne.—A
Snake in the Grass.—Fern-tree Gully.—Boating.—Driving.—
Racing.—Two Men and a half left in Town.—Recreation generally.—Suburban Villas.—Dingo and Dinginess exchanged for
Beauty and Buildings.—The Shark Story.—Trip to Geelong.—
How the Geelongites drew away Melbourne commerce . . 49

CHAPTER VI.

Ballarat.—Tom Tiddler's Ground without the Silver.—The Central
Avenue—Taken in and done for.—The "Lake."—Bulls and
Bears.—The Chinese Quarter. "Johnny Chinaman welly much
Seas Over."—The Pleasures of Opium.—Gambling more suited
to Johnny than Gambolling.—Shark Soup and Puppy Dogs at a
Discount.—The Chinaman's Character.—Europeans, Australians,
Natives, and Blacks.—Corn-stalk and Gum-sucker.—The Band
of Hope Mine.—Treading the Air.—Charging the Rock and
Charging away.—The Process of the Gold-mine.—Economy
versus waste.—A Touch of the Acid and a Thirst for Knowledge.
—Suiting the Action to the Word.—The Out-put and the Put-out of the Mine.—A Journey around Ballarat.—The Early Days
revived.—Tipperary Boys.—Where was the Law when the Light
went out?—The Welcome Nugget.—The Eureka Stockade—
Sunday "at Home."—The Champagne Magnum.—Extremes
meet.—Prospecting as it really is.—The Technological College
abused 59

CHAPTER VII.

From Ballarat to Melbourne.—Scenery at a Premium.—Rabbits and
their Doings.—The Caudal Tax.—Dinner for One.—Marvellous
Melbourne again.—Finance.—The Law and the Bar.—Melbourne University.—A Peep into Pentridge Gaol.—Solitary
Confinement.—Harmless-looking Convicts.—Escape to Sydney
from Temptation.—Up the Coast to the Harbour.—"Look at
our *chef-d'œuvre*."—The Capacity of the Harbour.—What you
may expect to see, and a great deal more to the same effect.—
Sydney in the Distance.—Smoke *versus* Landscape.—Sydney
Docks.—Middle Harbour.—Why is not Everything provided?—
Solitude in the midst of Bustle.—The Inner and Outer Domain.
—The Arum.—The Aloe. 76

CONTENTS. vii

CHAPTER VIII.

A Bird's-eye View of Sydney.—The Paramatta River.—The Hawkesbury must be taken on Faith.—George Street.—High Houses and Narrow Streets.—Hansom *versus* Waggonette.—Tramways *versus* the Train.—The Sea Coast from the Town Hall.—Rosa Gully.—Botanising in Botany Bay.—The University.—Parks.—Church Spires in the Minority.—The Roman Catholic Cathedral.—The Houses of Legislature like the Lily of the Valley.—The Lower Form gets Unruly.—The Mint.—The Library.—The National Gallery.—Australian Artists at a Discount.—Government Offices.—Sandstone *versus* Bluestone.—Hotels and Clubs.—Sixpenny Dinners.—Poverty unnecessary.—Employment for all.—Domestic Servitude of the Mistress to her Servant.—Scarcity of the gentler sex.—St. Andrew's Cathedral.—Mayoral Sanctum.—" Walk across the Crossings."—Adventures in Cabs.—The Governor and Loyalty.—Beverages 90

CHAPTER IX.

The Weather Topic.—Keep clear of the Outside in a Shower.—Thick Blood *versus* thin.—Up the Paramatta River to the Town.—Bush still around Sydney.—Advertising extraordinary.—Benevolent Asyla.—National Park.—Shanks's Mare must be used to get there.—Taken in and done for.—It was a Maiden without her h's.—Port Hackin River up from the Lodge.—Down to the Sea.—A Feast of Bivalves.—We pass on to Bulli.—Wayside enterprise.—Surveying extraordinary.—Accommodation Houses.—Coalfields.—Bulli Pass.—A Leap in the wrong Direction.—" Show us your patterns, mister."—Wollongong Butter.—Quicksands and the Insurance Company compete. 111

CHAPTER X.

Boot-cleaning extraordinary.—Off to the Blue Mountains.—New South Welsh Civility.—" Everyone goes First Class."—Aboriginal Nomenclature.—Rolling Stock.—Penrith.—Scaling the Little Zigzag.—A Feast of Nature.—In the Ranges.—Wentworth Falls.—Katoomba.—Mount Victoria.—Mount Piddington.—Sunset from the Summit.—" Creep in after Dark."—Govett's Leap.—Mermaid's Glen without the Mermaids.—Mount York and Hartley Valley.—Nothing about the Fish River Caves.—No Inquest or Waste of Ink.—The " other side."—Paint-boxes at a Premium.—Similarity of the Scenery.—Bathurst passed through.—The Line to Dubbo.—Bribery and Corruption.—The Bitter Cry of the Overladen Coach 129

CHAPTER XI.

From Dubbo to Coonamble.—The way we pull up.—The Imbibing Capacity of a Driver.—The Driver's Creeds.—Pure Liquor wanted.—Bush Scenery.—A Heaven-forgotten Spot.—" Hold hard inside."—Bad Roads and Worse Roads.—Matters of Passing

Interest.—The Strong-flavoured Scents of Nature.—Australian River-bed.—Topsyturvydom.—Coaching at Night.—A Sight for an Old-Country Coachman.—'Possums.—Dawn and Differences.—Accidents by Flood and Field.—Drivers' Mistakes.—Passengers' Foolhardiness.—Our Destination.—Coonamble.—Hats of a Pattern.—The Ubiquitous Chinaman.—Stores, Banks, Hotels, and Barbers.—A Good Clip.—The Silent Meals.—No Beauty in the Township.—Life in the Verandah of an Inn.—A would-be Purchaser.—"This old hors'll drink and think on it."—Epithets more Gay than Grave.—The Black fights his White "Brother."—The Blacks. 142

CHAPTER XII.

Station Life.—Making a Plunge.—Salt Bush in the Bush.—From Bare Earth to Gay Verdure.—Perfumes not of Barbary.—Timber.—Twenty Mile Paddocks.—Slabs *versus* Sawn Timber.—The Homestead or Station.—Its Kitchen and Cookery.—"A fast feeder works fast."—Mutton *et id genus omne*.—A Week's Work and Play.—Look to your "Leathers."—"That's not the way to mount a Bush Horse."—An Equestrian Pupil.—Out on the Plains.—Murder of the Innocents.—Five Hundred dead Bullocks.—A Kangaroo Hunt.—The Finish.—The Prosaic Overseer.—Capitation Fees.—Why the Kangaroos are so thin.—Paddocks baptised.—Clearing the Paddock.—The First Essay.—Breaking Back.—"There he goes prop."—A Hasty Dismount.—The Rendezvous.—Kangaroos and Emus in sight.—The Emu's Extermination drawing near.—The Stockwhip acts unfeelingly.—The Mob in motion.—The Wethers weathered.—Bush Riding.—Drafting the Sheep.—Counting them out.—The End of Day One 157

CHAPTER XIII.

Another Day's Work and Play.—Out after Scrubbers.—Blue Sky *versus* Clouds and Fogs.—Praying and Whistling.—Jim's Yarn of the "Parsons."—The Visitation of the Clergy.—The Scrubbers smelt and sighted.—"Well done, Jim!"—The Squatter Ejaculates.—The Bull-fight barring the Saxpences.—The Execution.—Don't dress Tripe.—An Old Scotchman and the Drink Question. A Squatter's Farewell.—A Cure for Snoring.—The Third Day. The Scrub-cutter and the Rams.—The Ants' Lesson to the Sluggard.—Ants of all Colours and Sizes.—The Danger of Attitudinising.—Another Kangaroo-hunt.—The "Old Man" shows Fight.—Pathos and Sentiment cut short.—The Tank-sinkers' Camp.—Their Board and Lodging.—The work of sinking a Tank.—The Pleasures of getting Bushed.—A True Story.—A Bushman's Memory.—Sundowners.—"Old hands" and "Roustabouts."—Rain at Last.—Spirits Within and Water Without . 177

CHAPTER XIV.

Fourth Day.—The Tanks and the Rain.—A Buck-jumper.—The Reality precedes the Romance.—Mustering, Drafting, and Examining.—"Culls."—Hair *versus* Wool.—Supper and Nightmare to follow.—Honesty a poor Bedfellow.—The Fifth Day in and out.—The Sleepers rudely awakened.—Rain and Work.—Swimming a Creek.—Retransformation from Dry to Wet.—Science fails at the Gateway.—Words heavy and Language of the Ornate Character.—Womenkind in the Bush.—Sport.—Ducks, Swans, and Teal.—Pelicans.—Native Companions lead off the Ball.—A long Shot at a Kangaroo.—The Pigeon brings its Fate on its own Head.—"Scalps."—The Dingo, his Tail and his Tale.—Wild Pigs.—Travelling Sheep.—The Drover's Camp.—The Drover's Artifice.—The Kangaroo drive.—Emus.—Natural History at a Discount.—Kangaroo Shooters.—Bushmen's Hospitality.—Their Occupations.—"Hatters."—A Bower-bird.—Wild Horse riding.—Horsebreakers.—Hydrophobia and Hydatids 200

CHAPTER XV.

Sunday.—How to Dress.—Various occupations.—The Mail-man and his news.—Soldier-birds and their fate.—Botany by a non-botanist.—Gums, Pines, Wattle, and Scrub.—Mallee.—Foliage and how it grows.—Galars.—Native Companions and how to shoot them.—Emus, how not to catch them.—The Sun's power.—Sheep-shearing.—Horseracing.—"Inglis bail good."—Treating a Pocketful of Apples.—Back to Sydney 228

CHAPTER XVI.

Colonial Steamboats.—"Heave to, and he hev."—Meal-time.—Coasting to Brisbane.—Fishing Question.—Brisbane River.—A Running Commentary.—Government House.—Law Courts.—Flowers and Trees.—Botanical Gardens.—Suburbs.—One-tree Hill.—The View of the Notice Board.—The Principles of Scenery.—A Sanguinary Conflict.—The Mosquito and the Sandfly.—Cockroaches and their uses.—Complexions.—Boots!—British-India Steamships a Stroke of Policy.—Wanted, a Free Library.—The Theatre and its Uses.—The Missionary Question and some of its Results.—King Billy.—Ventilation!—Drafting Cattle under Difficulties.—The Cattle have burst the Rails.—An Aboriginal's Civilisation.—Is that a Black or a Kangaroo? . 241

CHAPTER XVII.

The Railway Policy.—Election Cries.—German Colonists.—Queenslanders: their Children and Education.—Up and away to the North.—The A.S.N.Co.'s boats.—Maryborough and Gympie *en passant*.—Bundaberg Streets, Hotels, and Chemists.—Plantations.—Cleared Ground.—Roads and their effects on the Buggy.—The Plantation—The Homestead.—Cooking.—Hot Work.—The lesser lights of a Plantation.—Tarantulas, Ants, and Fleas.—The Fourth Plague out of Egypt.—Plum-duff for Dinner.—Locusts.—Lady-birds.—Iguanas.—Centipedes and Scorpions.—

Snakes.—Carpet-snake-catching Extraordinary.—Sugar-planting a Sticky Story.— Sugar-growing Lands.— Jungle-clearing.— Plantation Fireworks.—Yarns about Cross-cut Sawing.—Crops. —Planting.—Rain and Sun.—Extremes of Heat.—Thrashing.— Cutting.—Chinese Contracts 260

CHAPTER XVIII.

Mill Work.—Feeding the Rollers.—Small Talk and Big Talk.— Crushing.—Clarifying.—Evaporating.—Vacuum and Open Pans. Drawing the Charge.—Coolers.—Drying.—Different Qualities.— Waste of Molasses.—Burning Trash.—The Kanaka discussed.— The Two Chief Objections.—Slavery?—State Supervision.— Before and after Service.—His Life in the Plantation.—Bright Colours.—Childlike Tastes.—The Second Objection discussed.— Revenge is sweet only when carried out.—Domestic Relations.— Washing.—Civilising the Kanaka.—Nomenclature.—Flirting.— Dusting the New Chum.—What he does with his Wages.—"This Fellow's sick."—The Reaper's Share.—A Corroborree.—Profits of Planters.—West Indian Negroes.—Singhalese.—Social Life on a Plantation.—Educating the Kanakas.—Missionary Work.— The Kanaka and the Copper.—Health on the Plantations.— Fever and Ague.—The Barcoo Rot.—Port Wine and Brandy a Specific.—Summary of Plantation Prospects 284

CHAPTER XIX.

Alligators.—A taste for Eggs and its consequences.—The Cassowary. —Paradise-birds.—Leave-taking.—Trip southwards.—The free and easy Squatter.—Sydney Harbour by Moonlight.—Railway to Melbourne.—The Murray.—A few inches of gauge-difference. —Inter-colonial rivalry.—Federation.—Albury Wines.—Doctors advocate their use.—Glenrowan.— Bushrangers.— Melbourne and Civilisation with a vengeance.—Queer Hotel Customs prevalent in the World.—Diet.—Leaving Melbourne for Tasmania . 305

CHAPTER XX.

Bass's Straits.—A Double Signification.—The Tamar.—The Boat walks ashore.—The Cabman and his Wiles.—The Sweetbriar, its Poetry and Prose.—Launceston.— Its Appearance.— The Devil's Punch Bowl.—The Falls of the Esk.—The Band.—The Wild Beasts of the Bush.—The Convict Curse.—The Railway. —Jericho and Jerusalem.—Consequences of Joking.—Nomenclature again.—New Norfolk.—Hell Gates.—Salmon.—Ladies to the fore.—Hobart Lasses.—Hobart Town.—The great Gums on the Huon Road.—Mount Wellington.—Jam-making.—Fruit-growing.—The Cow in the Streets.—Government House.—Houses of Legislature a Barrack.—Tasmanian Progress: does it exist?— Immigration.—Mining Industries.—Wheat.—Agriculture.—The Prisoner at the Australian Bar pleads Not Guilty.—The Australian "Case."—Climate.—Great Expectations 317

LIST OF ILLUSTRATIONS.

	PAGE
HOME OF THE LYRE-BIRD	*Frontispiece*
PORT SAID	9
A STREET CORNER, VALETTA	10
SEA BEACH, POINT NEPEAN, VICTORIA	21
FLYING-FISH	23
VIEW ON THE YARRA-YARRA	35
PORT PHILIP, FROM THE HEADS	38
FITZROY GARDENS, MELBOURNE	50
GOVERNMENT HOUSE, MELBOURNE	51
SNAKES	58
LAKE WENGAREI, BALLARAT	61
EFFETE CIVILIZATION	75
BATTERY POINT, SYDNEY HARBOUR	85
GOVERNMENT HOUSE, SYDNEY	88
GARDEN ISLAND	89
BOTANY BAY	95
SYDNEY UNIVERSITY	96
SYDNEY CATHEDRAL	110
ON THE PARAMATTA RIVER	113
WARRATAH AND ROCK LILY	119
PORT HACKIN RIVER	121
GOVETT'S LEAP, BLUE MOUNTAINS	136
OVERWEIGHT	141
SCENE ON A BUSH ROAD	145
COACHING BY NIGHT	147
AN UP-COUNTRY COACH	156

LIST OF ILLUSTRATIONS.

	PAGE
A Squatter's Home	160
Stockwhip	176
Pines and Wattle	182
Pething a Bullock	199
At the Dam	209
Laughing-Jackass and Snake	227
Wool-shed and Wool-room	236
A Bushman's Hut	240
Scene on Brisbane River	248
View of Brisbane	259
A Queensland Sugar Plantation	269
A Kanaka's Hut	283
Screw Pine	304
A Fallen Giant	316
Mount Wellington	326
Gums on the Huon Road	327
Government House, Hobart	332
Absit Omen	339

THE "NEW CHUM" IN AUSTRALIA.

CHAPTER I.

Self-Introduction.—Leave-taking.—The Bay of Biscay.—The Fatal 29th.—Tea and Coffee.—Gibraltar.—Artists' Colours at a discount.—Char-à-bancs.—The Galleries.—Voyage to Malta.—Fortifications at Valetta.—St. John's Church.—Milk.—Interior of the Island.—A Big Draft-board.—Ride to the Catacombs.—The Traffic Returns.—The Catacombs.—A Maltese Cabman.—Voyage to Port Said.

AN egotist is the world's abhorrence, but a man who can write of personal travels without occasionally using the first person singular, is too good for this life, and should hastily convert his securities and make his will. Therefore, readers, whoe'er you be—and I trust, for your own sakes, you are numerous, gentle, and patient—do not blame *me*, so much as Dame Nature, who has not conferred plurality upon me as upon the Siamese twins, if " I " occasionally appears in the following pages.

For those who wish to find themselves in Australia without the preliminary voyage this book begins at the third chapter, while to those who are contented to take the more regular course, and do not wish to dismiss six or seven weeks with their varied scenes and experiences in a line, these first two chapters are dedicated.

On a certain Wednesday in February, 1884, the good ship

Kaisar-i-Hind swung off from Tilbury, gradually broadening the distance between the misty shores enveloped in an incipient winter fog, and our misty eyes enveloped in what, to a close observer, might have appeared like the pearly drops that Niobe shed. However, as this piping of the eyes does not occur every day, the captain makes certain allowances for us all, and, cautioning us not to do it again, bids his "bosun swab up the decks," and tells us to leave the main deck to dry while we ourselves take care of the main chance in the saloon where our first P. and O. meal is to be served in smooth water.

Down we glided, and for the next few days the cold weather, the strange motion of our floating hotel, and various other causes not herein specified but well known to tempters of the Channel and the dreaded Bay in winter, caused our tables to be somewhat more roomy and less lively than was that first and well-remembered meal.

Certain lady friends on board had received strict injunctions from my well-meaning relatives to guard me safely from the dangers of Leap Year, but fortunately there wâs no need to tax their quickly made but speedily broken promises, for they, in common with all the other ladies, fascinating and quiet, grave and gay, kept mysteriously within their cabins, and only struggled up in small quantity and very poor quality as we were nearing the shores of Portugal.

Meal-time, on which so much interest centres on board ship, has its special features. Not alone that every one seems to find it such an engrossing occupation on a long voyage, but that it continually suggests reminiscences of the vagaries of the galley.

I do not set up for an epicure or a gourmet, but I cannot let the opportunity slip of venting my wrath against the more innocent liquors that "do not inebriate" that one finds on board ship. It would be a heresy very often to say that they "cheer," for their state is aptly represented in the old, old story of the man who, travelling once on an Atlantic liner, called back his retreating steward with the following remark:

"Steward, I asked for coffee; if this is so, bring me tea; but if tea, bring me coffee : the other liquid, whatever it may be, can only be as bad, and may by chance be more appetising."

The fact is, that tea and coffee on board ship generally remind one, by some undefined channel of association, of the beverages they bear the names of, but no farther does the overwhelmingly greasy, sugary, kettle-flavoured liquor resemble those godlike drinks which to have lacked must have been one drawback to the jovial life of a god of Olympus. Let Mr. Plimsoll see to this.

Six days after leaving London we were anchored off Gibraltar in that very bay beneath whose waters so many of our own and foreign seamen have found a grave; and though many of my fellow-countrymen have attacked the Rock with more success, I have sufficient presumption to say a few words of what we saw there that bright morning in March. In Gibraltar, as one lands from the small row-boats that ply between the big ship and the shore, one immediately notices the great variety of coloured skins clad in garments which in turn combine all the prismatic colours, and if possible something more. From the swarthy Moor, through successive grades of mulattoes, Turks, Spaniards, to the pallid-looking English soldiers—new-comers—the chromatic scale is carried on. The colours of the garments are so vivid as are only permissible under Southern and Andalusian skies, and serve as many a picturesque "arrangement" against the delicate-toned lime-wash and paint on the houses which, with their cool verandahs and emerald-green jalousies, line the streets.

Our artist went with us, but at the first attempt at depicting the scene before him, he was peremptorily challenged by an English redcoat, who demanded to see his permit allowing him to sketch before proceeding any farther. Not having one, he was forced *nolens volens* to put up his plant, though, had there been time, he would have found no difficulty, as he was assured, in getting the necessary permit franked by the proper authority

—the military secretary—allowing such apparently innocent amusement.

So the artist had to comfort himself with observation, for which there was plenty of scope in this model, clean-kept, neat garrison town.

Besides the more respectable-looking houses of the wealthier residents there are many little picturesque cottages and cabins, which are gradually stretching up the western slope of the rock; and even at this time of the year the gay flowers that here and there decked little gardens, or reached over from garden walls, tended to make the recent arrivals from the bleak, flowerless February of England realise the decided change for the better that had already taken place in their condition.

Of vehicles in these streets there are various forms, from the garrison officer's smart equipage to the humble "growler" or to the *asinus solus*, the patient, hardworking mule, who, carrying burdens double his own size, plods along, unheedingly endangering the safety of "other" passengers in some of the narrower streets. The "growler" is called so more from association of its use than its resemblance to our London jarvey's instrument of torture, for it much resembles a pony-chaise, with an inverted child's cot on the top, and a driver's seat just fixed on by some extraordinary means in front. The whole affair looks as though it would come to pieces with a gentle wrench, but appearances here, as elsewhere, are deceptive, and from the many wrenches that some of these vehicles received without apparent hurt, I came to the conclusion that even here "new chums" were doomed to be deceived in more ways than one.

As some of us wanted to see the far-famed Galleries, we had first to get a permission from the military secretary's assistant's deputy's clerk, an official who, though occupying such a lofty position, yet was most condescendingly civil and obliging. Such are the ways of the truly great!

Armed with our permit, we were taken all over the galleries

—great passages and ante-chambers hewn out of the solid rock, bristling with guns, which run round from the western to the eastern side of the rock. The climb—for such it was—was well worth the trouble, for of wild flowers there were many here and there where we emerged on to a platform from one gallery before entering another; and on such a fine day as we had the views over the sea, the bay, and the Spanish territory, with the doll's house-like town at our feet, were most beautiful. Our guide, companion, and friend, a non-commissioned officer, gave us a running sketch of the history of the place and its contents, and I can only hope that future visitors may have the good fortune to enjoy the guidance of our intelligent and courteous chaperon.

Across the neutral ground one can see from the north end of the rock a constant stream of men, women, and children going and coming, most of whom, we were told, would deem the journey across of but little service if they could not at the same time manage to smuggle some contraband through the lines. The neutral territory is given over to a cemetery and a race-course, and withal is such an arid-looking plain, even in this the spring-time of the year, that one cannot help admiring the sense of either nation that would "have none of it."

The far-famed monkeys of Gibraltar had, for reasons best known to themselves, retreated before the approach of their human brethren, and now were reduced in number to three or four, who were occasionally to be seen by a climb to the summit of the rock near the signalling station, perhaps showing, by assuming such an elevated position, their contempt for their so-called superiors.

The Indian boats anchor but for a short time at Gibraltar, so after about six hours of open-mouthed admiration of our Spanish rock we were off again, bound for Malta, which we reached, after alternate fine and stormy weather, four days after leaving the Rock.

Here the P. and O. boats go into the quarantine harbour of

Valetta, this being their convenient station for coaling, loading, &c., and as we stopped there for some twelve hours, and the weather was fine, those of us so minded spent the day in looking over this sunny possession of ours. Here, as elsewhere, the boatmen who ply between the ship and the shore made harvest out of the too indulgent passengers; but for those who want to verify their fares police officials are ready at hand to assure them that they are paying a hundred per cent. too much, which is, according to my experience of the Maltese, a preposterously low demand above the right and proper sum that they will eventually take. Tradition says that a Maltese shopman looks down on a customer who pays him what he asks without any bargaining as a poor creature hardly worth dealing with.

At Malta the show places are the harbour of Valetta, with its fortifications, the church of St. John, and, as I am informed, the catacombs. I have seen all three, but cannot conscientiously endorse the assertion so far as the catacombs are concerned.

The fortifications of the harbour require to be seen both from above and below. Some of the forts enclose gaily-kept gardens, full of the most blazing colours of the peony, rose, poppy, and other gaily-blooming flowers—indications of peace, which agree but strangely with the panoply of war, in the form of guns, breastworks, and turrets, which bristle all around the harbour. From below, floating on the harbour itself, one gains some idea of their height, impregnability, and their commanding positions.

In the harbour itself there is a lively scene of bumboats of varied hue, laden with fruit, fish, and other products of this sunny spot, and navigated by handsome, gaily-clad Maltese. On the quays are men and women chattering and posing incessantly in picturesque groups, with their wares and merchandise to hand, and lighting up with blazes of colour the clean, well-kept streets, which are lined with their inevitable pale-painted and washed houses and green jalousies.

At the street corners one sees wooden and stone statues of Our Lady of Valetta, St. John the Baptist, and other saints, many of them merely studies in black and white, others brightly —nay, gaudily—daubed in crude reds, blues, greens, and yellows. Vehicles cannot climb up and down the steep streets of many parts of the town, but one sees instead a few mules, and the milk-seller gets over the difficulty of transport by driving his flock of goats up to the customer's door, and milking them into the customer's own milk-jug. The only means available for the Maltese milkman to dilute his milk is to induce his goats to drink an abnormal quantity of water just before the delivery of his living and lively milk-cans.

Everybody knows of the church of St. John, its pavement of tombs of the knights of that order, and its silver and bronze gates, its English and French chapels, its wonderful wealth of decoration, carved iron, wood, and stone work, so I do not mean to describe it. As a reckless criticism on the interior of the church, I would say that the prodigality with which the ornamentation is lavished on almost every square inch of glass, stone, wood, or metal, fatigues the eye, and makes one feel that the church is too florid to be artistic; there is no repose, no restfulness, all is distraction; and visitors feel a pleasant relief in the plain, straight lines of the exterior of the church and the surrounding buildings.

The catacombs are reached by a ride by railway through the centre of the island, or, if the adventurous traveller prefer it, let him hire one of the many char-à-banc drivers who clamour for patronage at every cabstand of the place. Passing by rail one gets a somewhat more elevated view of the country, which for the whole distance is divided up into little paddocks, rarely exceeding ten acres, by walls of that white stone of which Malta has a surfeit.

In certain conditions of season I have been told that the country looks like a land of ruins, but in spring, seen from the somewhat elevated position of the rail, the little squares of bright green grass, crimson clover, and newly sprung wheat looked beneath the warm rays of the spring afternoon a peculiarly novel and pleasing sight, such as Walter Crane or Kate Greenaway might well depict. Here large groves of oranges showed the dark green of their leaves above the garden walls, and there the prickly pear, with its curious trellis-work of straggling branches covering the stony fences, afforded a pleasant retirement for the numerous bright green lizards that darted in and out playing hide-and-seek with the approaching visitor.

The chess-board aspect of the country is rather broken up by large white stone aqueducts, which, supported on arches high above the paddocks, convey the precious material to the thirsty mortals of this or that village, for a few villages and isolated houses glow here and there resplendent in the blaze of the afternoon sun.

In summer the island assumes one intolerable glare, radiation of heat from the white stone is overpowering, and all the crops are harvested before this scorching influence renders them more fit for the fire than the barn. During this season the tired land lies fallow in readiness for the ensuing crops of next winter and spring.

The traffic receipts of the railway from Valetta to Citta Vecchia, the station for the catacombs, could not be very heavy, for I am prepared solemnly to state that at the four or five stations we passed in three-quarters of an hour's run only one man got up and down, and that man was the conductor. So melancholy did it seem for him to be doing all the work alone, that I took pity on him, and at one station jumped down to keep him company, being rewarded therefor by a wild flower or two hitherto unknown—though full of interest—to me.

I intended when reaching Citta Vecchia to secure a guide to take me to the catacombs, but I had no need, for *he* secured me, and marched along, trotting with ragged garments and bare feet to a cabin close to the grated entrance, where an old Maltese with unshaven beard and ghoulish expression produced a few composite candles, and led the way down a few steps to the barred gate covering the mouth of the cavern.

This gnome-like guardian of the cavern, looking almost weird by the flickering light of our candles, with grim and terse phraseology, consisting of broken English, almost pulverised, so small were its fragments, pointed out the curiosities of the place.

The catacombs themselves are no longer in use, and by far the largest and most interesting portion is now shut up from the prying eyes of tourists on account, so one is told, of a lament-

Port Said.

able calamity which took place some few years back, when a number of tourists were lost in the mazes of catacombs, and perished miserably from hunger. I was told subsequently on good authority that, had they but known it, a few yards beyond where their bodies were subsequently found, they could have reached an entrance to the vaults and gained the upper air.

What remains to be seen consists chiefly of ledges and shelves carved out of the solid stone on the sides of these uneven passages, which were successively used during the Saracenic occupation for beds, and under the Christians for burial-places. In some few of these niches there were, to complete the morbid reality of the place, bones and dust, both of which the guide informed me most irreverently to be those of Christians, stirring up the dust, as he spoke, with the bones, and filtering the crumbling fragments through his fingers.

We "adjourned the house" then, and moved along to a great hole in the side of a rock-hewn cavern, in which the Saracens are said to have insinuated malcontents and malefactors, and left them to meditate on their offences until their spirit should fly away, defying alike the solid rock and the great stone placed before the hole.

On settling up with my host of the underground, some altercation of course ensued, during which my good friend tested my ideas of propriety by telling me that "*gentleman* give four sheeling." As the standard of gentility was too high in that neighbourhood, I had to content myself with occupying a lower rank, and although that dignity is conferred on me by virtue of an Act of Parliament at home, I found that out here in Malta the natives had a much more practical method of testing one's right and title thereto.

As we had lost the last train back to Valetta, it was necessary to hire a jarvey, who, with the promise of a double fare, sent the soft Maltese mud flying from the carriage wheels in Catherine-wheel-like displays, much to the amusement of bystanders and the no slight bumping of myself. Again I must confess my astonishment at such crazy vehicles standing such bumps and crashes that they are forced to bear, and ascribe their safety to the principle that protects the lives of threatened men.

Malta has other sights besides those I have mentioned, such as the Opera House, of finely sculptured exterior and gorgeous interior, the markets, cleanly and interesting to a stranger, and the Palace, which with its armoury attracts many; but these and others are sights such as the guide-books explain too well to be described here; and so, bidding adieu to the gentle Maltese, whose dark gleaming eyes peep coquettishly from beneath the deep shadow of their great black hoods, with a fair wind and smooth sea we steamed away for Port Said.

CHAPTER II.

Nearing Egypt.—No local Colour.—Port Said *versus* the Pyramids.—Local Companions.—Olive Wood from Jerusalem.—Through the Canal.—A Mirage.—French Gardens.—Suez Hills.—An Adventure with boatmen.—The Red Sea.—Hot Weather.—Aden.—The Tanks.—Hotel Eggs.—Flying Fish.—Ceylon's Spicy Breezes.—Colombo.—The "Columbines."—Washing and Tailoring.—A Blind Guide.—Cinnamon Gardens.—Public Char-à-bancs.—Catamarans.—Singhalese have been libelled.—Voyage to Australia.—Our Passengers.—Quarantine Regulations.—Humour and Pathos.—At the Quarantine Station.—Trip to Melbourne.—Landing at the Quay.—Melbourne Shipping.

WE were steaming for four days from Malta to Port Said, and, with the exception of an afternoon of gymnastic sports, which as usual broke the monotony of the way and afforded both spectators and spectated much amusement, our four days were uneventfully passed 'neath a kindly sun and blue sky.

Port Said is not the most romantic or reassuring spot from which to gaze over this land of the Lotus. A low mud bank, turned by some wondrous means into a hybrid town, comprising, amongst others, the Turkish, French, Italian, Greek, and English elements, and possessing a multitude of strong odours, and not over-clean streets, hardly suggests historic ideas of Tothmes and the Pyramids, or romantic thoughts of the Nile and the houris of the ancient dynasties. The odours, many of them, were so strong as to suggest to our artists (we had two or three amateurs on board) Tom Hood's jocular attempt at sketching a strong scent near Bath.

On shore here, as in Malta, Aden, and Ceylon, the globe-trotter will be accompanied by a retinue of would-be guides and attendants, all more or less shoeless, and not so reputable as they might be. They receive opprobrium and praise with one and the same sweet smile, and the biggest "swear" is only thrown away, as is the most caustic oratory assuring them that, like "Hanner Marier," one is "not allowed followers."

The bazaar here at Port Said is a miserable little place compared with those in large Turkish towns, and had we not wanted to get some fruit there I fancy we had never penetrated so far, for a perfectly unique scent met us just as we got there which would have completely routed anything other than Anglo-Saxon energy and persistence.

Here we were offered the curios of the place, in the shape of fans, imitation amber, olive wood, and the like. Some of the straw fans were fancifully made, in imitation of lace and tapestry. The so-called amber partook somewhat of the character of the Chinese celebrity Tay Kin, for one unlucky wight who smoked a cigarette in a "guaranteed amber tube" was surprised on reaching the end to find the mouthpiece literally melting away in burning drops. Of the olive wood, judging from the quantity said to have come from the Mount of Olives —as all these articles with Jerusalem inscribed purport to have done—one must infer that those far-famed groves stretched at least all over the country known as Palestine. A heretic on board suggested that a large number of paper-knives were made in England from wood grown in the Grecian Archipelago.

At Port Said we waited but five or six hours, quite long enough to get tired of the low mud bank, with its spick and span hotels and shipping-offices on the canal bank, and its yellow lighthouse beyond; and then steamed for the next two days through the canal, through which ships move but slowly, as the water-wash would otherwise prove too destructive to the banks.

The stoppages to permit other boats to pass are frequent, and at night-time no boats are permitted to proceed. Taking advantage of our stability of an evening our would-be actors gave two performances, wherein the ship's carpenter and the prompter gained most notice.

The first day of our passage in the canal we were favoured with the sight of a mirage—an appearance of a quantity of jagged rocks standing up out of a glistening sea—the sea and rocks being in fact but one stretch of sandy desert. It is hard to believe that your eyes are deceiving you, for the appearance is perfect, and obstinate, hard-headed, matter-of-fact people, of whom we had a few on board, would not believe that their senses were playing them false.

One or two spots on the canal are picturesque—Ismaila, with its minarets and domes, its white walls and mosques, for one; the signalmen's stations for others. The signalmen, who are mostly Frenchmen, show their national love for flowers by producing plants and shrubs out of the arid-looking soil and sand around their little cottages, often themselves objects of some interest.

On the morning of the third day of our passage through the canal as we neared Suez the artistic beauties of the scenery opened up. The colouring of the hills around was delightfully soft, the warm pink haze that the sand seemed to give out enveloping the rocky hills in its embrace, and serving as a foil to the intense blue atmosphere that filled the shadows. The sky was cloudless, of that clear almost violet tinge that loses itself in a gentle mauve on the horizon, and the sea a most exquisite sapphire, deepening near the shore, and verging to an intense Mediterranean blue near the ship's side.

Indolently gazing at such a wealth of colour was sufficient occupation for all but our artist, who seemed to find it necessary on all occasions to libel nature regardless of her own feelings on the point.

One of our passengers had an amusing adventure coming off from Suez to the steamer at night. After the boat was some distance from shore, his two rascally boatmen *refused to take him the whole distance* unless he doubled their fee. His measures were prompt and successful. Gripping one of his antagonists by the throat he sent him into that portion of the other where he kept his lungs, and then seizing the tiller in his own hands quietly steered the rest of the way himself, thereby earning rather the respect than the hostility of his late assailants, who became quite effusive when he gave them their bargained fee. Our artist being engaged next day in putting in the Suez hills in oils, felt highly aggrieved with the captain for starting in the midst of his operation, thereby, as he said, subordinating the interests of art to commerce. He received much sympathy from his lay brethren, though the only tokens of art as yet visible were the blue daubs, more or less shaded, representing sea and sky.

Our passage down the Red Sea was uneventful. The heat was not so overpowering as it would be later on in the season, and punkahs and ice-creams kept the thermometer below boiling point.

A story went the rounds that one man incautiously walking about on board with a fuzee-box in his pocket was observed to be in a state of combustion, and was extinguished summarily by a hose being turned on him; but it was only a part of a deep-laid scheme to get a shower bath without the trouble of providing it for himself. The more responsibility of action you can shift on to a fellow-passenger going down the Red Sea the happier and easier your lot.

At Aden we stopped for a few hours, and had an opportunity of inspecting the tanks and the show-place of this sunburnt volcanic rock, being about the only spot on the peninsula where you will find green trees. The water in some of the tanks was of a mixed character, supplying food as well as drink, for there appeared to be considerable body in it; but in others it had not this advantage, being only ordinarily clear.

Here I would warn folks who take breakfast ashore from ordering Aden eggs. One of our party asked for two at the hotel at which we tried to get a breakfast, and when one was dropped into an ordinary egg-cup the article so completely disappeared in the gloomy abyss, that the would-be partaker got frightened and thought somebody was practising the Black Art. However, when her eyes got accustomed to peering into the inmost recesses of the cup she took heart again, for there like a pea in a soup-tureen lay that egg waiting to be manipulated. How the contents were extracted we never knew, for we were otherwise employed contenting ourselves with an omelette which prevented a similar catastrophe and display of ingenuity, though its flavour forcibly reminded us of the old adage *ab ovo usque ad malum*, and the hotel-keeper mistranslating *malum* for bad, had deemed it wise to join the *ovum* and the *malum* in one *pièce de resistance*.

From Aden we steamed with little event, though delightful weather, calm seas, and hot sun; the usual flying fish tracing out geometrical diagrams on the placid surface of the ocean, or, flying into our open ports, alternately amused and annoyed those who knew not who their nightly visitors might be.

As we neared Ceylon one passenger seriously informed "whomever it might concern" that we should really smell the spicy breezes blowing off from that isle "where only man is vile," but he was treated with contumely, and being an humble ease-loving individual, urged his point no further. His triumph was to come; for assuredly as we neared Colombo one morning just a month after leaving the old country, we were greeted with the odour of an all-spice box which the scoffers could with difficulty help swallowing as a savour to their words.

Colombo is not at first sight so picturesque as it subsequently appears when one has landed and has opportunities to unravel its natural beauties. The surrounding scenery for many miles is so flat that if a man wishes to have a good view he just puts on a pair of high-heeled boots, and from this lofty eminence scans the country.

But the ordinary wayside scenery, even in the town where the chief hotels, shipping offices, and banks stand, is picturesque in the extreme. The dull crimson-coloured earth that forms the roadway, sandy and flat as a billiard table, wide and often fringed with a broad belt of grass, thus divided from the pathways themselves, edged with bungalows of wood and stone surrounded with cool colonnades and verandahs, often shaded with palms, banyan-trees, lettuce-trees, and many other flowering and beautiful trees and shrubs—all are to the new arrival a source of admiration and wonder. Here one does indeed see tropical foliage to perfection, for nature has been assisted by art, and all around the suburbs the loveliest tropical flowers and trees are scattered with lavish hand collected from far and near, yet growing like weeds in this congenial and moist climate.

The inhabitants are worthy objects of observation by the new arrival. Labour is very cheap. The first sign one gets of this truism emanates in the offers of half-a-dozen neatly-robed Singhalese, with tortoiseshell combs in their hair, who, with grinning teeth, offer to do your washing at very low rates, or bring you a suit of white drill in a few hours for a " couple of shillings."

Of course such workmanship either in the laundry or in the tailoring line is not of the best, but what can you expect for the money you pay? If your white shirts come back with frayed sleeves and fronts considerably " frilled," your other garments minus a button or two and provided with more than the usual number of apertures, you just have to pay and look pleasant, comforting yourself with the reflection that your disbursement is small, and this new method of washing has a certain novelty, which serves as a foil to the monotonous routine of the irreproachable laundry woman at home. The clothes too, referred to above, are delicately put together and naturally require delicate use, so that if you expect them to stay out the trials of a sea voyage of any length, you had better lay in a store of sticking-plaster or postage-stamp-margin wherewith to repair split seams.

The Singhalese are said to be mild and inoffensive. Mild I believe them to be; but after an old hag of a Singhalese (and these islanders know as well, nay, better, than any other race how to produce the ugliest of old hags) has been indulging in the frugal betel-nut she certainly cannot be deemed absolutely inoffensive. From the colour of the teeth of those who chew this dainty morsel, our jocular man suggested that in future it should be called the blackbeetle-nut.

Here as elsewhere the globe-trotter is made the object of cruel deception by the native; for example, desiring a guide to the Cinnamon-gardens, I selected one laughing, good-tempered-looking Singhalese, who assured me he could "spik mush Eenglis." After having inquired of him many things (being desirous of looking upon him as a Gamaliel), I found that his English seemed to consist but of the three above-mentioned words—a discovery which I shortly tested by addressing to him a series of vituperative epithets, the whole of which he with self-satisfied smiles took as complimentary.

Now if there is one test of a native's knowledge of English it lies in this, does he or does he not understand the import of such words? For the heathen, wherever he be, first picks up our "swears" and "epithets," and if he be ignorant of them you can count that he is innocent of all knowledge of the English tongue. Instead of propounding Shibboleth to him try him with a "big big D," and watch the effect. If by his manner he indicates no knowledge of the meaning, then is his ignorance deep indeed, and fraught with no bliss for you; if, on the other hand, he manifests comprehension, you may then test his knowledge in the higher branches of the art of "epithetising," and thus gain the desired end.

The Cinnamon Gardens, a mile or two out of Colombo, are well worth a visit, being a perfect paradise of tropical flowers and trees. Formerly actually used as cinnamon plantations, they are now partly left to nature and partly planted as public gardens, with crotons, orange-trees, oleanders, poinsettias, and hundreds of other plants and shrubs, which in the spring seem to be a joy for ever. The Mahometan mosque one passes on the way to the gardens forms a superb picture, its white walls and minarets, cool, deep colonnades and doorway, contrasting vividly with the lovely setting of palms, bananas, and other foliage all around it.

The public conveyances here are something like those of Malta, only more so. I could but wonder that the driver ever consented to get on the box without first having insured his life; and I had serious misgivings once or twice whether I ought not, in fairness to the crippled condition of the vehicle, to have offered to help him by lifting it over any spots less smooth than usual.

The water conveyances that the natives possess—well known as catamarans—are the most extraordinarily shaped craft that human ingenuity ever went out of its way to construct. They are in two pieces, a hollowed boat-like portion and a solid outrigger attached to the boat by arched sticks and spars, and ordinarily glide along so slowly that a tortoise might give them fifty yards start in a hundred and emulate the hare at the end. The occupants do not sit on seats athwart the boat, for in most cases the width of beam does not allow of this, so either they range themselves along the gunwale, or the place where it ought to be, or sit on a slightly elevated platform erected above the boat, allowing a leg or two to dangle down either in or outside.

I left Ceylon with the idea that the gentle Singhalese had been libelled by our friends the missionaries when they referred to them in the well-known words of the poet. I presume that it hardly suited the purpose of these learned gentlemen to except also from the 'vile' catalogue the poisonous snakes, the twenty-foot sharks, and the towering rogue-elephants, indigenous here like man. Perhaps these exceptions might have spoilt the metre, or the learned gentlemen may really have been pleased with the condition of the wild things of the field.

Some of us transhipped at Colombo, taking the Australian boat, which had arrived a day or two before, and was awaiting our arrival, and on our setting foot amongst the passengers, who had come all the way from England in her, we were most properly received with the cold reserve and get-out-of-my-way-if-you-please air that forms one of the noblest traits of our

English treatment of strangers. Strangers forsooth! "intruders" is the proper expression, and as such were we for some time treated.

Our run from Colombo to Melbourne and Sydney was marked by no adventure. The weather was hot for a great portion of the journey, and the boat was crowded for a still greater portion, and so good spirits were at a premium.

All through the hot weather we had punkah-boys to keep our temperature down at meal-time, but as we neared our destination we lost the breeze, which was fast becoming too cooling to be pleasant. One of our melancholy-visaged passengers apostrophised the departure of our punkah-boys in terms most poetic and heart-rending.

"Good-bye," said he, "oh punkah-wallahs; Othello's occupation is gone! No longer will ye put on your best robes and sashes, no longer waste time on cleaning your hands and faces to grace our festivals with your presence! Good-bye gentle though ofttimes ugly punkah-wallahs, good-bye! Why is it that my lachrymose glands exude the dewy pearl! Think ye that it is because one of you has touched my heart? Alas! I fear not. I weep because I cannot help it, having caught a cold through your confounded over-fanning!"

During this voyage idle rumour, represented by the old classics as—

"Mobilitate viget, viresque acquirit eundo,"

had been spreading abroad an announcement that we had disease on board, and sure enough we steamed into Australian ports under the tragic ensign of the yellow flag, and were quarantined at every port where we landed passengers.

The arrangements for quarantine are not uniform at all Australian ports, so that at Melbourne the passengers who got off there got off best, at Adelaide second best, and at Sydney third and last best. The operation of disinfecting the luggage of all the passengers was of a most laughable description. Boxes, portmanteaux, and bags, all were supposed to be placed in a small room where pans of sulphur were occasionally burnt;

but inasmuch as many of the bags and trunks were never opened, any lively germ stood the best chance of passing through unscathed, and of testifying to the perfection (!) of sanitary arrangements.

The heading of this chapter might have been tragically termed Under the Yellow Flag, for it certainly waved over our heads for a great portion of the time that lapsed between Colombo and Sydney. The tragedy was, however, one in name only, for there was actually more comedy than aught else in our detention in quarantine.

Sea Beach Point Nepean Victoria

We were provided when on shore with an ample supply of victuals, to which we first-class passengers sat down as at table d'hôte, but quantity was so much in excess of quality that for months afterwards I felt ashamed to look a sheep or bullock in the face, when remembering the enormous chunks and cubes of meat which were dispensed to us. Our eyes were also somewhat charmed on the spit of land allowed to us infected ones, or on the sea-shore there are one or two pretty pieces of cave scenery with names such as London and Blackfriars Bridge, suggesting home thoughts and comparisons.

This quarantine ground of Melbourne is at one of the extreme points of the crescent of land surrounding Port Philip, so that we had the conveniences of both the sea-shore and the bay, if one may talk about convenience where so many folk seemed to find nothing but inconvenience.

On the day of our being released from quarantine a small paddle-boat came down to take us across the port up to Melbourne, some forty miles distant. The passage was rather rough, and the small boat dived occasionally, upsetting her own centre of gravity while increasing the gravity of a large portion of the unfortunate passengers, who declared that they were certain that the Government of Victoria was to blame for their present unpleasant condition, in fact, wholly responsible for the bad weather and every individual's *mal de mer*. Poor Government! when last I heard of it, it was trying to get over the blow caused by such base ingratitude after the generous way in which the grumblers had been supplied *ad lib.*, if not *ad lip*, for the past seven days with the fat of the land and house rent free.

There were not many of us in a fit state to appreciate our approach to Melbourne that April afternoon, but those who could brave the terrors of the deep, without feeling as though they were turned inside out, had a very bustling view before them as we steamed up to Sandridge, one of the shipping sub-burbs of this metropolis of the South.

Although I had read in handbooks and books of travel of the size, population, and other statistics of this city, I confess that mere figures gave me no idea of the bustle and size of the docks, wharves, and forest of shipping that met the eye as we steamed up to our berth. A slight mist had settled down on the water, and the whole scene, fog included, bore such a realistic semblance to the scenes at home on the Mersey or the Thames, that for a brief moment I could not help thinking that somehow, though I had thus been travelling six weeks in search of the Antipodes, I had as a matter of fact been brought back to my starting point. The custom-house officers who inspected us and our baggage, the very dock labourers and officials, all reproduced their brethren in the old country, and I gave my friend who kindly came down to welcome me some anxiety by asking when the next train would be along for Fenchurch Street.

The colonials who watched us disembark had not their respect for the mother country much increased, for a more bedraggled, sickly-jaundiced, water-washed crew never, I do believe, stepped off the channel steamer at Folkestone or Dover than did our unhappy band of pilgrims that day at Sandridge Pier.

CHAPTER III.

English Language at the Antipodes.—"New Chums" and Colonials.—"It's a 'New Chum's' Trick."—Taking the Train to the City.—Hangers-on.—"The City" and the Suburbs.—Mixed Nomenclature.—Broad Streets.—Sanitary Arrangements.—Cologne rivalled.—Novelties in Odours required.—Climate of Melbourne.—The North Wind.—Melbourne's End.—Architecture.—Hotels and Living.—The Block and the Blockheads.—Eight Hours Labour System.—Fashions in Melbourne.—Protection and Free Trade.—Books.—Newspapers.—Colonial Literature and Art.—National Gallery—Museum and Library.—Buying Pictures by the Square Yard and Books by the Cartload.—Burke and Wills' Monument and History.

MANY visitors to the Antipodes express "astonishment" at hearing their own language spoken as the vulgar tongue so far as twelve thousand miles from "home." I tried hard to experience some of this astonishment, as it seemed the right and proper thing to do, but found that the whole of the stock had been consumed by former astonishees. Having failed to procure a sample of this "astonishment," I naturally adopted Æsop's foxy example and deemed it an unnecessary and unpalatable commodity.

If when a man went to the Arctic regions he wrote home saying he was astonished at such a quantity of ice or such a degree of cold, would other men think well of his intellectual powers or his application to the sources of information? To be astonished at finding English spoken in Australia does not tend to heighten my respect for the persons so astonished, any more than would my veneration be much exhausted for a man who wondered that a pond of water was so damp. I can appreciate (who cannot?) Mrs. Towser's wonder at the Parisian street Arabs knowing French and speaking it so fluently; but I cannot sympathise with those who are surprised to find Englishmen in Australia speaking their own tongue.

As my friend led me away from the throng of reviving sufferers who were trying to forget their recent pains and qualms in the excitement of chasing another sufferer or a porter who might be making off with their ill-sorted baggage, one of the first expressions that met my ear was, "I say, Bill, here's a couple of new chums."

The expression "new chum" is a colonial term for new arrivals to the colonies, and includes a vast proportion of the population of the colonies, as the new chum does not graduate as a full-blown colonial for some years; but the virulence of the epithet lies not in this, but rather arises from the fact that the new chum is supposed to be in a state of dense ignorance, possessed of a mind resembling in vacancy that of an idiot, and so is rather deserving of pity and contempt until he has had his ignorance cleared up and his vacant mind stored with "colonial experience." Every one, however new to the colonies, glories in calling a fresher arrival a "new chum," not of course to his face, if the new chum has muscle and sinew wherewith to back up his "new-chumism." The term implies contempt and pity for the poor creature's ignorance of matters *per se* of a colonial nature, and therefore (mark the logical deduction) of all things worth knowing. A man often means by it, "There's a poor weak-minded ignorant fool, we must teach him everything *a priori*; all that he has learnt is but of little avail to him, nay, perhaps may hinder his graduating as an old chum; he's got to be educated all over again, and begin at an age when our boys have long passed through the Alma Mater and taken the senior opt. in the Colonial-Experience-Tripos."

A wharfinger throws a rope badly or hauls something out of the way awkwardly; it's immediately called a new chum's trick; and if you could pierce the bronze on the sturdy fellow's cheek you would see the blush of conscious shame for having merited such an opprobrious epithet. A cart is put together in an unworkmanlike fashion; it's a new chum's trick. A man rides badly who never could ride anywhere or anything except perhaps a hobby; he is disgraced by being likened to a new chum.

Formerly new chums could be more easily detected by colonials than at present. Up country the strangeness of the scene and life makes the "new chum" declare himself in a thousand actions; and he betrays himself by speech and by the cut of his clothes. Down in the towns, however, where Britannic fashions arrive in all their Britannic folly almost as soon as they come out in England, a new chum is more readily told by the colour of his face. The colonial has seen a few summers and his hide has become tanned; by the fresh complexion of the newly arrived Englishman the colonial appears often sallow.

Of the practical jokes played on a new chum in order to break his new-chumism and give him "Colonial experience" I shall have something to say later on.

The docks at Sandridge are some way removed from the city itself, with which they are connected by railway.

The twelve thousand miles of separation from the old country was annihilated that night by the English-like reception in an English-like suburban villa by an essentially English-like matron and children, and the full tide of civilisation was at its height, I felt, when I had an odd half-dozen or so of these charming little ones covering every square inch of my person.

After having settled myself in my new quarters, I began to look around me and make general comments on the city of refuge I was in.

Melbourne appears in a great many points to be aping her mother metropolis of the other end of the globe. She has a city *stricto sensu* which is just as much a commercial portion of the town as is the City of London.

Suburban railways bring up their thousands of a morning from all around in orthodox style. The carriages are built with regard to warm seasons, of frequent occurrence even so far south; they have Venetian shutters as well as glass windows throughout. Victorians also adopt the well-ventilated roomy cars which we in England still look upon as luxuries, and their suburban stations would cause many of our own to blush with shame, particularly on consideration that these copyists of the South have copied the names without the dirt and meagreness of their prototypes of the North.

The mixture of English and Australian names strikes a visitor as being rather comical. Kew, Richmond, Prahran, Balaclava, Brighton occur in close connection, irrespective of association and of distance, in many cases.

The noticeable feature in the "city" when you arrive there is the breadth of its streets, as all the principal streets are two or three chains wide, that is getting on for a couple of hundred feet in width, the effect being somewhat calculated to dwarf into insignificance all but the principal buildings; and a visitor from London or any other of the large English and European towns cannot at first help being struck with a sense of this disproportion.

The advantages are, however, very soon apparent, both from a sanitary and spectacular point of view. So far, the traffic does not adequately fill up the streets; in fact, after busy narrow streets of London and our large provincial towns, Melbourne seems to be far from brisk. In the lapse of time of course this will be an additional advantage when, as she bids fair to do, Melbourne begins to rival the *Great Metropolis*. They are said on good authority to have been thus laid out in the early times some fifty years ago in order to facilitate the movements of herds of cattle and sheep, bullock-teams, and the like. Whatever may have been the cause the result is eminently satisfactory; with broad open streets and the sea-breezes from Port Philip, Melbourne for generations to come need have but a very low death-rate.

Air they will have in plenty to penetrate into their inmost recesses. Again, from a globe-trotter's point of view, they possess great advantages in enabling him or her to maintain a graceful position when sight-seeing, and to be free from that "ache in the neck" from which sight-seers in less favoured towns suffer; and here in Melbourne there are banks, offices, and government buildings which are well worthy of observation by the observing one.

Why guide-books should tell you that all the streets in the city of Melbourne run at "right angles to one another" I may not say, for, as I tried to convince an infatuated friend, such an observation would reduce the streets of the city to two. The fact is that the city itself is built in square sections like the newly built cities in America, surveyed as for a draughtboard; and though the streets are thus deprived of some picturesque qualities which curves and convergent lines possess, their utility is much increased, for a man cannot very well lose his way, that is to say, always providing he has not partaken too largely of the River Yarra water, which is decidedly heady, abounding, like our Thames at home, in a full rich "body" flavour.

Although their city is well ventilated, with its broad streets and parks and gardens, of which I will speak hereafter, the Melbournians somewhat qualify this advantage by running most of their water-sewage down open gutters along the streets. These seem broad enough to serve that purpose, but since the city is built on slightly hilly ground, the gutters in the lower parts during a heavy downfall of rain get overcharged, and transfer their contents gradually across the road, until instead of a roadway there is only a broad swift-flowing river visible.

Down the centre of one of the chief commercial streets of the city a friend had seen within the last few months, as he solemnly assured me, the comical sight of a barrel carried along on the bosom of the deep.

The late Earl of Beaconsfield would indeed have been in his element here, for when he applied the term "gondolas of our streets" to our cabs, he little thought how aptly he could have applied it to Melbourne conveyances during an extra heavy shower of rain. This chance, however, of getting a wetting to one's nether limbs or the basements of the houses is a minor disadvantage, far outweighed by the fact that these open gutters in all weathers, and more especially in warm weather, are a source of a series of odours which run those "two-and-seventy stenches" that Coleridge smelt in Cologne very close indeed for first place. However, as far as my experience went, they had a peculiarity that those of Cologne have not, for since there are but three distinct odours in the most odoriferous street, after the first day or two the monotony of coming across the same old friends again and again induces a familiarity which breeds contempt and a hunger and thirst for a novelty even in this line, and causes one to fear that, notwithstanding all their vaunted enterprise, the colonials are deficient in inventive genius.

As Melbourne stands some thirty-seven miles by nearest land route from the open ocean, and the capacity of the bay or Port Philip for reception of the waste of the town is not unlimited, the question for future generations of an efficient cleansing of their city is not so easy as it might generally appear. At present typhoid fever is far too common a visitor, both to high and low, rich and poor, to cause the question to be shirked, notwithstanding that Melbourne boasts a death-rate lower by two and a half in the thousand than our "healthy London."

In her weather Melbourne varies very much. One morning the thermometers will find it so cold that they will get down off their hooks and lie on the floor as a sign of disgust; by midday their sulky fit will have given over, and they will have climbed to the top of the lightning conductor or weathercock, and lie there gasping for breath. The cause of this sudden change of temperature is in nine cases out of ten the hot north wind blowing from the interior. As it passes along it seems like a blast of a furnace, and scorches up the tender vegetation in much the same way, so that if an artist start out in the morning to sketch a green field, by afternoon he will have to change all his tones to yellows and browns.

It is said by the profane that once during a hot wind a very wicked old man died. (Even here in Australia there are some bad ones, otherwise how extremely monotonous life would be.) Well, for a bit things were quiet, when all of a sudden the whole of the telegraph operators in the country were summoned by the hoary old sinner to "send along his blankets."

One objectionable feature of this wind is that it is often accompanied by such a cloud of dust as to cause a man, woman, or child to consume in twenty-four hours an appreciable portion of that peck of dirt that we are all allotted to get through in a lifetime. As little of this dust is ever carried away, the fate that awaits Melbourne is certain: its river, docks, and streets will gradually be filled up, so that men will have to leave their houses in time-to-come by their top-floor windows, and live the greater part of their indoor life like moles and earthworms beneath the surface. Melbournians do not see it themselves, and actually laugh when a man prophecies such a fate, but such is always the prejudice that truth-tellers meet with.

I have spoken of the buildings and show places of Melbourne, and confess that notwithstanding I had read of the size and population of this city I was much surprised to see the extensive manner in which new buildings in the city and suburbs are being put up. Many of the banks and offices would do credit to large European capitals. The Public Offices and Houses of Parliament, when these latter shall be finished, will speak volumes for the elasticity of ratepayers' pockets, and the suburban mansions and villas are both within and without so charming that the tenth commandment just has to be scored out of the list, otherwise a conscience would be a burden. In many of the outlying suburbs the roads want metalling, so much so that it is dangerous for an unbetrothed couple to ride together in the same vehicle, for the bumps and jars and jolts they will receive will be constantly throwing them into one another's arms. One has to take especial care in this direction, for Melbourne ladies are already too dangerously enchanting without such additional assistance as this.

Hotels in Melbourne there are in legion, but as I am not an authorised tout I do not intend to specify any as being over good. They compare in accommodation and charges very favourably with those in England and in the rest of the colonies, and are considerably cheaper than in America. Food such as is produced in the colonies is considerably cheaper than at home, and imported foods are but little in advance of home prices now that rival companies have reduced the freight.

At one eminently respectable restaurant in one of the principal streets of the city, namely Bourke Street, one can get a lunch nicely served, of three courses, with a large menu to choose from and the usual accompaniments, for the sum of one shilling. The waitresses are not only forbidden to accept tips, but many of them would scorn the base insinuation of a coin, and probably give it back to the donor. I have not found attendants throughout the colonies so universally independent of tips and vails, but in the majority of cases they were so, and many of them would really feel offended if offered a *pour-boire*. There is a sturdy spirit of independence in them as in all the working classes which brooks not this species of patronage.

Melbourne has its West End as well as its City, but on account of its relative size the two are much closer together than those of London. Certainly some of the shops in Collins, Swanston, and Bourke Streets would do credit to Regent and Oxford Streets, and although the "dude" male and female is not so strongly developed in the colonies, yet there are a certain number of these butterflies to be seen every afternoon "doing the block," as the process of parading along these streets is technically called, a term of increased significance from the fact that the principal actors are often blockheads.

One evening, being in this quarter of the town, I was surprised to see a vast crowd filling the pathways and extensively dotting the roadway. As there was no attraction in the shape of a fire or any other especial amusement, I pondered long on the reason, until I perceived on another occasion that the scene represented the exodus of shop assistants on their way home.

The eight-hours labour system is much favoured here, that is from ten to six, and especially in the cities, where at the first stroke of the hour of six innumerable counter-jumpers dart out with shutters in hand, and before the last stroke has ceased to reverberate every man and woman serving in the shops appears to have jumped, like the versatile Duval, into his or her walking costume and to be hurrying homewards. Woe to the unlucky wretch who is purchasing when the tocsin goes; better were it indeed that he had a milestone at his back between him and the avenging shopman than that he should be cast into the sea of discontent his prolonged stay causes.

As far as purchases are concerned, I fancy that one can get anything one could get "at home" here in Melbourne, though often at greatly increased prices, the result of freight plus Protection. Good clothing is very dear, both for the investiture of males and females, so that a constant answer from clerks and others when a visitor congratulates them on having salaries in advance of what they would have at home is, "Ah, but we have to pay almost twice as much for our clothes."

It is comical to see how on a broiling hot day the black coat and tall hat should be considered as indispensable here as in London. Comfort in this case is made entirely subservient to conventionality. Many a time did my acquaintances cast envious eyes on my tourist garb as the moisture ran in great creeks down their faces.

Protection is doomed, so those in the running say. When Sir Charles Dilke paid a visit to the colonies in '67, he found, he says in his "Greater Britain," the colonists patriotically advocating Protection frequently at their own individual expense and self-sacrifice. THEN he found the masses desirous of the retention of the system; NOW a process of leavening is going on, and I was informed by one high in office that public opinion is slowly but surely veering right round to Free Trade. I speak

THE "NEW CHUM" IN AUSTRALIA. 33

feelingly concerning the evils of Protection, for it cost me at least six shillings on a hat which I had to get in Melbourne. Many labour under the delusion that the customs in Victoria tax "goods brought in by passengers for personal use." Some are particularly annoyed at the idea of guns and revolvers being thus saddled with an import-duty. This is a mistake, as all goods which can reasonably come within this definition are passed duty free.

One redeeming point in a system which taxes the importation of almost everything, from a steam engine to a pin, is that books and music come in duty free, so that they can be purchased here almost as cheaply as at home. The discount allowed off published prices in England is absorbed, so the booksellers say, by the freight, so that the books are generally sold at the published prices, and one cannot complain at this, when one finds standard works at such a low rate thousands of miles from their source. One bookseller, who advertises his "emporium" in all the colours of the rainbow, boasts the possession of over a hundred thousand volumes, and contends that his book arcade is one of the sights of the world.

Sir Charles Dilke again and others have doubted the capacity of local manufacturers to hold their own if Protection be withdrawn, but evidences are not wanting at the present day that in this event many colonial manufactures would be locally supported and flourishing.

The reason commonly given that so many colonial productions are dearer than home manufactures, is that labour is so much dearer there than at home. Some doubters are inclined to insinuate that the colonial manufacturers are actually making very large profits, and think that this apparent overcharge is really of benefit to the colony, for in time the people's eyes will be opened by these very means, and they will see that Free Trade implies increased prosperity.

One is surprised to see what a number of newspapers and

periodicals Melbourne supports. Seven dailies, including the *Argus* (the *Times* of the colony, and almost as old as Melbourne), the *Age*, and the *Daily Telegraph*, nine weeklies, and some round dozen monthlies, form the solid and respectable portion of the newspapers. There are also a few rags which splutter like an ill-conditioned catherine-wheel for a space and then go out ignominiously. The matter to fill all these papers is as varied as it is at home. The latest news, foreign, colonial, and home, comes by wire or cable. American and English quotations figure on Melbourne breakfast tables within a few hours, and the Australian larrikins are as well up in the latest horrors as are the street Arabs at home who dispense special editions for a bronze equivalent.

Local literature is at present considerably in long clothes here, except the periodicals; books are written by native-born prodigies, but not often read. As with the fine arts, there has not been much time or opportunity for the encouragement of *les belles lettres;* but nowadays a strong feeling is growing up for a native art and literature which will probably meet with a supply as the new world shakes down more and more into the higher paths of civilisation, and further and further from that most delightful of primitive modes of living "when Adam delved and Eve span, and nought was known of a gentleman," in the words of John Ball, one of the lieutenants of the famous Wat Tyler.

The fine arts have made a very good start at the National Gallery and Museum, where both painting and sculpture of first-class character serve to educate the eye of the would-be Rembrandt or Michael Angelo. The paintings hanging on the walls here are, as to many of them, first-class specimens of the modern English school, as the names of the artists will testify, such as Leighton, Pettie, Long, Leslie, Herbert, and others of fame at home. Some few pictures there are of colonial scenery by colonial artists, but at present these form a decided minority; still whenever the muse favours a native, colonials are ready to give him substantial patronage, although there are those who deny this assertion.

The National Gallery is under one and the same roof as the Museum and the Public Library. The building is after the Grecian style, resembling a somewhat broadened Parthenon, and occupies a very good position in the city.

The Museum has unfortunately often coupled with it a term calculated to frighten all but very strong-minded persons, namely the word Technological. However the ship was found sufficiently stout to bear this word out to the colonies I know

View on the Yarra-Yarra, Melbourne.

not, as I do not seriously entertain the idea that such a monstrosity was produced spontaneously and is indigenous with the gum-trees. Notwithstanding its awe-inspiring name, the museum is one of those goodly places where there is much to interest and instruct; it is essentially the museum of a practical country.

The Public Library up above is a place fit for a king. The apartments are lofty, and so thickly stocked with books that tradition has it you cannot ask for a book ordinarily known which you will not be able to procure. Anthony Trollope says in his work on the colonies that it contained every book heart could wish for; but then Anthony Trollope wrote at a time when hearts were content with less than they are now, and I would not vouch that the modern article would be content even with the hundred and twenty thousand volumes to be found there. I had much courtesy shown me by the Library officials while in Melbourne, although I had no especial recommendation to them, and gave them some trouble, so I have pleasant recollections of that booky sanctum.

In private life the wealthier classes have their own libraries and pictures as at home, and much advantage may they derive from them. I fear very often that, as with us, they are only purchased for the look of the thing, and that the parvenu who ordered his bookseller to send him in about a couple of cartloads of good works in handsome bindings is not unknown on the southern side of the line. One gentleman showing me a drawing-room full of water-colours, some of them of very fair merit, on my examining them individually, begged me not to trouble to do so, as he himself had "chosen the whole lot in half an hour when over in England," having asked the picture-vendor to give him a few of the high-priced articles.

In the way of public art-works Melbourne also boasts the possession of what she delights to call a "Colossal group" of some of her greatest pioneers. The monument to Burke and Wills, the two stout hearts whose lives were forfeited through the carelessness of their subordinates, occupies a central position in this city. The sculpture of the figures is certainly noteworthy, though not of the most refined character, and the bronze relievos on the four sides of the large pedestal look rather the worse for wear. They, however, represent four of the most striking events in their ill-fated exploration, and as far as the conception is concerned are pleasing.

On the first side is portrayed the setting out of the expedition, armed and accoutred in readiness for the trials and obstacles before them, camels laden with goods, and men on horseback, all testifying to the thorough way the expedition was taken up. On the second relievo is shown the disappointment of the two leaders when after having gone to the extreme north of their travel, and been the first to cross the great continent from south to north, on returning to their depôt in the far interior they found not even a sign to show that their attendants with fresh supplies had been there but a few hours before, and, in disobedience of instructions, had left before they should. On the third side there is represented the finding of the mortal remains of the heroic explorer Burke, dead for the want of the very supplies which were buried within a few feet of the ground he had dragged his weary limbs over, but without a sign to tell of the presence of safety—starved to death, all tattered and torn, when there was plenty of food and clothing within a measurable and procurable distance had he but known it. The fourth relievo brings to an end the pathetic story by representing the discovery of the one survivor of the expedition which had started with Burke and Wills, an attendant named King, living a bare existence among the friendly though debased aborigines in the interior.

I have lingered round this monument because it illustrates one of the most striking incidents of Australian history, bright with the good-nature, amiability, and heroism of the leaders, and contrasting thus forcibly with the untimely and sorry fate which befell them. However, to have perished thus in the service of one's country would be the envy of many another Australian or Englishman, who deem it thus grander to die in a good cause than rub along without a cause at all. You do not come across many other such monuments in Australia; a nation that has only of quite recent years had time to emerge from the toil of the field or the counting-house and cultivate its higher faculties, has not had many men whom it could single out as exceptionally worthy of being immortalised where all have been heroes in one way or another, and finds something better to do with its public moneys than to expend large sums in erecting a griffin to obstruct traffic, and to be the laughing stock of all save its designer.

CHAPTER IV.

Churches.—Bells *versus* Bed.—The Pro-Cathedral.—Not a Thing of Beauty nor a Joy for any Time.—"Why do you go to the Cathedral?"—St. Patrick's Cathedral.—Ambition of the Children of the Emerald Isle.—Music.—The Hurdy-gurdy.—Salvation Salvoes.—The Drama.—Passes.—The Houses of Legislature.—The Edifice.—A Debate.—The Upper Form set a Good Example.—Is it Marble or Paint?—Lint at a Premium.—The Medical Fraternity.—"You've forgotten to call for your Brains!"—Fearful Feud on the Franchise Question.—"Who shall say between the Two?"

A GOOD and righteous commencement goes a long way with some people, just as a good plate of real turtle helps to soothe the alderman and render him blandly pleased with everything yet to come. So to propitiate this section of my readers I commence this time with a learned disquisition on churches, denominations, schisms, and heartrendings, as pretty a dish as any *chef de cuisine* can evolve.

Of churches Melbourne has a very fair show. If a man be stopping at an hotel in the city I fancy he will pretty soon realise that he has got everything denominational, from the Chinese joss-house to the Protestant Cathedral.

Bells high and bells low, bells loud and bells soft, assail one in strophes and antistrophes on all sides, and evil were it for that listener if he still courts his couch after the warfare of sounds has commenced. He will find that the brighter climate of Australia has revived his old enemy long lost sight of in the liver-compelling clime of the old country, and there formerly called "the conscience" (and now known as the Fourth Party), and perforce he will have to leave his habitat and seek safety either in flight or in fulfilling the conventionalities, and entering one or other of the many buildings from which the clamour issues and whose existence they advertise.

The Church of England Cathedral is as yet only half finished, and the Pro-Cathedral is really in great need of being replaced, for there are few uglier and less convenient churches than this St. Paul's of the South. The roof has for some time been freely though unnecessarily ventilated by cracks, which afford an entrance to little rivulets of water during rainy times, and thereby afford the congregation a chance of diluting any matter they may imbibe from the pulpit. A colonial told me in my private ear that no one would go to the Cathedral as it exists now were it not that it is the thing to do. Just fancy coming across conventionalities like this in a land until lately wholly given up to nature! The idea was preposterous, and the wicked colonial was promptly lent half-a-crown, and of course did not trouble me again.

The Roman Catholics are most ambitious in the building of their cathedral. Its site is elevated and commanding, and when it is finished the building will be the same, but, although commenced some time back, scarce a quarter is as yet finished, though indeed it already covers a considerable area. The name of St. Patrick suggests immediately the nationality of those from whom it will derive its support, but although Pat is ubiquitous in the colonies, his generosity and liberality will have to be considerably fostered and cultivated before this massive building is finished. The division of the finished portion into three sections—one for the worshippers of St. Joseph and a second for those of the Virgin Mary—suggested the regretful question why the worshippers of the two should be thus separated; although the *duo* were *juncta in uno*, their followers here as elsewhere seem determined to separate them.

The bright yellow glass with which the windows are glazed produces the effect of perpetual sunshine or thick fog, according as the weather is bright or dull. In the gloaming the interior appears dim and ghostly, and the few statues and pictures hazily suggest the reappearance of their originals, and when the notes of the distant choir or the gentle echoes of the organ fall in soft cadence on the ear the charm of emotional worship is complete.

Salvation salvoes are loud and long throughout the colonies, for "The Army" is doing its best to knock in its own drums and the drums of all its hearers.

Now and again that *rara avis* over here, the street organ-grinder, has been seen. Like the sea-serpent, many people disbelieve in his existence, but many trustworthy pairs of eyes and ears can testify to the infernal machine having begun its work over here. When the first street organ was heard a colonial was seen to retreat to a distance for fear that it was a dynamitard's trick, and when, having gained courage, he permitted himself a closer inspection, he remarked that "If the Blood-and-Thunder League, talked about in Ireland, really wished to coerce the English Government, their path was as plain before them as could be. Let them flood the country with a few thousand of these infernal machines, and the whole nation must to a man grant them any request on a promise to withdraw."

Reverting again to the sublimer paths of Melpomene, the Opera House sometimes gives its visitors a treat, and concerts and organ recitals at the City Town Hall are of common occurrence and warmly supported.

The drama receives considerable patronage in Melbourne at the three principal theatres, but of local talent comparatively little is known. The artistes who conjure the shillings and half-crowns are generally from England or America. On the principle that a prophet hath not honour in his own country, the imported article fetches a higher price than the home-brewed.

The most favourite performances seemed to be those of the farcical or comedy type, but even that musty and fusty old gentleman, Shakespeare, has been known on occasion to fetch long prices and applause for the actors who have translated him for the benefit of the Melbourne world.

One desirable feature, as on the Continent, connected with dramatic representation in the colonies, is that from *any* part of the theatre one can get a pass, so that during the intervals of the performance one can adjourn to the cool and refreshing breezes or other cool and refreshing matters in the neighbouring streets without forfeiting place or precedence.

Speaking of the drama, my thoughts naturally turn to the "House" where the great State performances are given—the two Chambers of Legislature of Victoria. The edifice that shelters the Upper and the Lower House, besides a number of lesser offices, is at present in an unfinished condition, and it is therefore unkindly to criticise it. A member of the House assured me that the building would be finished in a few years' time; and I was shown the architect's model, whereby one can see that the building bids fair to have an imposing if not grand exterior.

The use of the material called "bluestone" for the grand staircase and for certain other portions of the exterior to some extent detracts from the appearance the building will present, for this stone, though hard and durable as our granite, has often the misfortune to be honeycombed like pumice, a failing which somewhat spoils the appearance of the work. Strenuous efforts are being made to open up quarries for a good white building stone in Victoria. In the meantime some of the best freestone comes from Sydney, but Victoria is not over pleased at having to depend on a sister-colony.

The interior of the Houses of Legislature is decorated largely with "Keen's cement." The facility with which this material can be moulded into the thousand and one delicate cornices and ornaments that cover the walls and ceilings, its intense whiteness, and its capability of taking a dull polish are noticeable features; but on examination of the composition ornaments in older countries after the lapse of a generation or so, one appreciates the truth of the fact that this decoration, though a thing of beauty, is far from a joy for ever.

The Chambers require to be seen by gas, not daylight, for by the strong rays of the sun the decorations in prismatic colours, the grooved plinths and columns, the gilded cornices and capitals, and the vast glass gaseliers which hang down with thousands of cut glass drops from the centre of the rooms, look somewhat overdone, and more gay than grave. Plain distempered walls and ascetic hangings and fittings somehow would be more appropriate to rooms where the weighty matters of the State are discussed than are these decorations, which savour of the ball-room or fashionable hotel and drawing-room.

Why make the Chambers gaudy and tinselly when, with the same materials available for decoration, barring the gaseliers, they might have been imposing and consistent? I always had a horror of cut-glass drops from childhood; perhaps it was from the remembrance of the chastisement I received once on a time for breaking open a drop to find out where all the pretty colours came from. However, though one has time for these reflections by day, at night, when the Houses are sitting, ears are more in requisition than eyes, sounds more attractive than sights; and by gas the colours look less crude, the gilding less glittering, and as the fittings are of dark wood, one almost begins to get reconciled to the elaborate decorator who tried his florid hand here.

The Legislative Assembly, which corresponds in many points to our House of Commons, affords, or at least some of its eighty-six members do, food for recreation and thought on occasion. To wit.

One evening the following scene took place. It appeared that a certain official had been dismissed in a way disapproved of by the Opposition, who had become rather exasperated by the refusal of the Ministry to grant an explanation. As the matter was dismissed the Opposition could not raise it again, but they adopted the time-honoured method of obstructing some Ministerial Bill for some local improvement.

One honourable member, in a jocular though unconvincing speech, told the House the Bill would not only fail to improve but would actually be noxious to the locality. An honourable member on the Government benches rose to reply, and in "vary brawd tônes" began to denounce the speech of the last speaker as "a monsterouse fabrication."

At which the first speaker rose to a point of order "whether the word 'monsterouse' was parliamentary, as he failed to find it mentioned in any dictionary, and whether if the honourable gentleman meant 'monstrous' he should not say so." Never was petroleum thrown on fire with deadlier effect; the second honourable member, incensed by this interruption, waxed loud, and forgetting his dignity, began to animadvert on the past political career of his honourable friend (?) opposite in terms the reverse of complimentary, and went so far as to shake his fist in the direction of the honourable member, who appeared to think the whole thing some great joke, for the louder his adversary stormed the more he smiled, and by goading the poor gentleman by various frivolous points of order almost brought his assailant to the verge of madness. When, exhausted with his efforts, the assailant sat down, a friend of the first speaker took up the cudgels, and jumping up as though ejected from his seat—to use the language of pugilists—began to send in his blows right and left straight from the shoulder.

"What did the honourable member who had just sat down mean by characterising his honourable friend's conduct as 'monsterouse'? Let him explain the use of such language before the Legislative Assembly. Had he ever been to school? No; he remembered the honourable member when he hadn't time to go to school, as he was making money out of other folk's misfortunes. [The home-thrust was lost on all save the victim.] Monsterouse, indeed!! He knew the time when the honourable member could not pay his washerwoman. There was a depth of degradation. Monsterouse, indeed!! Let him take care again before he vituperated an honourable member on the Opposition benches who was an *honest* man, and who had more sense in his little finger than the honourable member had in the whole of his body. Why, he knew the time when the honourable member opposite would lie and fawn at the door of a Minister in office, and flatter and cajole until he could get some appointment to keep the pot a-boiling."

And so forth did the debater continue for some time, until foaming at the mouth with efforts Herculean but speech inarticulate, the honourable member vented all his spleen in a culminating stretching forth of his fist. After that affairs became complicated, strangers had to leave, and the Premier had to be sent for to keep his debating-class in order.

A Victorian Minister assured me that such a scene had not been witnessed since the early days. It is said that in the early days the debaters would, if argument failed, adjourn outside, and see which "was the better man of the two" with coats off in orthodox style.

I do not think that an exhibition of this sort is much to plume one's self on having seen, but as an Englishman, with the recollection of the recent Irish scenes in our own House of Commons, I cannot resist the temptation to heave a brick at a neighbour's cucumber-frame, knowing well that he either has paid or is about to pay me a similar attention.

The Legislative Council preserves a more dignified bearing, as the Upper House had need do. There, in place of excessive fervour, there almost appears to be a lack of general interest, and from various sources and my own experience I gather that these sage thirty-six* never damage themselves, their cause, or their constituents by the use of that lowest form of discussion, *i.e.* the substitution of vituperation for argument.

While exploring the Legislative Houses I ran against a bust of her gracious Majesty, executed in white marble, standing on a pedestal which at first sight appeared to be one of the highly ornate marbles that our Devonshire quarries produce. On closer acquaintance, and on the application of his cane by one of our party, it was found to be a clever imitation in oils.

* Though one can hardly say thirty-six minds with a single thought.

We explained to the watchful attendant that the investigation of our friend with the stick was in the interest of truth and art, but he did not accept the explanation, in fact would not stick at anything, and vented his righteous indignation—however the rest is too painful. The poor investigator's doctor's bill for lint and bandages is remembered in the doctor's surgery and in the victim's account-books to this day. Those of us who advocate the entities and consistency of art in our own heart of hearts rather sympathised with our bolder and more practical friend, but we could not afford the luxury of a doctor's bill, so we "passed."

Talking about doctors, you would not fancy that Melbourne is such a healthy place if you were only to notice the way in which the brass plate and red lamp are dotted around. As a matter of fact, its death-rate is low and its birth-rate high, and the medical men must get their fees like the Chinese medical men are said to, that is so long as the patient is well, and when he gets ill then nothing; for certainly many of these Melbourne Æsculapii look fat and flourishing.

American practitioners seem to make a good hit here as elsewhere, their spryness and 'cuteness captivate men who care more for these characteristics than the solid consideration and grave deliberation of many of their English brethren. It is said of an American M.D. here that he gave out that, by a new method of trephining, he could remove the rusty brain, cleanse and restore it. Men were incredulous, as they always are at the first appearance of some grand truth. But one more adventurous than the rest went to have the operation performed, as he complained of his brains having got confused and out of condition. The whole of the brain was successfully removed, and the patient was told to call in a day or two, when the brains would be ready cleaned. The surgeon chanced to meet him in the streets some six weeks after.

"Why," said he, "my dear sir, have you not been for your brains? They have been lying at my surgery ready for you these five weeks and more."

"Oh, thanks," replied the other, "but the fact is I don't want them now. Since calling on you I have got a nice Government appointment!" This is not a true story, *verb. sap.*, and the joke loses some of its point against Government officials since it is rather inapplicable to them. I think in very few places or countries will you find more courtesy and attention combined with intelligence than among Government officials in Melbourne, or for that matter throughout the colonies. However a wit must have his target to aim at, and the broader the mark the easier the hit.

While travelling around I presided at a discussion between two gentlefolks of opposite opinions on the question of franchise, which fairly well illustrated the prevailing opinions with respect to this vexed question. One, an advanced Liberal, by chance referred to the grand element in colonial politics that manhood suffrage gives. To which the other remarked that he looked on this so-called universal franchise with dread.

"America," said he, "is a standing warning to us of the decline in purity of the politics of a nation entirely ascribable to this manhood suffrage."

"Granted," said the other, "that this be the case there, your conclusion does not apply, for here we have at once started by educating our lower classes with an education such as many a middle-class boy or girl does not get, and that I count the very groundwork and foundation-stone on which to erect your universal franchise. You will at least agree that the highest ethical theory of legislation is that where the people is its own ruler."

"No," replied the other, "not so fast. Supposing for a second that that question of self-government which many good men and true have argued for and against be granted you, can you say that the experience of the past few years in countries such as America and England, where education has been making giant strides, justifies you in claiming for education the virtue of being a specific for the ills of corruption and impurity which are even now so prevalent at home and in the United States?"

"Yes, forsooth," replied his friend, "for although this improvement of education has been so recent that it is still being proved in the rising generation, its influence is indirectly felt in politics, and things are taking a turn for the better both at home and in the States."

"And yet," observed the other, "how are you going to get over the fact that there are many ignorant men now entrusted with a vote who are not fitting recipients on the score of their not appreciating their responsibility or understanding even the most elementary principles of the theory of legislation?"

"Here in the colonies this is hardly true, for the vast majority of the voters are such, by the very nature of their being here, as are more than ordinarily 'cute for their station in life and have received considerable advantages of education. Besides, to counteract the effects of an entirely democratic legislation, you have the aristocratic body of electors, the landed proprietors who return the Upper House, which forms a sort of governing check to hasty legislation and to republican tendencies." The subject got too dry here for the two disputants to tackle it any further, and as it may have become so for those of my readers who have waded so far through colonial politics, I will ring down the curtain for a few minutes— *an argumentum ad hominem* of a practical nature.

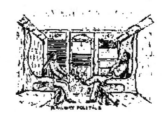

CHAPTER V.

Public Gardens.—The Era of Beauty.—Botanic Gardens.—The Mosquito and his Remarks.—Government House or Barracks. Which?—Reserves.—Cricket and Football.—Bicycling *sans peur* but not *sans reproche*.—Country round about Melbourne.—A Snake in the Grass.—Fern-tree Gully.—Boating.—Driving.—Racing.—Two Men and a half left in Town.—Recreation generally.—Suburban Villas.—Dingo and Dinginess exchanged for Beauty and Buildings.—The Shark Story.—Trip to Geelong.—How the Geelongites drew away Melbourne Commerce.

OH for another peep at the Public Gardens of Melbourne. Adopting the tone of the head waitress at "Mugby Junction," could you believe that there is a people so benighted as to spend considerable care in beautifying their public gardens, keeping them in splendid order, full of flowers, well planted with tree ferns, English timber and foreign trees, interspersed with models of Italian statuary?

When our great novelist Anthony Trollope visited the colonies, he would have us believe that this loathsome and servile state of affairs was not *in esse*, that the same proper air of weedy neglect, broken branches, and trampled grass and absence of flowers prevailed in the orthodox fashion which we know so well here at home; but now another era has come, and beauty has taken the place of ugliness, care of neglect.

On a hot summer day you can walk from the centre of Melbourne to beautiful oases of flowers and shaded walks in as many directions as you like within a few minutes, and there within easy reach of your office or club, almost within stone's throw of the busy mart, you may feast your eyes on avenues of oaks or elms, varied with rows or fine isolated specimens of fern-trees and exquisite glimpses of giant convolvuli climbing some twenty feet up trellis-work or trunks of trees, dotted with pure white or purple trumpets. Here even nature herself might take a hint or two in artistic arrangement and harmonious concord.

Then just over the river you step into one of the best-kept and loveliest Botanic Gardens you ever saw, emulating Kew in

Fitzroy Gardens, Melbourne.

the fineness of its lawns, and exceeding Kew in the multitude of plants and trees of a semi-tropical nature which grow in the open air. An artificial but extremely handsome lake attracts both your attention and that of the mosquitoes, who give unmistakable notices to you that you must quit the neighbourhood of an evening. Here indeed all in nature pleases, and only this insect is vile. A recent writer on Australia calls the Australian mosquito a poor meek-spirited, blasé creature after its American brother. If the author of this libel had placed himself for half an hour with palette on thumb in a shady nook of these gardens he would have withdrawn the libel with ample apology, and I am sure have had to confess that the "Australian bird could fix him pretty tarnation tight."

Beyond and above the mosquitoes another nuisance in these gardens is the proximity of the Government House, than which a more barrack-like building could scarcely have been conceived. It does not even do of an evening "in the dusk with a light behind it," like the attorney's elderly daughter. I should be sorry to disappoint Victorians, but I must confess that I should firmly refuse the governorship on the occasion of

Government House, Melbourne.

the next vacancy unless they promised to rebuild the Government House in better style.

The difference between the two incompatibles, the mosquitoes and the Government House, lies chiefly in this, that the former only affect the new chum (according to tradition), whereas the evil architecture of the latter sends both old and new chums into a fit of apoplectic contempt and dyspeptic disgust.

Besides these gardens there are a number of open spaces in and around the city called Reserves, where the grass and the trees grow in the orthodox fashion as in our parks at home; only sometimes the life of adventurous nurse or child receives a fillip of excitement from the close proximity of a centipede or a tarantula in the grass.

Wherever practicable of a fine afternoon or holiday, in these parks or reserves, you may see the good old games of cricket or football going on according as the season permits the one or the other, and besides this guerilla warfare, the chief clubs carry on pitched fights on their own grounds, often in the presence of many thousands of spectators.

Of a Saturday afternoon in winter you may see as many as twelve thousand folk looking on at *forty* lusty young fellows kicking a ball about and applauding freely and audibly. The method of playing this *bête noir* of careful mothers is less dangerous in appearance and effect than the methods of play in vogue in England, as the element of running with the ball is omitted, and consequently a man does not stand the chance of the ground coming up and hitting him on the nose so often as happens at home through his being "collared." The absence of touch-downs, of a string across the goal posts, and of scrimmages, and the presence of a concurrent umpire whose life does not seem to be a happy one, and the presence of a species of outer goal, some three times broader than the inner goal, were the most notable differences to an English eye. One writer on Australia asserts that this game was played in his presence in such a way as to afford considerable opportunity for spite and horse-play, and the indulgence of these objectionable intruders into sport was rather applauded by the spectators than otherwise. Though on the watch for something of the sort, I cannot say I ever saw anything approaching thereto, and old colonials confirm me that roughness is not a necessary, common, or belauded element in the game.

Cycling men in all stages may be seen in and around Melbourne, though at first sight one fears to think of the spills and shakes a man ought in fairness to get passing over some of these Australian tracks and high roads. I am assured that the bicyclists get the considerable advantage of their many-wheeled brethren, for they can get into a rut, and although their gaze is limited from the depth to which the rut plunges them in the bowels of the earth, yet they do at least find a fairly level bottom to ride on, and their only fear is of being buried alive by the masses of earth piled up on each side of the rut like a railway embankment.

The flatness of the surrounding country is rather an advantage than otherwise to cycling, and when the roads look less like ploughed fields in winter, this sport may be extended considerably beyond the vicinity of towns, though cyclists will ever lack one of the chief pleasures of the sport in the old country, namely rural and beautiful scenery as it is understood there.

After having passed through a hundred miles of gum-trees (many perhaps leafless all the year round through being ringbarked, and stretching up their white, ghost-like, gaunt arms to heaven as though invoking curses on their destroyers), and never seeing a cottage or a garden, a corn-field, or aught but grass, a few sheep here and there, and a horse-team or so, you begin to feel that, like the musical-box with its one tune, it is all being wound over again, and you long for a bit of hedge to replace the inevitable post and rails, and a warm-roofed and picturesque cottage or garden to replace the bran-new-looking corrugated-iron sheds that often serve well-to-do folk up country for habitations.

This is the dullest side of the picture I confess. As a rule the weather is finer than in the old country, the sun behaves in a respectable fashion and shines during his working hours, and the climate is more stimulating to the spirits than is our ofttimes rainy, muggy weather at home.

Then, again, within twenty miles or so of Melbourne, after passing through this dead-alive country of grass and gum-tree, you come in one direction to the extreme edge of the spurs of hills and gorges that run away from the Dandenory ranges, and here your eyes will be gladdened with such delightful nooks and glens, waterfalls and fern-trees, that you will forget the gum-tree altogether, and feel that life is worth living after all since you are permitted to rest beneath the shade of fern-trees fifteen, twenty, and twenty-five feet high, with great fronds often fourteen feet in length and of the most exquisite lace-like elegance and beauty. Besides, you will here have the excitement possibly of finding a snake which may be, and often is, really poisonous; just conceive the zest that the discovery gives you when you find yourself sketching the locale or picnicking at your ease with a viper crawling out of a rotten trunk or a hole at your feet.

One gully or glen in particular is a favourite resort for Melbourne folks, and is well worthy of its popularity. Fern-tree Gully, as it is called, is a wonderful wealth of moss-grown boulders, fern-trees, miniature waterfalls, and charming effects of light and shade, and is only one of a vast series of somewhat similar gullies that are said to run up all the gorges of the Dandenory ranges. The road thither is one of the broadest you may come across, and you feel as though you were driving through a broad field rather than a road, with the long stretches of grass on each side of you, and the only care you have to take is not to get lost and stray around looking for the track.

Of other sports and recreations in Melbourne, boating on the harbour and the river Yarra is in high favour, but in neither case do the disciples enter on their pleasure free from risk. The wind at Port Philip is treacherous and gusty, and often catches men at a disadvantage, and the Yarra is for a long distance from its mouth sluggish in flow, dirty in colour, and laden with strong odours not of the lavender-water kind.

The word Yarra means Plenty, and in its native origin was repeated (Yarra-Yarra), partly from a regard to poetry, partly also perhaps to impress on hearers the overwhelming fact of the magnitude of its waters. Comparatively with the little creeks around it is a river, but its name of Plenty is still appropriate even in these times of latter-day misapplication of terms; for in that it has plenty of smells, if the native word for smell were only added to the original Yarra I am tolerably certain the name would be more pleasing than the reality.

Many parts of the river are pleasant to look upon, fringed as are the banks with weeping willows of great size and delicate colouring, and with the gardens of some more adventurous townsfolk. Lower down near its mouth it has been broadened and dredged, but affords no very healthy spectacle when the steamboats leaving or arriving stir up the thick black mud unctuous and greasy from the bed of the stream.

Riding and driving are by no means such cheap luxuries in this city as we at home imagine they should be. Although horse-flesh is cheaper than at home, labour is much dearer; fodder is much about the same in price.

Should Harry wish to take his sweetheart for a spin he will have to pay as much here as he would at home, perhaps more, because there are not so many grades of conveyances here to suit everybody's purse. Of course our friend need not complain of the high price he may pay for his treat, for the dearness of labour —the high rate of wages—is the very factor which most likely enables him to provide his lady-love with this luxury. If he is worth his salt as a bricklayer he may earn eight or ten shillings a day; if he be a skilled artisan, or labourer, or miner he may make his four or five pounds a week; and even as an unskilled drawer of water and hewer of wood he may command his two pounds. If he be a clerk he is probably not much better off than the skilled artisan *mutatis mutandis*, for over here there is an excess of would-be gentlemen and a comparative dearth of skilled manual labourers.

Whatever our friend is he will probably go out to the horse-races when they take place, as the principal races involve a public holiday. Talk about an exodus, why on the Melbourne Cup day (and who has not heard of that?) you will hardly see two men and a boy in the city. On one occasion recently 180,000 people attended races at Flemington race-course, near Melbourne, and the city itself boasts only a population of 300,000 or thereabouts. Fancy more than two and a half million people from London going to the Derby, and you may gain some idea of the fact that when the Britisher removes himself to the Antipodes he is determined to make his life a fairly pleasurable one.

A book on Australia would not be complete without a chapter on the sports and recreations, even when written by a non-sporting and melancholy author. Why, it would be better to publish it minus a binding than to omit the catalogue of amusements shortly referred to, and the mention of the twenty-two regular legal holidays and numerous half-holidays that Victorians in the towns enjoy.

And they do really enjoy their holidays. The Frenchman who thought that John Bull took his pleasures sadly should see the Melbournians on a Saturday or general holiday. A brighter tone must necessarily prevail where the air is so much clearer than in London, and it is certain that the general feeling among the lower classes is lighter and healthier than in the old country. The only fear is lest the recreations should absorb too much of the time of these brothers of ours. They live in a climate which is warmer and more conducive to ease than that of England, and therefore it would be dangerous for them to go within even a measurable distance of the indolence that characterises the ease-loving South Europeans or the lotus-eating Egyptians, whose holidays and climate respectively have not tended to educe steadiness, progress, or great application.

If a fresh arrival or "new chum" go anywhere in the immediate vicinity of Melbourne he will find such handsome villas, mansions, and cottages, festooned with flowering creepers, shaded by deep, delicately latticed verandahs, and ensconced in handsome gardens, as will astonish him over and over again. Talk about the colonials only looking after money, he will say, why that must be rank heresy and *scandalum magnatum*, which all these big-wigs in handsomely built and furnished houses and gardens daily and hourly traverse.

As you peep through the elaborately decorated iron gates of a house at Toorak—the fashionable—or Kew or Brighton—the homely and comfortable—you get a glimpse of receding lawns set in beds and banks of flowers, verandahs with screens of abutilon, jessamine, magnolia, and a thousand and one flowering plants and shrubs, that only whets your appetite for more; and should you be fortunate enough to get the *entrée* of one of these little paradises you will be able to feast your eyes on a wealth of colour and verdure that will veritably transport you.

It is not so very difficult either to get this *entrée*, for Melbourne folks are proverbially hospitable and open-housed, and are pleasantly proud of showing the new chum how they can "fix things up" near the South Pole. And all this wealth of art and culture, beauty and ornament, now stands in the place of what the pioneers fifty years ago called a "howling wilderness" of grass and gum-trees, presumably called howling because of the native dog or dingo, which can freeze your marrow-bones with the noise it makes.

Brighton, which is a suburb on the bay of Port Philip—that inland sea—offers a very fair apology for the sea-side. The distant though narrow inlet from the ocean is not perceptible, and you can fancy yourself on the sea-shore with the greatest sense of realism, particularly when you are out bathing and a shark has a *penchant* for the lower half of your body. Accidents in bathing with these pirates of the deep were not at all uncommon until enterprise erected palisading around bathing spots, and so baulked the fish of their meals.

While I was in Melbourne, on cutting open a shark that had been caught the fisherman found a human head in the fish's interior, which, to add to the horror of the episode, was recognised by a gentleman as the head of a son who had gone out boating a day or so previously. Connected with the identification came a ghost-story of the spirit of the drowned lad appearing to his father and telling him of his fate; but as this happened after the finding of the remains, and as the spirit was too watery, the majority of well-thinking colonials, who like their spirits above rather than under proof, couldn't swallow it, in which they appeared to have fallen short of the shark.

Brighton is to the east of Melbourne on the bay shore, and deserves all due praise; but the railway ride to Geelong along the western shore of the bay is not one to inspire any but the ultra-enthusiastic with lofty sentiments; for flatness is the most noticeable feature after West Melbourne smoke is left behind.

As we spin along a chatty colonial tells us the "yarn" of how the Geelongites compassed within their minds how they should build a railway, and thus draw away the wealth and commerce of Melbourne. While thus thinking about it Melbourne folks built the line, and, sad to relate, drew away what little business Geelong had. Thus saith a Melbourne man. Like most yarns, one or two discrepancies occur in it, the chief being that Geelong is a flourishing town with a trade all its own in the woollen line, its factories turning out many a yard of " protected colonial tweeds " of wonderful wearing capacity. The town itself is quiet after Melbourne, but in other respects partakes of Melbourne's characteristic features.

Snakes!

CHAPTER VI.

Ballarat.—Tom Tiddler's Ground without the Silver.—The Central Avenue.—Taken in and done for.—The "Lake."—Bulls and Bears.—The Chinese Quarter. "Johnny Chinaman welly much Seas Over."—The Pleasures of Opium.—Gambling more suited to Johnny than Gambolling.—Shark Soup and Puppy Dogs at a Discount.—The Chinaman's Character.—Europeans, Australians, Natives, and Blacks.—Corn-stalk and Gum-sucker.—The Band of Hope Mine.—Treading the Air.—Charging the Rock and Charging away.—The Process of the Gold-mine.—Economy *versus* waste.—A Touch of the Acid and a Thirst for Knowledge.—Suiting the Action to the Word.—The Out-put and the Put-out of the Mine.—A Journey around Ballarat.—The Early Days revived.—Tipperary Boys.—Where was the Law when the Light went out?—The Welcome Nugget.—The Eureka Stockade.—Sunday "at Home."—The Champagne Magnum.—Extremes meet.—Prospecting as it really is.—The Technological College Abused.

IF you are in Melbourne of course you must go to Ballarat. If you do not, one of those unpleasant "know-alls" will tell you that it was the one place worth seeing, in fact the most noteworthy spot in the whole of the continent. At this point your patience will be exhausted and the consequences varied.

The railway journey from Geelong to Ballarat is not worth lingering over. One feels, as one passes through the interminable forests of gum-trees and long stretches of yellow grass, that it would be a fitting punishment for some heinous crime to have to look on such a prospect for ever.

Once at Ballarat, the excitement of walking over streets paved with quartz, and lined with handsome shops, houses, banks, and buildings of all sorts and conditions, within easy reach of the precious metal, overcame the feelings of our critic so much that he omitted to speak caustically for once. The greed of gold filled his breast, and expelled all ideas of cynicism and attempted wit. The artist rushed to the first shop he could light upon and bought a great piece of india-rubber, which he keeps to this day in memory of all he did not sketch at Ballarat. Not that there is a surplusage of beauty; I cannot say I have seen an excess in that line in any Australian town; but of curiosities on all sides there was more than enough to transfer to black and white.

The principal street, that stretches right through the town, down one hill and up another, is almost one continuous double avenue of gum-trees of a most respectable size.

As we hesitate on our course of action, our time being limited, a friend comes down, puts us into a waggonette, of which there are a surprising number plying for hire, and whisks us away up to his house to dinner. After dinner off we go for a sail on the lake, as pretty an artificial bit of water as you might wish to see produced from its parent—an uninteresting, unhealthy swamp.

Botanic gardens, as in most colonial towns of importance, there are here, though as yet in their childhood. However, the enterprise and love of beauty displayed by the good folk of Ballarat in blocking up the swamp, building fine paths all around, and planting willows, gums, and ornamental trees as a deep fringe to the lake, speaks well for the good taste and foresight of the civic fathers.

Now again for a stroll through the town, where we see the knot of brokers and merchants standing out in the street outside the building called an Exchange, rather for the sake of euphony than aught else, buying and selling gold shares and stocks. This custom, of which an exact counterpart is seen even in busy Melbourne, attracts the new chum's attention, and he naturally lets drop a sort of holy doubt lest the familiarity of the populace with those fearful animals bulls and bears might not make them irreverent. Fancy Capel Court coming out during 'Change hours in a body, and standing around in Cornhill or Threadneedle Street; no longer would the laity preserve that holy respect for "firm stocks" and "falling operations," that now fills their minds, as, with half-lifted eyes, they hurry away from the *sanctum sanctorum*, for fear of being supposed to have listened to the noisy proceedings within and being ejected as " No. fourteen hundred."

Past the Exchange we come to the Mechanics' Institute, where the librarian shows us through his realms of 40,000

Lake Wengarei, Ballarat.

volumes, almost one book per head of the population of Ballarat, discoursing to us of their scientific, historical, and generally useful character.

Here, too, is the monument erected by the mechanics, clerks, and others of Ballarat to their eight-hour labour deity.

Now as we proceed through the town in the gloaming our nostrils scent quaint smells, not pleasing, yet not unpleasant. We soon find out what it all means. We are coming to the Chinese quarter, where opium is being smoked and various articles of food of an extraordinary character sold and consumed. Here we are joined by a police inspector and Chinese interpreter, and thus reinforced make our way into various queer holes and corners.

This quarter is quiet, and as the night gathers in is quite hushed; so few lights seem to be burning that you would fancy all the inhabitants are gone to bed. We soon found out that this is not the case, for, walking into one hostelry kept by Li Hung Shi, we get a strong sniff of the sickly odour of the opium, and pushing aside a heavy curtain at one end are fairly in the midst of the operations.

The room we are now in is small, and the couch that extends across it almost fills it up. A couple of topers stretched on the couch are enjoying the enervating poppy juice; though they are not yet in the thraldom of sleep, their glazed eyes and slow movement and utterance betoken that they are some "half seas over." One has finished his third pipe, and the host is preparing him another. He takes a little portion of the thick gummy juice out of a bottle, winds it on a long needle, and, ever turning it round over a flame, after three or five minutes melts it into a fluid of the consistency of treacle. He then scrapes the pill of heated juice off the needle on to the small orifice of the pipe, and hands over the pipe to the smoker, who then takes up the running by holding the pipe vertically over the flame of the little lamp by his side, making the opium boil and seethe, and leisurely and appreciatingly, so as to get the full value for his money, does he suck in the insinuating opiate.

A few minutes and all is over, although the vapour is economised in the large bowl of the pipe and very little is expelled from the mouth, and with a grunt of satisfaction the smoker sinks back on the far from cleanly couch, and if he has had his fill retires into realms of bliss, or if not, awaits stolidly and patiently the refilling of his pipe; or perhaps, and we are told this is a very general custom, many so-called respectable Chinese come nightly for their whiff or two, and go away again long before they are muddled, just as the honest English tradesman goes to the village tavern and quaffs his half-pint, and returns a merrier though still sensible man.

The next hostelry was serving the double purpose of an opium den and a gambling hell. One of the gambling tables was in full swing as we entered, but the presence of the inspector was a signal for some confusion, as when schoolboys are suddenly found doing something unorthodox by their pedagogue. But the inspector reassures them, and the merry game of cards and dice goes on.

We are told that the method of gaming is too hard to be explained, and the Chinese guide says that if he tried "he should take all night about it," so one of our party with delicate nasal organisation prays for a release from such an impending purgatory. My European friends, resident in Ballarat among the Chinese as they had long been, had not the remotest conception of the method of playing, as they too had always been told it was too complicated to admit of explanation.

However, this was not the striking point; it was not the play but the players that attracted our observation. What a contrast to the self-satisfied greasy fat face of the Celestial who acted as croupier were the haggard, lean, often half-starved faces and dirty garments of the Chinese diggers who were gaming with their hard-earned pile of gold-dust with the hope of increasing it, a hope, in more cases than not, futile. The feverish hollow eyes and thin yellow scarred cheeks of some of them pointed a stronger moral than ever did goody-goody book, and one felt more than half inclined to pity the poor fools who after working with the sweat of their brow all day for a week or so, had thus laboured only to fatten the bulky pockets of the sleek and shining Celestial who presided.

The purpose of these hostelries in the way of providing food seemed to be subordinated to the opium and gambling interests; but the accommodation for would-be diners was comically secluded; each one was provided with a separate little cupboard-like partition, where one man could just get in and sit down to a table in front of him, like a prisoner in a cell, only more so. Sociability and chop-sticks don't seem to agree over here in Australia.

The kitchen of one Chinese inn was interesting from a nasal point of view. The numerous pots and pans that stood on a stove some five feet square in the centre of the kitchen gave forth ancient and fish-like smells, which in many cases heralded the nature of their sources or sauces.

The Chinese tea made *à la China* was of a most delicate straw colour, delicious aroma, and so superior in taste to the European decoction that one could hardly credit the identity of the two articles.

In another inn, again, a lottery was being drawn, and our conclusions that the Heathen Chinee outside his own country, at any rate, delighteth in games of chance were confirmed by our Chinese guide, who assured us no man was too poor to buy a chance or a share thereof in one of the many lotteries always being promoted.

The food in the Chinese stores, at least such as consisted of non-European articles, was neither pleasant to the smell or sight. One leather-like-looking odorous substance was dried fish, we were told, and required to be "muchee boil." To our smiling inquiries for puppy dogs, our guide and his compatriots expressed themselves in terms the reverse of complimentary to the gastronomy displayed in the selection and mastication of these immature canines; and as for bird-nest soup, that was far too great a luxury in these hard times and dear markets.

The Chinese here, as elsewhere in the colonies, have the character of being a mild, inoffensive, hardworking race, seldom if ever directly giving the police trouble, though the assaults by the jealous whites on these honey-sucking bees have been frequently the cause of magisterial judgment. They are physically as well as mentally below the mass of the whites; nay, in many cases the Chinaman is a most ignoble coward; but that is no reason, as magistrates wisely say, why the assaults committed on the Celestials should be dealt with less severely than those on their less heaven-favoured brethren; on the contrary, in some cases the pains and penalties for such offences are made harder than ordinarily as a lesson to such cowardly assailants.

There is even now a considerable prejudice entertained against the weavers of pigtails by the whites, which is partly derived from the old standing prejudice generally entertained by civilised nations to a Chinaman on account of so-called barbarous habits and customs, and it is also due to the fact that a Chinaman will take a job and thrive on it at a rate of wages on which a white could barely exist.

One noteworthy feature is the absence of Chinese women. Among so many thousand Chinamen that inhabit Australia alone the Chinese women can almost be counted on one's fingers, but these wily "Johnnies" seem to see charms outside the almond-eyed, small-footed female Celestial, for in many cases they have European or English-speaking wives of unimpeachable respectability and notable good-looks, yet the Chinaman is not as a rule half so pleasant to look upon as the average Briton. "Why then," folks ask, "do these girls, who are in great requisition as wives for the whites, go and marry the yellow-skinned ones?" Rumour hath it that these white wives are accorded a liberty and a position by their Chinese marital admirers which they would never receive at the hands of those of their own race, and that this is one if not the sole reason for the mixture of the races.

This mixture of Chinese and English blood is looked on with some amount of apprehension by the "know-alls," for they say it is plain that the physical cowardice and want of stamina of the Chinese being such as it notoriously is, their progeny must to a greater or less degree partake of their ancestors' qualities, and thus the race of Australians must seriously degenerate.

In speaking of Australians at the present day is meant those who are by birth or naturalisation subjects of any of the Australian colonies. The vast majority of these are sprung from English-speaking forefathers, but if born here in Australia are generally termed natives, or Australians pure and simple.

The aborigines are commonly called "blacks," not "natives," and it is the confusion of these terms, Australians, natives, and blacks, that has formed the subject of many mistakes outside the colonies. For instance, the other day a lady friend at a fashionable dinner was telling to her neighbour that a native of Australia was present, and was astonished at hearing her neighbour say, "Oh, you are laughing at me, there's no Australian girl here, for one could easily distinguish a black face."

In different parts of Australia the natives are variously nicknamed; thus I heard a New South Welsh shepherd call a Victorian "a corn-stalk," while the Victorian retaliated with the epithet of "gum-sucker." These terms are not, however, apart from other circumstances, to be taken as opprobrious epithets. Far from it; a Victorian will proudly boast that he is a cornstalk, and a New South Wales man glory in *his* cognomen, while a Queenslander is equally distinguished by the title of "banana-man."

Some travellers assert that there is a very observable difference between the native and the European colonist. They say the men grow slimmer and taller, the women rather plumper. Although I set out with the determination of finding out all I could, I could not discover any very marked indications in this direction. As in the old country, so here, you come across all sizes, thin and stout, long and short; the only difference so far as I can see between the colonist and the native being one of complexion, which in the new-comer speedily loses its pristine delicacy, as a few years of the Australian sun thins his blood and tans his face.

Being at Ballarat of course we had a peep at the gold-fields in and around the city. This a man cannot well help doing, for here and there in the township itself an old deserted claim warms up the side of the road with its strong gravel colour, and from all positions of the city of any height you may see mounds—great hills of pounded rock of varied hue, with the poppet-heads close by indicating the mouth of a gold-mine.

Our kind host introduced us to the manager of one of the most famous deep gold-mines in the township, namely the Band of Hope and Albion, and after peeling our outer garments and assuming the canvas articles provided for the purpose, big water-boots, an old hat, with a candle in hand, we adjourned to the poppet-head in such a guise that our own mothers would have passed us by. There are three of us to go down, and the cage certainly doesn't look over big to hold us; but being re-assured by the manager saying that four are frequently, nay usually, accommodated, and blessing ourselves that we are not aldermanic in our proportions, we step in, fetch in all prominences, such as toes, noses, or elbows, likely to get caught by the sides of the pit, the signal is given, and for a second or so we feel as though we are being lifted from the ground, so rapidly do we fall.

The sensation was in no wise disagreeable; but on nearing the bottom the sudden checking of our downward course by the engineer up above caused us all to feel as though we were ascending. The engineer has in front of him a little weight, which runs up and down a scale with the various drives and seams indicated on it, the little weight showing the exact position of the cage in the shaft, so that he can regulate the movements of the cage to a nicety.

Arrived at the bottom, some eight hundred feet from the surface, we wended our way along the white "drive" or passage, which was throughout headed up with timbers and cross-pieces, and after having, notwithstanding the caution of our guide, repeatedly tried the solidity of our heads on the roofing, we came across two men at work, one holding the drill and the other hammering it home, preparing for a charge. The work was monotonous in the extreme, but hard and warm for the employed, as the moist drops on their brows proved, for although ventilation was carefully attended to, the temperature down below here was considerably higher than up above at that time of the year (namely winter).

No gold was visible in the shining quartz rocks that lined the gallery here nor in the rubbish that strewed the ground; but farther along excitement reached a high pitch, for after having climbed through and up ladders with imminent peril of a lump of quartz coming on one's head from a shoot up above, we espied a speck of gold in the surface of the quartz wall. But to no purpose; the rude hammer of the workman broke down a large section of the rock, and the speck was lost like a needle in a bottle of hay. As the miners in this "stope," a sort of a branch or upper drive, were charging their work with a few ladlefuls of blasting powder within a foot of their candle, we stood and contemplated the picture of this wondrous foolhardiness which in the operator seemed intended skill. However, as the charge was likely when it fetched away to have filled us with something more than wonderment, we stayed no more, but hastily retreated in time to hear the dull boom of the explosion some yards away.

A shaft descended some eighty feet still lower than where we then stood, and down we went. The only novelty was in the method of descending, by standing on the rim of a great bucket, with a plentiful shower of water dripping all around and fighting with the candle for very life.

Our inspection of the lower drive revealed no further signs of the precious ore than the above, and so we were fain, after picking up various specimens of quartz, pyrites, and the drift rock, to reascend to the surface and shake ourselves free of the ton and a half of clay and water that seemed likely to change us into terra-cotta figures. After having assumed our proper clothes and brushed our hair with a venerable comb containing three and a half teeth (actual computation), we were guided around, and followed the quartz through the various processes to which it is subjected.

Here it comes up the shaft in the little truck, of which we saw some specimens below; now it runs down an inclined set of rails to the crushing shed, where it is disposed into huge funnels or feeders, which lead down to the mills or enclosed pans, where the stampers make it look very small indeed.

The din of these fifty stampers all working together, added to the rattle and noise of the machinery, required one to talk in language above a whisper; in fact, so loudly did our guide explain all things that we could almost distinguish the words falling from his lips in big capitals. A stream of water running through the mills mixes with the crushed quartz, and carries it through the sieve-protected side over a mercurial plate and a series of blankets, one below the other, which serve to catch most of the particles of the precious metal not caught by the amalgamating mercury. The blankets are taken up at certain periods, and the gold collected by shaking and scraping. The rest of the muddy liquid, after depositing the iron pyrites in great troughs, runs out and away into the valley below, carrying, it is said, often as much as one-third of the gold, which cannot be saved by the present process.

The iron pyrites is roasted to free it of sulphur and arsenic; the latter is condensed and deposited, and the remaining product, red oxide of iron, sold for paint or knife-cleaning. This last operation has of course nothing to do with the extraction of gold from quartz; but it conveys some idea how carefully and economically the mines are worked nowadays, in comparison with the mode by which they used to work them formerly, when some 20 per cent. was lost of the possible earnings by carelessness. That a vast quantity of the gold thus crushed has been lost is proved by the fact that the creeks down which the old rubbish and quartzose water used to flow yield from their beds sufficient gold to pay the Chinese for their working, and, according to all accounts, would make the fortune of any one who could extract all the gold from a few hundred yards at a cheap rate.

After collection from the amalgamating plate and the blankets the gold is melted, the mercury redistilled and condensed, and the precious metal is turned out of the plumbago-pot and assayed. The assaying work seemed so easy that one member of our party burned to turn assayist there and then.

"Only a scrape of the metal and a touch of the acid, and there you are, don't you know."

He was *not* all there, however, when *he* got a touch of the acid instead of the gold; he seemed to be aching for higher branches of knowledge, for he jumped about and danced around most enthusiastically, invoking the mythological deities. A lump of gold had just been turned out of the cooled pot, and was wrapped up in a shred of brown paper and weighed, to find its value, on a pair of scales such as a grocer uses to weigh his sugar. Here was an anticlimax.

Having got back to the office at the entrance of the mining property without any piece of "colour," we naturally clamoured for a piece of quartz showing a strong streak of gold which we found within. The old Scotchman in charge assured us it was not in his power to give us anything, but if while his head was buried within his desk searching for articles to show us (here he suited the action to his word), we ran away with the lump aforesaid (we suited the action ditto), why, it was no fault of his!

The mine at that time, before we ran away with the lump, was yielding fourteen pennyweights to the ton of quartz crushed, and could be carried on without a loss with only a return of four, so we learnt. Queensland miners affect to despise these figures, since they aver they can turn out three, four, or six ounces to the ton from their mines. Ballarat may, however, affect to pass over these "nouveau-riche" remarks, for she has all the solidity of nearly thirty years' production, whereas few of the Queensland mines are out of their teens, and many of them have not yet got into them.

If any one of my readers has a kind friend at Ballarat who wishes to take him for a "pleasant" drive round this El Dorado, trust him not, he's fooling thee. Once you are out of the town and on the old gold-fields, you see before you a far-stretching graveyard with all the graves dug ready and the yellow gravel heaps flung up by their sides, little herbage, and even scantier foliage. The heaps of "mullock" lie there just as they were left some ten, twenty, or thirty years back when their weary diggers, after having well-nigh broken their backs and hearts with continual digging and grubbing for the gold grains that came so fitfully into their pans, left the place with a sigh or a curse (more often the latter), saying to their partners, if they had any, "Ding this hole, it's a duffer; let's try another."

Oh the "yarns" I heard about the gold-fields of '51 to '58, with their tent-city of 20,000 gold-diggers,* their excesses and their depressions, their feuds and their riots.

Here on the sandy plain a series of little holes, not more than a yard cube, stretch out from a larger one like the spokes of a wheel. These form an example of the "shepherding" that took place twenty and thirty years back. Perhaps it was bruited about that "two coves had made a good venture just above the far bend of the creek." Down came a mob to see the hole and hear for themselves, and if the hole looked promising they pegged out their claims and dug little holes where they fancied that the streak of gold would run, supposing the parent hole turned out really good. A certain amount of work had to be done to warrant the retention of a claim. This work was thus carried out by the speculators, who sat dangling their legs in their infant pits "shepherding their claims," awaiting with anxiety the course of events, which in this case meant the run of the vein, which too often resulted in no further nourishment being given to their premature progeny.

Who has not heard of the "new chum" being taken in with a "salted claim," a "pit" sold for a £10 note in which a

* The population of Ballarat gold-field has been variously estimated from 20,000 to 80,000; the difficulties which meet one and prevent an accurate estimation of a shifting population are obvious, and at Ballarat were rendered greater by the hostile feelings of many, even the better class of diggers, towards the authorities by reason of the excessive license fee and its collection. It is stated on authority that the mining population of the gold-fields of Victoria in 1855 was 100,000, of which one-half may be estimated to have been located at Ballarat.

nugget worth a few shillings had before been "planted"? Who has not read of the stirring scenes enacted when a night fossicker attempted to wrest with a loaded five-shooter the hard-won dust of some lonely digger? Who again has not heard of the Eureka stockade with its melancholy history of needless bloodshed, for which the then premier, Mr. Latrobe, cannot be held irresponsible?—where scores of lives were lost in asserting a principle afterwards conceded by the Victorian Government, when the excessive licence required to be paid by a gold-digger of 30s. per month was replaced by a gold duty of 2s. 6d. an ounce, a "miner's right" being, however, still required, costing 20s., now 5s., per annum.

Who again cannot picture the Tipperary boys, a gang of ruffians, mostly convicts, who borrowed their name but naught else from the Emerald Isle, as they wandered around seeking a more fortunate but lonely digger who perhaps had just discovered *colour*. As he is eagerly bending over, with the flush of long-delayed pleasure, and the thoughts of home and what the gold would bring him, scraping away in the corner for his dear life as the golden grains and nuggets come tumbling out, he sickens as he hears—

"I say, mate, you seem to have struck luck; here, just tumble up out of that and let your betters in, or we'll smash your brains in." Should he resist they are four to one, and he is lucky if he gets off without the threat being executed. *Sic transit gloria auri.*

"Where was the law to cope with all this lawlessness?" our kind friends in the old country say. The law, in the persons of magistrates and police, was gone a gold-digging too. What was the good of a man taking a salary of a few hundreds a year when he might make that with a single stroke of the pick. Wages were so high, for labour was so scarce that a carpenter or bricklayer might earn £8 and £9 a week.

Who has not heard or read of the "Welcome" nugget, found close by a disused claim upon this very gold-field, which weighed over 2,196 ozs., or, for that is more intelligible to every-day folk, was valued at £8,000? All these things you might have heard or read, but there we had the advantage, for we were listening to the narratives of men who had experienced all of them. My host had run against the Tipperary boys, had had a narrow squeak of receiving his *congé* from a night fossicker, had seen the Welcome nugget carried down to the Bank in a horse-feed bag, and had joined in the joke at the expense of the cunning finders, who did not realise that as a rule it doesn't require three men to carry a bag of horse-feed.

Another friend had witnessed the slaughter at the stockade, and with care did they point out the place where once stood the tent of the head police officer who ordered the shot to be fired at the offending light after the *couvre-feu* had sounded, and thereby shot a digger dead. Another had been robbed of his "dust," taken when in charge of the military escort who were attacked on their way to Melbourne and killed to a man at a place we were shown not long after.

One friend, a staid and steady supporter of the municipality, told me with glistening eyes of the watch he and his mates had to keep for a few days armed to the teeth, because they were making a "big haul." Sunday was as a rule a day of rest, but one memorable Sunday they had to turn to and clear out as on ordinary days, as they had struck "colour" in plenty, and could not risk leaving it. Day and night had they to work without rest or wink of sleep until all was safely lodged in the Bank, and then—the most "rational" method of enjoyment at that time seemed to be a quiet "spree," when in a few weeks or days, according to the nature of the "spree," the dust would all be "knocked down," and a fresh start would have to be made. Some "irrational" modes of enjoyment were to run-a-muck with a loaded revolver, making flying shots at all or any. Or again, a favourite method old diggers tell of was for the fortunate one to empty a number of bottles of champagne, probably at 20s. a bottle, into a bucket, and invite every passer-by to drink. Should he refuse, his head was forcibly ducked therein, and the bucket offered to the next comer.

The ways of the world are strange! One of the chief leaders of the Eureka riot, who was much "wanted" by the police on the defeat of the diggers over this wretched licence business, now holds a most respectable position in the colony; instead of leading men to break the laws, he now leads members of the Legislative Houses to make them. Many, too, of the leading men in Ballarat, from the mayor downwards, lawyers, doctors, architects, storekeepers, preachers, and others, had once walked, with pick and shovel on shoulder, and pan and cradle in hand, over the self-same spot where their villa residences, their offices, or shops now stand.

Do not fear that a colonial magnate will be ashamed of retailing these earlier passages of his life. As you ask him the pertinent question, "Did you, too, make a pile?" he will say most probably, "Ay, and lost it too," and then will discourse with brightening eye and smiling face of the hundred and one incidents that made that happy-go-lucky life such a memorable, in many cases such a pleasant, one. One friend assured us that, though a happy husband and father, respectable, and respected by his neighbours, and in comparative affluence, he was never happier than when his only goods were pick and shovel, his only shelter a canvas tent, and his credit at the store fallen down to zero.

All this gloss and this excitement is gone now, and in its place is an untenanted gravel plain which resembles as aforementioned a gigantic graveyard which the sextons have left incomplete. Here and there you may see a man, perhaps a Chinaman, *prospecting* for the leavings of his predecessors, probably many of them dead as well as gone.

If you do catch sight of a few diggers, go along and have a look; the subject has lost some of its interest, and almost all its excitement certainly, but as you watch the digger gradually swilling out the dirt in the pan until nothing remains but a little mud, which with a clever sweep of the hand is jerked out, and leaves the gold dust behind, you will begin to realise something of the feeling that actuated men to throw up good positions and search for this precious metal with such eagerness. I declare if you stop long enough you will get an incipient desire to seize a pick and shovel and prospect for yourself, and talk as learnedly as did the digger just now of the average from this dirt being, as near as he might guess, about ten penny weights to the ton.

Here, too, are one or two of the Chinamen we saw last night retrieving their losses at the gaming table by washing over some of the dirt already perhaps washed over twice by their less careful predecessors.

At Ballarat there is another of those stumbling-blocks to the illiterate in the shape of the Technological College. However, its name is the only frightful part about it, as its exhibits in the mineral line are many and varied, and its assistant secretary most courteous and attentive.

Though I advise a visit to this seat of learning, I should warn visitors against leaving under the same circumstances as we did, for most of our party had a firm conviction that we were now in the Palæozoic period, and that gold was but a fossil form of the *Platypus ornithorhynchus*. In fairness to the secretary, I should say that it was no fault of his that "things got mixed" in this way; the fact was that at dinner-time some of our party, unaccustomed to strong drink—but there, we must speak gently of the sins of others, and ascribe it to the fact that it was their boots only that were tight.

CHAPTER VII.

From Ballarat to Melbourne.—Scenery at a Premium.—Rabbits and their Doings.—The Caudal Tax.—Dinner for One.—Marvellous Melbourne again.—Finance.—The Law and the Bar.—Melbourne University.—A Peep into Penbridge Gaol.—Solitary Confinement.—Harmless-looking Convicts.—Escape to Sydney from Temptation.—Up the Coast to the Harbour.—" Look at our *chef-d'œuvre*"—The Capacity of the Harbour.—What you may expect to see, and a great deal more to the same effect.—Sydney in the Distance.—Smoke *versus* Landscape.—Sydney Docks.—Middle Harbour.—Why is not Everything provided ?—Solitude in the midst of Bustle.—The Inner and Outer Domain.—The Arum.—The Aloe.

FROM Ballarat we took the coach towards Melbourne to "see the scenery." The driver of that identical coach must to this day think with bitter anathemas of his fellows on the box seat. For the incessant question was "Where is the scenery?" Let us hope the face of the country was then at its worst, certainly the weather had been until quite recently very dry, and foliage had suffered.

The one point noticeable was not of beauty, but of singularity. As we neared Melbourne, being then some thirty miles off, we approached a rabbit-overrun country which the vermin had cleared of every blade of grass and leaf of tree as high as they could reach up the branches. The bare brown earth was indeed a scenic variety after the yellow dry-looking grass and monotonous gum-tree. Regarding these devastated tracts of country from a wider point of view, one cannot help sympathising deeply with those squatters whose runs are thus ruined, and appreciate the terror of those who see the army of pests advancing nearer and nearer every year. The tragedy of Bishop Hatto and the rats is being reproduced in Australia with almost an equally tragic termination. The squatter, the Bishop Hatto of the colonies, is beset by millions instead of thousands, and has the poor consolation of having fellows in affliction.

The Victorian Government has adopted various and strenuous measures to stamp out the pest, such as offering a capitation bounty, the appointment of regular rabbit-destroyers and organised destruction of an advanced type. Of course in time these measures will bear fruit, but at present the frisky little vermin perks up its tail in contempt at the tax laid on its head; its contempt for organisation is not to be wondered at, as a pair of rabbits under favourable circumstances will before the lapse of ten years increase to *a million*. Melbourne housewives as a rule are rather averse to stocking their larders with the little rodent, as poison is commonly employed as a means of killing off the pest, and by chance a poisoned rabbit may get mixed up with some more wholesomely killed.

When the coach stopped for dinner at an inn or "hotel" (as these unpretentious-looking weatherboard houses-of-call pretentiously style themselves) on the way, a rather noticeable feature was that all the passengers of the coach had to eat off one and the same plate, which, had I not been prepared for colonial fashions, might somewhat have perturbed me had I not also been the only passenger. This coach was a kid-glove article compared with the usual type of up-country Cobb's coaches; its entrance was from behind, its springs were steel, and its paint was tolerably fresh; its work was of a quiet kind, as the surface of the road was comparatively even as colonial roads go, and little holding on was necessary. A cyclist could have enjoyed a run over a considerable portion of this road, an unusual enjoyment in the colonies on roads any distance from large towns.

Back in Melbourne, the last twenty or thirty miles being

travelled by steam, I made the most of my time in taking another look around. One begins to appreciate Melbourne after having been even for a short time up country. Marvellous Melbourne art thou called? Well in good sooth raise me up any town in fifty years from a couple of log huts to such a city as she now is, with her population of nearly three hundred thousand, and no one would or could justly deny her the title.

Gold is generally said to be the lever that has made her what she is. Gold has established the banks doubtless, and they who bought an ounce of gold at fifty shillings and sold it in England for nearly four pounds may certainly live on their past achievements, and think that their bank rate of 6 per cent., overdrafts at 8, and good wholesome securities at 7 or 8 are but trivialities compared with past glory. But something else has had a hand in making Melbourne, and that is wool, not as with the Scotchman is it *aw 'oo*, but *'oo* has had a vast share in the building of the palatial buildings and charming mansions that dot Melbourne as thickly as currants in a Christmas plum-pudding. Why money should be so dear when this same colony has exported over two hundred of the two hundred and seventy millions of gold sent from the whole of the colonies of Australasia since the first gold discovery, this riddle forsooth is for financiers, not for ordinary globe-trotters, to solve.

Colonial banks have a character for "grabbing;" whether founded on fact or no I may not say, as I was never grabbed. Folk say that the fly is *got* into the parlour and never gets out again. Let this be some consolation for the fly that the parlour is a very handsome one and its cage is ornamented both within and without in a most artistic manner, and the spider is most engaging and gentlemanly.

The fable of the spider and the fly naturally suggests the law courts. Here too should the unhappy fly ever get landed he will in Melbourne at least have the pleasure of knowing that he is in one of the most noteworthy edifices of the city, and has the pleasure of feasting his eyes on airy courts and offices, handsomely fitted benches, with ceilings and walls profusely decorated with mouldings and Keen's cement. If he still grumble at the six and eightpences he is incorrigible; rifle his pockets and turn him loose in the law library, where the few odd thousand volumes on Coke upon Lyttleton and *vice versâ* will so confuse him that he will never have the spirit to grumble again.

The profession here is not in such low water as their brethren of Pump Court at home would have one to understand *they* are. The bar is strongly represented, and is commonly said to be the best bar in the colonies (except by noted topers, who "back Menzie's hotel against the world").

A junior has a better chance of making his voice heard at an early date than at home, and should he acquit himself at all passably is bound to succeed. For one reason, a very small one I admit, the courts are easy to find, and the bewigged orator comes to the case fresh and ready, not with brain and body bewildered and exhausted as at home by the labyrinth he has had to thread to reach his destination.

From *lex* to *alma mater* does not necessitate a great jump either mentally or physically. You can take a waggonette or tram up to the college in a few minutes. A short walk along a pathway through grounds which might show more care, brings one in front of a battlemented building already covered with ivy, looking quite venerable. Small indeed; but then Oxford was once a mere four-roomed house, while at Melbourne they have started a long way in advance of that.

The University buildings are on three sides of a square, and do not provide for residence, which is afforded by the affiliated colleges in the grounds near at hand. In these buildings lectures are given and examinations held, while in the Wilson Hall close by, a fine lofty building with handsome groined roof, hammerbeams, and stained-glass windows, are held examinations and prize distributions. I have to record my thanks to the courteous and kindly registrar, who caused me to be conducted around and trusted me alone within the sacred precincts of that booky sanctum, the library. Such confidence could not be abused, and I left without bringing away any usual memento of my visit.

A visit to the colonies without inspecting one of their convict establishments would have been futile indeed. I meditated on the course to be adopted to inspect an interior. Two courses were open: one to get an order from the Home Secretary, the second to commit some offence against the law. I adopted the former, which procured civility and courtesy for me throughout the mazy precincts of the gaol—a most dungeon-like and forbidding building, standing "with its walls so stern and cold" at Pentridge. I will not weary the reader with an account of the armed sentries, the patent locking gates, the men's cells, their books, and so forth. The whole gaol is managed on English lines, the discipline being if anything a little less strict in certain reasonable directions, and equally severe where necessary.

One great consolation consisted in this, that if by the adverse hand of fortune one ever became "cabinned, cribbed, and confined," ventilation was most efficiently provided for, the diet was good, and the prison library varied and of easy access.

Solitary confinement is carried somewhat further than in the old country. My accompanying warder told me that a prisoner could receive half his term in solitary confinement, each term, however, not to last more than six weeks. A prisoner thus confined spends twenty-three hours of every twenty-four in his cell, seeing no one but the warder, the doctor, and perhaps a clergyman, with nothing to do, but a Bible to read, and a pound of dry bread, and as much water as he likes to drink. The remaining hour he spends marching up and down a small enclosure where he can see nobody, and can be seen only by the warder. What wonder that the man's brain becomes affected. The wretched felon may have been guilty of fiendish acts of brutality, but this requital is equally fiendish in its effects. As a rule, the terms of solitary confinement are short, seven or eight days at a time being found amply sufficient for its purposes, and the term is always determinable at the doctor's discretion.

As a rule the prisoners were very well fed—bread, meat, vegetables, and hominy porridge, being served out in ample portions, and they seemed to thrive uncommonly well on such diet. The dark cell for punishing refractory prisoners, with its darkness that might be felt, was pointed out to me, but is not often called into requisition for any length of time, as the most unruly "become amenable to discipline" in a few hours at most. The warders were all unarmed, save the sentries on the walls, this, according to their own account, being their safeguard rather than a source of danger.

"What would be the use," said one "of my having fire or side-arms? They could be turned against me in an instant. Whereas now if a row occurs we all use our hands and no much harm is done, the quieter prisoners as a rule coming to our assistance, with the motive amongst others of getting good-conduct marks, and thus curtailing their own incarceration."

As a matter of fact good conduct serves to deduct a portion off the term of every prisoner; even one sentenced for life has his life computed for him according to tables similar to an insurance company's, and thence is deducted a bonus of good marks, if he earns them, whereby he may leave before "the term of his natural life" actually expires.

On the whole the convicts were plain-looking, ordinary men. Their shaven faces made them appear somewhat at a disadvantage, but there was little of the Bill Sykes look that we at home hear so much of, and few were repulsive. I was somewhat struck at the liberty allowed the prisoners in the shape of conversation, though this license is rational enough if the conversation be of a wholesome character.

A second feature in the management of this gaol which exists in the old country establishments, is the separation of youthful offenders from their maturer brethren, thus preventing the deteriorating influence an elder in crime invariably has over his juniors.

Escape from the gaol without the complicity of the officials would be virtually impossible, as a lofty wall surrounds the whole building, towering some thirty feet high, on which are the cages of the armed sentries before referred to, who thus command a view of the whole prison, and can "pick off" a man, while themselves secure in their armoured boxes. Escapes are often attempted, but unsuccessfully according to the authorities and the press.

It is a fitting termination to the description of the glories of Melbourne, to describe the spot where the rights of its citizens are vindicated in actual fact, and as after Melbourne one naturally thinks on far-famed Sydney, the decree went forth that with bag and baggage we should travel thither. Two ways you may adopt to get there from Melbourne—by sea or by rail. The former course, if by steamboat, occupies about forty-eight hours, and probably acts as a corrective of high feeding and friendly hospitality, while the latter occupies by express about eighteen hours, and probably acts as an incentive to further high feeding, which the railway refreshment-rooms adequately provide.

If you want to see Sydney at its best, arrive there at early morning or dewy eve by sea. The country round from the heads of Port Philip towards Sydney lack in interest, as the boats go at a sufficient distance from the coast to render the hills only formless masses of sombre-looking greys. As we near Sydney, however, the heights of the Wollongong country show more distinctly, for we are steaming nearer into the coast, but even as yet no scenic features would warn the passenger innocent of all information thereon, of the charms that Port Jackson, the Sydney harbour, is going to open for him.

The day is gloriously fine, and as we near the white lighthouse of the south head of the harbour, the pilot boat glides out, and the ship rounds to and makes straight in for the open cleft between the "frowning heads"—frowning, indeed, very placidly to day under the genial influence of the autumn sun. A chatty colonial, who had been imbibing too freely of the cup that cheers, calls out, "There, me boys, now you may die in peace: you've seen the greatest achievement of the English race, the invention of this harbour." Far be it from me, an Englishman, to detract from the doughty deeds of our countrymen, but this seemed to the innocent bystanders rather a stretch in the way of "blowing," and their vanity was less tickled than their sense of humour.

Should a globe-trotter try to expatiate on the scenery of Port Jackson after so many and more powerful pens have tried, and only half-succeeded, he would probably call down on himself the wrath of all the visitants to this charming spot. But he who clothes himself in the inflated gas-bag of his own privacy can develop to his original dimensions after every adverse criticism he may receive.

To say that the harbour is the finest in the world for scenery as well as capacity, as some have said, is to make a statement implying an accurate acquaintance with every existing harbour, which few possess; but to say that in quiet romantic scenery it surpasses every other harbour in Australasia is, I think, quite within the bounds of truth and the paths of virtue. And when this is said it must be taken into consideration that it is as a harbour that it so surpasses other inlets in the coastline of these countries. Other inlets of the sea there are of vast size and depth both in Australia and on the west coast of Middle Island, New Zealand, and some of these far surpass in grandeur of scenery Sydney's placid haven; but these are not yet actually utilised as regular havens, and have no wharfage or other accommodation for shipping beyond bare anchorage.

In the harbour of Port Jackson all the navies of the world could lie without crowding, so local sailors say; and certainly if they did their seamen would have a very pleasant time of it, for Sydney folks make much of the advent of a man-of-war, British or foreign, and give the officers and crew substantial welcomes in the shape of entertainments and banquets.

As you enter this noteworthy piece of water from the sea, two great arms stretch up, with countless indentations, left and right, running amid tree-covered slopes and hills, bending here and there in an endless series of convolutions. These little coves which cut into the land in all directions, form some of the most pleasing features of the scenery, for from their excessive number and variety of direction it is impossible to see more than a very few at one time, and when you think you see the whole harbour you are by no means doing so; thus as the steamer glides by a fresh surprise awaits you at the turn of every headland.

It is a pity that travellers "blow" so much about this harbour, for even this scenery can be exaggerated, and if one has read many over-glowing accounts of a spot, the reality often does not receive the full due of appreciation it merits. However, there is a wide margin in Sydney Harbour for admiration; and though the colouring of the foliage (the gums) is not so charming or varied as it might be in New Zealand or England, the meeting of blue rippling water and tree-covered slopes, broken here and there by abruptly terminating rocks of varied hue, or here again in the shelter of a cove by the warm tones of a sandy beach add those features to the scene which call for the painter's pencil and brush almost as soon as he sees them. Even the sunken battery that commands the entrance to the southern arm of the harbour, where lies Sydney itself, smiles down to us with its grassy slopes and rocky surroundings as we move past its range; and as we stand up a straighter portion of the harbour and catch sight of Sydney in the distance, with its spires and towers standing up out of its green environment, its suburbs stretching on both sides (especially the southern) far down to the mouth, with villas embosomed in varied hues of Moreton Bay figs, Norfolk Island pines, and the like, and Government House with its embattlements shrouded in the lovely and variegated foliage of the Botanic Gardens, and see its shipping stretching down towards us on the placid bosom of the harbour, a sense of keen appreciation of the luxuries afforded the palate comes over one and all.

This tranquil enjoyment of the surroundings is doomed to be disturbed as we near the city by the scores of boats, from the ordinary row-boat to the respectable paddle conveying two or three hundred passengers, which shoot across our slowly advancing bows, freighted with men and goods. Men of Sydney, you must dispense with that hideous black smoke that issues from every funnel in the harbour, throwing often a thick roll of dirt across the landscape; you must also, amongst other matters, paint your villas in less prominent colours, as they stare in too

Battery Point, Sydney Harbour.

glaring a fashion from out the environment of their gardens. On the south side of the harbour this is especially noticeable, the north side being left more to nature and oysters.

The islands in the harbour have little to recommend them now, whatever they once had, for they mostly serve as military points of fortification, and so have lost their picturesque qualities. Garden Island looks at its best when seen through a fog with the sun behind it, according to the writer's experience, and the other islands follow suit.

Sharks are a prominent feature 'tis said here in the harbour, and when the new drainage works are completed, which carry

Sydney drainage to the sea direct some four miles overland, instead of emptying it into the harbour, these sharks will be its sole detracting feature. If all that is told about them be true, their nature must be as evil as that of "a certain elderly gentleman" himself, and an army of bishops is required to convert them and bring them to a sense of their evil ways. Not content with having a congregation of sharks of other seas, Sydney Harbour boasts a shark of its own, called the Port Jackson shark, a small though ferocious creature some three or four feet long. Other sharks have been captured twelve feet long and six feet in circumference, notably one in 1858, whose memory the fishermen still cherish.

Fortunately, the jolly tars who land at Sydney are not the prey of those legions of landsharks who disgrace our civilisation and docks at home. Of course where such confidence is displayed in fellow-man as by the man of the sea, there will not be wanting those to make capital out of him, but in the colonies generally there is much less excuse than at home for Jack's foolish and childlike though abused confidence; and at Sydney special provision, in the shape of a seamen's mission-hall hard by the docks, is made for his special guidance and comfort.

The quays and docks of Sydney are, after the harbour, the boast of the marine community, and in their dimensions and activity, crowded as they are with the ships of all nations, deserve the praise they receive.

Before we leave the harbour to the placid influence of the indrawing evening and the on-coming night breeze, which is cutting up its gilded western surface with gentle ripples, it were as well to explain what the right or northern arm has been doing all this while. It just cuts into the land similarly to this southern arm, and then goes wandering about in a delightfully unconventional fashion, until it gradually loses itself in coves, bights, and bays, and finally a little stream. It is called Middle Harbour, and is considered to comprise the finest—as it certainly does the wildest—portion of the harbour scenery.

Here, gentle readers, you may take a boat, disembark on a sandy shore, and then send your men-folks away with picks to knock off the luscious oysters that cover the rocks all around. Little crinkled shells have they, but to the lover of bivalves, the insignificant outward appearance in no way detracts from the flavour of the toothsome morsel to be found within on applying a hundred horse-power pressure. Picknickers grumble now that the oysters are supplied to them thus gratis, that "brown bread and butter and bottled stout does not grow around promiscuous-like." Was man ever satisfied?

You may take a ticket for a few pence, and be conveyed by a little steam ferry to a dozen spots all over the harbour, and alighting when, where, and how you please, rove around amongst natural scrub and flowers, ferns, waterfalls and rocks, within a few minutes of the seething mass of humanity in Sydney, as far for all practical purposes from the madding crowd, as though you were in the "backwoods of Canada." You have also the excitement occasionally of meeting a snake face to face, and engaging with the enemy in deadly battle, when "look out for squalls," if he be a black foe; if he once dig his fangs into your nether limbs, you will have but little time on this earth left in which to attack another of his brethren.

But you can bury yourself in the solitude of nature, without even crossing the harbour should you please, for the Botanical Gardens are within two or three minutes' walk of the busiest thoroughfare of the town, and are not yet affected by the bituminous coal used throughout the city. They comprise some of the most tastefully laid-out gardens in the world, and though in general care and keeping they do not equal those of Melbourne, their natural position, sloping down to the waters of the harbour as they do, gives them great advantages over their Melbourne rivals. Stately palms, tree-ferns, stags-horn ferns, wind-torn bananas, and various semi-tropical flowers, shrubs, and trees, as poinsettias, hibiscus, and the like, grow here like weeds at home, side by side with their English brethren, which contrast their deciduous and changeable foliage with the vivid greens of many of these their strange bedfellows who ne'er "forsake their garments for a while." Come any day but Sunday and a public holiday, and you will get such perfect solitude as would make the heart of the hermit of Malea to rejoice.

Here too, even nearer, stands Government House, with its park-like grounds, in which, if you have impudence enough, you may wander, notwithstanding the "bold milingtary chaps" at the gates, and perhaps catch a glimpse of the Governor and

Government House Sydney

Governess—I should say his lady—driving in or out in a neat and quiet landau. Or, again, close by, if you will not risk being bayonetted, you have the Inner and Outer Domain, the first a well-laid out garden with terraces, lawns, carpet-bedding, and a sprinkling of statues copied from the best works of art, showing their graceful, or as Aunt Towser might say, disgraceful forms, in pure contrast to the verdure all around.

The Outer Domain is timbered like an ordinary London park, and is sacred to the same purposes—a grand breathing-place, should Sydney ever become abnormally increased and choked for air, situated within a stone's throw of the centre of the city.

Speaking of Sydney vegetation suggests that the suburbs abound with American aloes and arum lilies. The uses of the first are manifold. The small boys around, unable to resist the kindred temptation that causes the English boy to whip his mate with a bramble, pull off the great fleshy leaves from their parent plants in the hedges and paddocks, for this purpose, reckless of the policeman's existence. The arum now grows wild; in many a wayside ditch it erects its glossy leaves and offers its lovely white cup to receive the refreshing showers of a Sydney October.

There are many other plants not indigenous growing around the villas and in the paddocks of Sydney, which testify to the fertility and equability of the climate. Palms and ferns grow cheek by jowl with poinsettias and hibiscus, abutilons, bougainvilleas, and many other flowering shrubs and plants, and render suburban roads gay for the larger portion of the year, while English deciduous trees strive harder and harder each year to dispense with their old-fashioned habit of hybernating.

Garden Island in a Fog

CHAPTER VIII.

A Bird's-eye View of Sydney.—The Paramatta River.—The Hawkesbury must be taken on Faith.—George Street.—High Houses and Narrow Streets.—Hansom *versus* Waggonette.—Tramways *versus* the Train.—The Sea Coast from the Town Hall.—Rosa Gully.—Botanising in Botany Bay.—The University.—Parks.—Church Spires in the Minority.—The Roman Catholic Cathedral.—The Houses of Legislature like the Lily of the Valley.—The Lower Form gets Unruly.—The Mint.—The Library.—The National Gallery.—Australian Artists at a Discount.—Government Offices.—Sandstone *versus* Bluestone.—Hotels and Clubs.—Sixpenny Dinners.—Poverty unnecessary.—Employment for all.—Domestic Servitude of the Mistress to her Servant.—Scarcity of the gentler sex.—St. Andrew's Cathedral.—Mayoral Sanctum.—"Walk across the Crossings."—Adventures in Cabs.—The Governor and Loyalty.—Beverages.

I CANNOT help thinking that the patient readers who have followed me so far may have recovered their breath, and be equal to the task of climbing to the top of the town hall with me, from thence to gaze over this Lisbon of the South Pole. The view well repays you for your trouble. It is a glorious Australian day, with the bluest of blue skies and the clearest of atmospheres. Far away to the westward you can distinguish the outlines of the range called the Blue Mountains, which rises as it were suddenly from the level country around.

Here to the north and east lies the harbour, a silver sheet busy with Liliputian craft. At this western end of the sheen a narrower but still indented expanse of water runs away to the westward in sinuous curves, winding here between low hills of foliage, broadening out there, with bright green mangroves as a bordering, and dotted with little toy-like steamers which are calling at the various outlying snugly ensconsed suburbs on either side of the river. This is the Paramatta River, famous for aquatic contests and orange groves.

Nearer in to the westward lie the wharves and quays, and the manufacturing portion of the town, which betoken great activity and business, but want in general pictorial interest.

Out away to the north the view is limited by the hills of the north shore, tree-covered to their summits, and as yet but sparsely built upon; beyond these hills lies the Hawkesbury River, that queen of all beautiful rivers in the estimation of the good Anthony Trollope, who beamed sweetly upon its waters and considered that it exceeded the Mississippi, which exceeded the Rhine, which exceeded the Dart, which exceeded all other rivers both small and great in beauty of scenery. You may see such scenery as you see on the Hawkesbury, however, *mutatis mutandis*, on all the rivers on this eastern coast of New South Wales, particularly to the southward in the direction of Wollongong.

A large portion of the city lies between the town hall and the western end of the harbour; and as the town hall stands in the principal thoroughfare, George Street, we can see a long distance down its busily thronged pavements.

We notice one or two points of striking contrast after Melbourne. The houses seem much loftier, the streets much narrower and more sinuous; in fact, we are no longer in a rectangular town, where we almost want a telescope to recognise a friend on the other side of a street; and if we were below and persisted in looking up to the tops of the houses, we should soon be afflicted with a disease comparatively unknown in Melbourne, *i.e.* a crick in the neck. That extraordinary creature called a "masher" would find his stuck-up collar deprive him of much sight-seeing here in Sydney.

Much of the effect of the good architecture of this city is lost to the observers from the fact that, as in so many European towns, there is no sufficient distance whence to gaze at the object. The Protestant cathedral next door to us suffers in this respect, as does the Post Office with its reputed carvings (the beauty of which cannot be appreciated) and elaborate facing in Italian style, and a number of banks and public buildings. Here too we see the exigencies of the case require underground sewers and wood pavement in many roads, not as in Melbourne, great open gutters and macadam.

The vehicles, too, differ essentially. Though you may watch for a waggonette, the gondola of Melbourne, you will hardly see one; but of hansom cabs there is no end. What is that puff of smoke and steam from one of the main thoroughfares? Not a railway? No, but something rather more dangerous, though otherwise more convenient, than the suburban lines of the sister city. A steam tramway, calculated to frighten horses by day and children by night! Rumbling along at considerable speed, often coupled together, the cars are pulled along by an extraordinary-looking little "motor," or engine, which bears the same resemblance to an ordinary locomotive that an abnormally fattened pug-dog does to a deerhound. The simile is borne out by the way it pants and puffs; but there it ends, for it climbs steep hills with a gallant rush, and can start off and pull up at the whim of the driver, passing over the ground at a brisk pace. The stations are generally at the cross roads, where sometimes a little awning is erected, protecting a few seats. At every cross road in the city itself is a guard or pointsman, who regulates the constantly passing tramcars and other traffic with considerable care and lofty surveillance. Accidents will, of course, happen on the best regulated tramways, and when the demon of steam and iron, with its great flaring eyeball at night-time, was first introduced some few years since, it would occasionally run over children; but as use is second nature, so the Sydney babes seem to have overcome their horror and their martyrdom at one and the same time, for now accidents are of rare occurrence.

Out eastward there is no railway system, so these trams,

which form a network in that direction right out to Coogee, Bondi, and Botany Bays, provide an invaluable species of locomotion to residents in those suburbs, and on the westward successfully compete, so far as travellers are concerned, with the railway which runs up to Paramatta, some fifteen miles distant. Both trains and trams are in the hands of the Government, and though the railways are worked at a profit, a practical engineer in the service of the Government told me that the tramways never would until the secret of pecuniary success in steam locomotion was applied to them; that is, until the maximum amount of cars were coupled with the minimum amount of motors. At present the tendency is in the opposite direction: the multiplication of individual tramcars towed along by motors which could reasonably be employed to do treble the work for the same amount of wear and tear, is opposed to all system of economy, though most convenient for the residents in the suburbs.

But to resume our bird's-eye view. When we look out to the eastward we see the lighthouses on the heads, farther south along the coast a series of bays and bights called Coogee, Bondi, &c., blue like the lapis lazuli, and sweeping out to the horizon in diminishing distinctness. They all repay a visit, and a walk along the shore from the South Head lighthouse, past the romantic dell of Rosa Gully, where the good ship *Rosa* jammed herself and thus saved her crew, past the numerous dells and clefts, bays and coves, will afford a lasting pleasure to the ordinary globe-trotter, geologist, botanist, or artist.

The ground-herbage all around these bays is in spring one mass of bloom—flowers small but pretty. When one comes nearer to the million-hued carpet that these shrubby little plants spread at one's feet, one distinguishes the delicate, wax-like, many-coloured bells of Epacrides of various species, those half-brothers of the Cape heaths that puzzle the unscientific haunter of botanical gardens. Of these the most curious though not the prettiest, is *styphelia viridiflora*, whose light, translucent green trumpet affords almost too delicate a contrast to its spiky leaves to be very noticeable. Here flourish the purple hovea, the yellow and purple bossiæa, the orange and scarlet plagiolobium, all of the pea or leguminous class. The grevillea which you may trample under foot is a prize in the greenhouses at home, where culture and care have deepened the rich crimson throats (which, like the honeysuckle, thrust forth their pistils) and enlarged the flower. See here again this lovely little pimelea, with its exquisite pink stellate blossoms, its flower-stem stiff and bristling with the thick glossy leaflets that cover its nakedness.

The atmosphere, invariably charged in Australia with strong scents of the gum or other trees, is sweet with the perfumes exhaled by the lovely golden balls of the acacia; and here, down in the hollows, growing best near the marshy "pockets," the orange, green, scarlet, and brown blooms of the banksia scent the air and beautify the scene. In this plant nature has tried to give as near a resemblance as possible to a bottle-brush, and her attempt has been most successful and praiseworthy; as it often measures three inches through and five inches long, it may be guessed that nature considers "magnums' quite small deer in her butlery. They were flowers similar to these which caused the great navigator, in 1770, to call the adjacent bay "Botany." The sandstone rocks too afford a variety of colouring unsurpassed, I think, anywhere on the seacoast, and these present a most cheerful contrast to the gum-tired eyes of a traveller from the interior.

Here again to the south-east lies Botany Bay, which from our eminence and distance appears to be a blue, but otherwise uninteresting piece of water surrounded on three sides of its coastline by low flat sandy mounds, and on the nearer side by a little ordinary scrub. Were it not so notorious from its past history but little interest would be centred in it, and unless a man wishes to lose his romantic conceptions of this old *locus in quo* so many stirring scenes in the good old days were enacted, I advise him not to go to Botany. He may still botanise scientifically or romantically there, it is true, but he may find the flora of Botany common to all the environs of Sydney, and I could not recommend the amorous botanist to go to a pleasanter spot than Middle Harbour. In the Botany scrub, if he has any curiosity, he will find a colony of blacks; but how they are fallen from their high estate, their good clothing and habitations, and their English language, testify!

If we complete the circuit of the horizon to the south and west we shall find nothing of remarkable note, as the wild bush-covered hills and valleys of Illawarra in that direction do not appear from this distance aught but sombre-coloured patches of green of deeper or lighter shades.

Botany Bay looking Eastward

As we narrow our range of vision we note that the thinly-populated suburbs of the south soon give way to the thicker masses of houses around the exhibition buildings, where the great exhibition of 1879—1880 was held. Nearer still is the main railway terminus; and close at hand thereto on a green knoll stands the University, with more pretensions to architecture, but built for similar purposes to that of Melbourne; it is also provided with affiliated colleges for the residential students.

Of parks standing out with vivid verdure, in contrast to chimney and roofs, we can see two or three besides the

Botanical Gardens, Government House grounds, and the two Domains. They are somewhat bare these Hyde, Victoria, and Moore Parks (though the latter is a large tract of country); none of them can equal the gardens of Melbourne in cultivation, care and beauty; but they serve their purpose as commonplace ventilators of this second largest town of the colonies in almost a purely utilitarian manner, Moore Park being the haunt of the football or cricket players.

As the circle of our vision narrows we notice that church spires more thickly dot the sea of roofs; but if one may gauge

Sydney University

the sanctity of a city by the number of these erections, Sydney must give first place to Melbourne. One church somewhat farther off than the immediate city, standing over the pleasantly environed Rushcutter's Bay in the harbour, wrapped in a feathery mantle of European foliage, recalls to memory the orthodox pictures of the old country.

The Roman Catholic cathedral calls for especial mention, for there you see a bit of Notre Dame joined to a fragment of Melrose Abbey. The fact is that the zeal of the builders has outrun the constable; some considerable portion of the building is a mere shell, and the authorities have not the wherewithal at present to satisfy their ambition. For artistic interior this cathedral even in its quarter-finished condition is far before the Protestant cathedral. The pillars in the Perpendicular style rise in clustering columns till they are lost in the dimness of the roof, thus giving a vast and mysterious appearance to this incense-scented church. The windows are small and glazed with that golden glass which produces a similar effect to that in Melbourne cathedral.

In the centre of the church before a dignified altar was lately raised a frippery article of gewgaws, which a Catholic friend deprecated even more strongly than myself; instead of the sedate subduing effect necessary, there emanated from this mass of inharmonious and discordant colouring a sense of irritation to the eye and distraction to the mind, which the worthy priest did his best, I will admit, to correct by his false quantities whenever he plunged into Latin verse.

It is to be hoped that this inharmonious eyesore is not a permanent institution in the church, for it detracted from the rest of the interior, which is extremely impressive. As the evening light throws faint beams into distant corners, the saints and crucifixes seem to stand out with the reality of life, a heaven or a hell to the impressionable, according as that little turbulent conscience directs. After all Southey's—

> "I to the woodlands wend, and there
> In silent worship seek the God of prayer,"

appears a more natural form of worship than that in temples, built by hands, possessing many emotional factors.

Not far away stands the museum, where a very complete collection of beasts and birds, more especially Australian, is on view. As we shall come across many of the originals in after pages in their natural haunts, it is not worth while lingering over their representatives here whose life-blood is sealing-wax, whose sinews are iron wire, and whose muscles are wool.

Close by we can see the domes of the Jewish synagogue—a Byzantine erection of most elaborate exterior and interior, which shares with the two before-mentioned buildings the advantage of being capable of being viewed from a distance, as they all abut on the park.

There again the roof of the Legislative Houses, more like a barn or barrack than a House of Parliament, cowers down in rightly-assumed shame behind the private buildings around. Inside and out the Houses offer a biting reproof to Melbourne for the Solomon-like glory in which gay Melbourne has clothed her Chambers, which are certainly *not* arrayed like one of these. Both the Upper and Lower House are ascetic in their unadorned walls, ceilings, and benches, though some of the language is sometimes hardly in keeping with this simplicity, unless it may be said that invective is that form of argument which approximates to the simplicity of our forefathers. As in Victoria, the Upper House sets the good example of gentlemanly breeding, which a few members of the Lower House, to the great disgust of the rest of the hundred and eight, do not follow. The excitement, if there be any seems to reach its climax after tea, for which an adjournment is made between seven and eight. Thereafter the stimulating effects of "the cup that cheers, &c.," become most noticeable in misapplied and unnecessary force of tongue and bitter dispute.

One night an honourable member was called to order by the Speaker in the midst of a heated oration, and promptly burst out with " I don't care a d—— for the Speaker." That this exceeded the limits of constitutional agitation, the shocked tone of the Houses themselves, the subsequent suspension of the member, and the clamour of the Press plainly testified. Except on field-days, the proceedings of Legislative Councils and Assemblies are of an uninteresting character, as you may see from the fact that the Strangers' Galleries, capable of accommodating more than a hundred, are occupied but by a handful.

The members of the Lower House being elected triennially, by what may be termed an approximation to a manhood suffrage, have, according to a venerable old colonial aristocrat, lost their high tone since the franchise was thus made non-exclusive.

"Yes, sir, with the introduction of the blatant gas instead of the mellow modest candle, we began to get gassy, but now that the electric light has displaced our gas we are going with lightning speed to the dogs." And wagging his head shrewdly, the dear white-headed old praiser of the early times, shaking off the dust of the "big big D's," *et id genus omne*, climbed on a tram and was whirled away into the night.

The reason why the fifty of the Upper House are so much quieter in mien and tongue than their brethren of the other Chamber is undoubtedly the same which causes a man sentenced for life to feel the gravity of his position more acutely than one with three years' penal servitude. These "upper ten" are appointed by the Governor, a kindly, white-headed old gentleman, and one of that old school of courtesy and good breeding which appears even in some of our higher circles to be fast losing its scholars.

Hard by the Houses stands the Mint, an equally unpretentious-looking building, established in 1853 (though not primarily in this building), nineteen years before the Victorian mint was erected. The machinery and operations are similar to those employed at home, including that most exquisitely delicate balance which rejects all sovereigns but those of exact and proper weight. We were told here the reason why the older coinage of the Australian sovereigns was so much paler in colour than that now in use throughout the Empire. The gold then was alloyed with silver, not as now with copper; hence a sovereign was worth more than it is now by a few pence. Everything cheapens in time, even money, as the overseer who took us round remarked.

The Court House close by rears its unsightly roof, covering equally unsightly courts, where an æsthetic lawyer would find it hard to be at ease. The building can hardly be said to have been erected for utilitarian purposes solely. The courts are small and inconvenient; they appear more than ascetic—absolutely undignified and far from impressive, and do not in the slightest degree uphold the dignity which the law really enjoys.

Not far off we see the large building of the Public Library, that noble institution of colonial education. It does not aspire in size, in accommodation, or architecture to its sister in Melbourne, but possesses one advantage over that institution in having a genial assistant librarian who is ever ready to assist ignorance and guide the faltering literati into the proper way. The sooner a larger and more fitting building is erected, and not merely talked about, so much the better. The present one is often unnecessarily crowded and does the colony little credit. Here, as in many similar buildings throughout the colonies, the fairer sex has a room set apart from the unfair, where in maiden meditation fancy free, they may study all and everything, from Shakespeare to Ouida, from Carlyle to Herbert Spencer, apart from the manly throng. A lavatory in front of the entrance to the reading-room significantly reminds one that here often come the great unwashed, whose study would otherwise be at the expense of the cleanly volumes which they thumb. At night-time—for the room is open from ten in the morning till ten at night—the larger number of the readers appear to consist of clerks and mechanics.

There is but one fault to find with the usual descriptions of this library. Many say that a broad flight of stairs *conveys* the visitor from the street to the rooms above; don't believe them! We waited, like poor Mark Twain on the glacier, at the bottom of that stairway a mortal five minutes, but had nevertheless to walk up in the usual way.

No great distance in association or reality separates the muse of literature from her sister of art. Close by the library Sydney National Gallery spreads its roomy though not highly architectural sheds, like a sheltering wing, over a collection of oil and water-colours, bronzes, and pottery, that serve both to educate the eye of the native and revive the memory of the visitor. Many an old Academy picture we come across here on the walls which we had lost long since, crowded out of memory by succeeding exhibitions. The modern school predominates to what admirers of the old masters would consider an alarming extent; but the modern evolutionary outcome of the nineteenth century, as represented in this Lisbon of the South, "wouldn't give you a rap sir, for your old fusty, musty masters, whose colours are dingy, whose drawing outrageous, and whose composition—well t'were better to say nothing about it."

The ordinary visitor will feel that the colonies themselves are not adequately represented, for but few views of colonial scenery grace the walls. Why should not Conrad Martens, Gully, Moreton, Chevalier, Hoyte, and others, by birth or adoption the natural expositors of the wealth and beauty of Australasian scenery, be patronised here as well as at Melbourne?

Continuing our omnivorous sweep of the eye, we can see the large brick and stone buildings that overlook the circular quay—Government offices towering aloft and hob-nobbing with the " largest wool warehouse in the colony." Banks, Exchange, and hotels all congregate in close union, many of them fine specimens of solid sandstone such as might make a Melbourne builder with his bluestone ill with envy. Oh ye dwellers in yon Victorian capital! how your hearts must vex within you when ye think that the men of Sydney may dig the stone to build their houses out of their very foundations, soft and workable, which the buffeting of the winds and rain and the scorching of the sun will but serve to harden, and ye have, beyond the prosaic baked clay, only the cold bluestone—hard to work, ugly to look upon, and withal no easy subject for the architect's skill! Melbourne hopes to crow in turn when she opens up those inexhaustible seams of white stone which " must exist somewhere or other in the colony."

Hotels? Yes, you can see plenty from here, but Sydney folk have little reason to be proud of them. The fact is, that Sydney folk are so hospitable, and visitors have so little need of hotels, that many are but drinking palaces or restaurants, which tacitly warn would-be boarders against trusting too strongly in such trivial matters as pleasant rooms and good attendance. Again, the visitor to Sydney may, should he wish it, generally be "clubbed." It's rather nice than otherwise. Clubbed? Yes, clubbed all over—the colonies. Should you be good-looking enough, any friend will "put you up" at his club, and you will be received with open arms, and if it be a good one the accommodation will be in better style, and at the same or more moderate charges, than at the best hotel in the place.

Hotel proprietors tell you that the clubs have put their noses out of joint, but the fact is that their noses were so much deformed before, that the clubs had in patriotic defence of their own and their visitors' comfort to emphasise this natural deformity.

Should you wish it, in most colonial towns you may find out restaurants where for a "square meal" you may have the melancholic pleasure of saying "Bang went saxpence." For the curious epicurean here is the menu presented to me by the beaming proprietor of one of these enterprising restaurants. The dining-saloon, which really deserved its name, was occupied by large tables covered with spotless cloths, on which were spread in readiness for dinner the usual table appointments. The display of flowers and of plated forks and spoons and the notes of an orchestra playing popular tunes, were sufficient to make one wish one's own dinner hour was at hand, a wish not in any degree diminished after an inspection of the food referred to in the menu, which was "quite up to sample." A man, woman, or child might have *each and all* of—

        Pea Soup,
        Steak and Onions,
        Roast Beef and Mutton,
        Boiled Mutton and Parsley Sauce,
        Corned Beef and Carrots,
        Stewed Rabbit,
        Stewed Veal and Pork,

> Boiled and Baked Potatoes,
> Cabbage,
> Jam Roll and Rice Pudding,
> Tea *ad lib.*,

the only bargain made by the proprietor being that the diner should be able to remove himself from his seat by his own unaided muscular exertions.

To suit the various classes—for even in the colonies class does not always mingle with class—another restaurant farther up the street offered the same or similar articles for ninepence, while another boasting a somewhat higher status charged one shilling. Here were merchants, tradesmen, and others, in the second were their clerks, and at the first-mentioned restaurant the music charmed the ears of tradesmens' assistants, artisans, and others. Every diner, even in the sixpenny region, had good clothes on his back, and was respectable in behaviour and appearance; not a single poor man could you see.

You may search through most of the colonial towns and see no such poor as we unfortunately know in England. Rags you may occasionally, though most rarely see, more perhaps in Sydney than in Melbourne, but even then such a *rara avis* is a tatterdemalion that you cannot help thinking he or she must be an original-minded person wearing the same for effect. I am confident that no one need be in tatters in the colonies; work there is, and usually plenty of it, though occasionally waves of slackness in trade, or bad seasons, will pass over the labour market and throw some few out of employment.

The "employment of the unemployed" is often raised as a cry in the chief towns in the colonies, but it usually comes from a handful of men who can't get employment because they won't take it, fostered of course by two or three acuter spirits who see their way to make capital out of their simpler brethren's misfortunes. Demagogues will sometimes hold a meeting of the unemployed to consider their grievances, and will with blatant phrases and inaccurate remarks work upon the feelings of their audience; but as a rule, when the inevitable "hat goes round" to further "the good movement, for which funds are earnestly desired," the listeners cautiously keep their hands and their coin in their pockets, preferring words to deeds.

On one occasion, the New South Welsh Government, ever ready to step in and relieve matters in a paternal spirit, sent a number of unemployed to some public works at Wâgga, where they were to receive 36s. a week. Some of the unemployed did not seem to like hard work at such a rate when some of their more skilful brethren were earning higher wages, and threw up their "billets" within a few days, preferring the indolence pitied by well-meaning but injudicious old women of both sexes to the honest sweat of the brow. As a member of the Legislature forcibly put it, "They went about the country seeking work, praying heaven they might not find it."

As a matter of fact, it is astonishing to any one, merely looking at the immigration figures, that there is not a larger surplusage of labourers than there actually is. The vast number of men, women, and children the colony receives through immigration every year would seem to justify the existence of a far greater number of persons without employment, yet as a matter of fact, except in bad times, the whole of the influx is absorbed, and the insatiable maw is still unsatisfied.

Colonial ladies sigh for good domestic servants. 'Tis true that the cook is often expected to be a laundrywoman as well, but for this she receives £30 to £35 a year, even though she be a very "ornerary critter;" and why should this affect the fact that Mary the housemaid, who perhaps receives £20 to £30 per annum, is always " givin' notis," and puts on the airs of a princess if she is not allowed to have her own way? She is very often far from magnanimous, wielding the upper hand as she knows well how to do; her threat of "Give me this or I'll give notice," has a meaning of ineffable dread to her mistress, which soon brings that poor lady to her knees.

A good domestic is bid for almost in the same way as a

piece of Sèvres china. The highest bidder ultimately gets the article, and then perhaps finds that she leaves him soon to marry, aye, and marry often into a very fair position, for "femails are skarse" in the land of wool and gold. At home mistresses often complain that their maids dress almost as well as they do themselves. In the colonies the fact is accepted. Complaint has long since died out, and mistress and maid not uncommonly patronise the same milliner and dressmaker.

Colonial-born servants should be the natural remedy for the unsatisfactory state of this portion of the labour-market, but here the education they receive in the State schools proves rather a hindrance than a help to the young women. For instance, a friend's wife, on applying for a servant had a girl sent her who, with the easy confidence of her race, said she could do " 'most anything." Somewhat suspicious of this open phrase, her would-be mistress catechised her as to boiling potatoes, cooking chops, and other elementary operations, none of which it turned out she had ever done, but probably could if she tried (like the Scotchman and the fiddle). Somewhat put about to find out what she could do, the lady asked, "Well, tell me something you really can do?"

"Oh, please mum, I can do algibrer, mum."

Talking about the scarcity of the gentler sex throughout the colonies reminds me that a common report goes around in New South Wales, that up in the interior of Queensland married women are open to take engagements for their second and third husbands, supposing their present consorts predecease them. This rumour lacks the confirmation of actual fact, for experiments in this direction by would-be suitors end adversely, the would-be suitor occasionally having the "old man" himself put on his track and having to run for it.

Again recurring to the labour question, visitors universally notice the excessive desire on the part of labourers, artisans, and others to make "gentlemen of their sons." The method they deem of all others the most speedy to attain this object is to get them into an office. The sons themselves having received an education that gives them a distaste and unfits them for hard manual labour, naturally fall in with their father's views, and help to swell the already overcrowded ranks of counter-jumpers and clerks, who are even now elbowing one another in their efforts to live and move and have their being.

I cannot conceive that the requirements of the colony for skilled artisans and the like could be better satisfied than by colonial-bred mechanics, who have this advantage over their emigrated brethren that they have no novelty of circumstances and unfamiliarity of surroundings to which to adapt themselves, nor have they any old-country prejudices wherewith to hamper the enterprise and invention of a new country. Young Cornstalk, take my advice, and instead of aspiring to the poor ambition of being snubbed by intending purchasers in shops, or driving a goosequill, so significant in name and suggestive of unchanged surroundings, be proud to be what your fathers are—worthy sons of toil, more or less skilled, with none the less a voice in the nation's welfare, although they are not merchant-princes or Crœsus-like tradesmen!

We have seen as much as we can of the outside life of Sydney, except, perhaps, the very object nearest at hand, and the chiming bells remind us of the fleeting hand of time.

St. Andrew's Cathedral, erected for the Church of England section, is a handsome sandstone building with an exterior in mixed style, having a decided leaning to the "Perpendicular," fortunately not from it. The average traveller will be disappointed with the interior. There the style becomes heterogeneous, and though it still affects the later Gothic, the encaustic tiles of divers inharmonious colours around the walls of the church, its ruddy pews, and its gaudy organ, do not harmonise with the rest of the architecture, which is ornamented tastefully with carving and stained glass.

Descending from our lofty perch on the top of the town hall, we come down below to the holy of holies; this is the council-chamber, with its polished floor and decorations of Keen's cement in the Italian style, where sundry pens and blotting-paper, and the elaborately-carved mayoral chair, denote the Corporation's occasional attendance and work. The assembly-room is just a step this way, and a fine-looking hall it makes, with its columns and statue-filled niches. But we cannot linger long here: you must come some day when the Art Society holds its exhibition, or the Corporation gives a ball, to appreciate the hall at its full worth. "Come, I say, you there; you mustn't poke at the marble balustrade as though you thought it were imitation. Nothing of the sort; they may put a bust of her Majesty on a piece of painted wood at Melbourne, but we in Sydney go in for the genuine article, and live in hopes of having the Queen's full figure in due course." Thus discourses the concierge, the while he shows us out, and we are in the road again.

Why do the drivers of all vehicles go at such a funereal rate just here? Police regulations! Don't you see the notices on the lamp-posts at the street-crossings to drivers, telling them to walk across? Just take a hansom down George Street to find out whether the regulations are observed. You're in a hurry to catch a train, and tell cabby so. He looks at you with a sort of mild pity, rushes along for a short distance, and just when you feel certain you're going to outrace a flash of lightning your vehicle suddenly halts and stops. If you look around, half fearing lest you may see some mangled corpse you have run over, you find no such material reason for this sudden proof of the law of inertia. The cabman is merely obeying the regulations in walking across the crossing. If you start from the quay end of George Street and travel its whole two miles' length to the station, long before you reach your destination you will be wondering why your liver is jogging around in your throat, what in the name of thunder has become of your breath, and why in the world you've got your right-hand thumb and index-finger sprained? N.B., the driver will not. He doesn't obey the regulations from an infatuated regard for authorities, but, as I am assured by careful observation, from a spirit of mischief and misanthropy. He will only be wondering why you have breath enough left to denounce the whole system at your journey's end, and chuckle to himself at your not being in a physical position to beat him down to his proper fare.

You may often see the Governor and his lady driving along in an open landau with powdered footmen. "The commoners don't seem to make much fuss," you say. Very true. "Hats off" would seem to involve too much exertion, so the old gentleman and his good wife are perhaps saved some trouble and back-aching themselves.

Did you hear that burly colonial grumble as he passed. "What does he do for his money, I'd like to know?" Oh dear no, the spirit is *not* at all unique, the feeling is very general, and oft-times expressed in the same or similar terms. He is not indeed overworked, but if he fulfils his social as well as his political duties, he cannot save a large portion of his £7,000 a year. He has to open Parliament and prorogue it, give his consent to bills, and so forth, as does her Majesty at home. Rarely is this consent withheld, and when it is, great is the outcry, terrible are the denunciations of the vulgar. His social duties are harder, though he does not always fulfil them *in extenso*.

"One recent governor gave," I was told by a Sydney resident, "no balls, no dinners, no nothing"—the double negative graphically pointing the acme of unsociability. He certainly was somewhat exceptional in his style and show of hospitality, and for a time so influenced Sydney society that visitors were treated with an astonishing and exceptional amount of coldness, so report goes. It is certainly true that the social life visible in Melbourne, which has received from her sister colony the epithet by comparison of "gay," is now almost entirely wanting in Sydney, and old residents say that in the good old times things were a great deal better and more sociable.

Talking about the good old times, a retired squatter vents his spleen against the republicanism, larrikinism, and socialism, with a horde of other "isms" more or less disreputable, which seem to have been sown pretty thickly in the colonies. Where they have taken root heaven alone knows, for every respectable person I have met disowns the whole fraternity, and will have none of them. Yet their organs are loud-speaking and blatant, and freethinkers lecture to vast crowds on Sunday evenings, with running accompaniments of music of all sorts. How in the world such disloyalty exists as many of the papers would have us imagine, in those very places which turn out on occasion loyal hearts shoulder to shoulder to fight the wars of the old country, is a problem exceedingly difficult, and apparently as little capable of elucidation as the phlogiston or the philosopher's stone.

If, after all this sight-seeing, the visitor feels hot and dry, I cannot conscientiously imitate Australian hospitality by suggesting any liquid refreshment, for here as elsewhere the worthy analysts and Æsculapiads hem you in at every point. Tea is too exciting and destructive to digestion, coffee too heating and seldom palatable, cocoa ditto, only more so; and if we mount to the more risky fluids, we find doctored wines and spirits, fiery brandies, methylated spirit instead of whisky, which will cause even such temperate persons as ourselves many an hour of disturbed digestion and headache.

How about colonial wines? Pure generally, but too new, yet eminently fitter to be consumed than the spirits and beer which the average Englishman drags away from his cold, damp climate to every other in the world, disrespecting altered circumstances with extraordinary short-sightedness. Water many colonials hold to be the most risky drink of all, as it may contain anything, from typhoid-fever germs to hydatids, and although here in Sydney the Botany Marsh-water is said to be beyond exception, 'tis rather excepted than accepted when undiluted.

The moderate drinker is often driven into a corner to find some innocuous potation, and without any innate tendency to or desire for firewater or malt liquors, is not infrequently told by authorities that those are his safest and *derniers ressorts*. From personal and other experience, I can say that if a man be moderately careful in his ways of living, he may drink even the turbid water of Melbourne, or the greenish semi-fluid in the up-country water-holes, without any severe consequences, and withal be able to enjoy a good digestion and consequently his life. Good Templars urge milk or effervescing drinks. Never practise what is preached. The milkman and typhoid seem to go hand in hand over here, and effervescing drinks—no matter.

Nevertheless the Blue Ribbon movement prospers, and is said to enrol large numbers of converts annually, and though backsliders are numerous, its work is profitable and necessary. The custom of the patient "shouting a drink" for his doctor, the client for the lawyer, the merchant for his *confrère*, on each and every occasion, is fortunately dying out apace, particularly in the large towns; but this notwithstanding, the amount of alcoholic drink annually consumed is astounding and deplorable, as thereby results much physical, moral, and social harm. Why not introduce the German Trink Halle and its enticing row of fruit beverages over here? A man of enterprise who thus worked in fellowship with the supporters of the temperance movement would make a fortune.

Sydney Cathedral.

CHAPTER IX.

The Weather Topic.—Keep clear of the Outside in a Shower.—Thick Blood *versus* thin.—Up the Paramatta River to the Town.—Bush still around Sydney.—Advertising extraordinary.—Benevolent Asyla.—National Park.—Shanks's Mare must be used to get there.—Taken in and done for.—It was a Maiden without her h's.—Port Hackin River up from the Lodge.—Down to the Sea.—A Feast of Bivalves.—We pass on to Bulli.—Wayside enterprise.—Surveying extraordinary.—Accommodation Houses.—Coalfields.—Bulli Pass.—A Leap in the wrong Direction.—" Show us your Patterns, Mister."—Wollongong Butter.—Quicksands and the Insurance Company compete.

THE true-hearted, patriotic Briton carries his weather-topic wherever he goes, so that here, as at home, it affords a vast fund and theme for conversation. Would you have the rainfall in figures? Let me assure you that should a man happen to be out in Sydney when one of the forty inches of rain is falling he will cut a pretty figure. What avails the macintosh or umbrella when the inch-per-hour water-jets are pouring down! Noah's ark would be at a premium. Cats and dogs? Such an old phrase gives but a faint suggestion of the situation. Rather speak of the clouds shedding kangaroos and wallabies! Most folk can boast about seeing drops as big as a tumbler's circumference, others can talk about sheets of rain or bucketfuls, but what would you say to a drop of rain broad enough to stretch across George Street, eh? What, don't believe it? Go and see for yourself; I wash my hands of the whole matter.

The great feature, however, about the rain is that it follows out literally the Spanish proverb about pouring, and consequently gets done with it. No beating about the bush, or rather the clouds; once it makes up its mind, the sky clears itself, and boasts once more the serene Australian azure. What a winter! A little brisk in the early morning, perhaps, but what glorious sunshiny days! what lovely evenings! Spring, too, is getting a trifle warmer, and autumn! How delightful is a dwelling in Sydney, or her sister city of the north, Brisbane! But come, if it's summer, we will away to the mountains. Too hot? You're just right; and a damp heat too, that makes you thin and sallow, and clears out the bright red blood of the more temperate climes, replacing it with a sort of thin, watery mixture, certainly not "blue," which will banish your roses, fair maiden, and leave your cheeks pale and sickly, giving you the new chum's "seasoning."

Melbourne lasses complain that the summer affects them in the same way, but you would never think so if you were there in any other season, while in Sydney you can see the dire effects of old Father Sol, even when he is passing the winter solstice. Never mind; do as many of the Australians do, and save your complexions by a trip to Tasmania for the summer. Move around in Australia a few degrees, and you will be able to have perpetual warm, genial weather; but you will not appreciate your good fortune, for what does a perpetual smile become but a smirk? and it certainly does *not* become you to have invariable blue sky.

Do you ask after mosquitoes? Let no one go on the water of an evening if he be going to propose to-morrow. They and the sand-flies make life a mockery of a summer's night. For their character refer to the remarks on Melbourne insects, which they resemble so closely that the difference is inappreciable.

As we are in Sydney, of course we must see the Paramatta River. For a few pence we get a ticket for one of the steamers journeying from these wharves behind the cathedral. Here we go dodging in and out, leaving the busy turmoil of streets behind, stopping here and there, now on one side now another, trending up this charming broad stream. Gums on the banks and sandstone cliffs, as usual, varied with the gayer foliage of climbing plants and the gardens of suburban residents perched now on the top of the cliff now on the sloping bank. Here the banks lose their bolder character, the river broadens out into wide reaches, mangroves deck the flatter shores with their bright foliage. We are on the Paramatta course, where Hanlan was beaten in 1884 by his Australian antagonist.

On the Paramatta River

A few more halting-places, and we land at the Paramatta Pier. The river is low here, and the steamer can travel no farther, so we take the steam tramcar up through uninteresting paddocks by the side of the river, shoot past the Benevolent Institution, as they call the workhouse here, and are fairly landed in the town. Take a boat and row up? Certainly, though we have to row some way before we find primeval beauty again. The scents that on occasion greet the adventurer are sufficient reward for any trouble. No, it is not the mud; that might certainly be healthier. Another whiff! 'Tis the scent of orange-groves grown here; but so capricious is the orange, that Paramatta all but has the monopoly of the orange-growing of Australia. Oranges as big as a lump of chalk can be seen any day hanging on the trees. 'Tis a fact; anyone may see them, and, by special permission of the growers, may eat them. These Sydney oranges are of great and deserved fame throughout Australia.

We have the choice of rail, road, or water to get back to Sydney. The railway stations along this line—which in the opposite direction goes right over the Blue Mountains—are noticeable, and would put the noses of many at home out of joint. In many parts between this and Sydney Station the bush grows just as it did when Captain Cook first surprised the savages of these parts, while here again it is varied by the well-kept lawns, flower-gardens, and shrubberies of some Nabob, whose homely and ornamental house, shrouded with verandahs and creeping plants, flashes out for a second as the train moves along.

The bush is *not* ornamental; gums would never, on their own soil, after the early down of youth is worn off, send a lover of beauty into ecstacies. In spring the tints on the young leaves of the younger eucalypti are varied and not unpleasing, but these small plants do not constitute a large portion of the scenery, except where the larger trees have been destroyed by the axe or fire. The grass close in here is green enough just now, and for two reasons: firstly, because a large portion has been grown from European grasses, and secondly, because the colony has lately enjoyed much longed-for rain. The ordinary bush-grass, after a few weeks of dry summer weather, becomes a tawny yellow, which is succeeded by a burnt brown tone, this succeeded—if the weeks extend into months—by an absence of all colour, for there is no grass to be coloured.

The paddocks that the road passes through are very unusually hedged. It is too warm for the honest old hawthorn to do well, and other shrubs that make a thick hedge often render themselves unsuitable by choking up the whole field. So here we have the crude post-and-rail fence; not bare, however, for the ingenious bill-poster roams around with a stencil-plate and paint-pot, and begs you to "Try Eureka Cigarettes," or "Go to Jones's Emporium for 50s. suits," or "Get Smith's Baking-powder," thus affording the eye variety and the *corpus vile* the anticipation of creature comforts. To be confronted in some romantic spot, far away, as you fancy, from the madding crowd, with these select phrases acts variously on different characters. The lover of his race feels glad to find vestiges of *animal* life, the artistic soul or the misanthrope aches for the gentle advertiser's gore.

Here, as we arrive at Sydney terminus, the dodging lights and ringing bells of the steam trams bid us look out for ourselves. If we are going down to the circular quay we cannot do better than jump on to one. Here we go past another benevolent asylum. What is the difference between a benevolent asylum and a workhouse? Many people "give it up;" but the close investigator discovers that the inmate of the asylum is looked on more as a State pensioner, and gives himself the airs of one, while the workhouse inmate at home has not much time or opportunity for airs, and doesn't get a chance of running riot on meat every day. Poverty is not so great a crime as at home, and the pauper feels this to be so, and rather looks upon himself as an exceptional and phenomenal character.

Of excursions around Sydney there are plenty: to Botany, Coogee, Manley Beach, the Hawkesbury, George River, and the National Park. The park comprises over forty thousand acres of land, but is rather difficult of access, a disadvantage about to be remedied by the new railway. To within eight miles of the accommodation house built in the heart of the park, you may ride by public conveyance for a shilling or so, through somewhat uninteresting country past Botany Bay; then we cross George's River on a ferry, which never seems to be on the proper (that is, your) side of the broad stream, and if you have not sent a note to the park-keeper to meet you with his trap you will have to tramp about six or eight miles along a bush track. Flowers of a few species grow here, chiefly epacrides, the undergrowth is thick and varied, and grass-trees (*xanthorrhea*) * throw up their bullrush-like spikes all around.

As we ascend the ridge we see to our right and left glimpses of deep wooded gorges, which soon open up when we reach the cleared summit of the ridge, where a most comprehensive view is obtained, from the glittering horizon of the sea to the east, the grand gorges up which the Port Hackin River and its confluents run to the south, wooded valleys and hills to the west, and Sydney far away to the north. As the evening gathers the effect from this summit on a fine day is marvellously lovely. The sunset glow up above, reflected from the timber on the eastern slopes of the hills, contrasts most vividly with the lovely "intense blue" of the gorges, deepening to their bottom and softening into the same extraordinary blue haze, so distinctive in Australasian scenery, in the distance. See here is a fine rock from which to take a sketch of the gorges, for two equally beautiful valleys, timbered throughout to the summits of the hills, diverge from this point, and there is no fear of snakes up here.

A massive boulder twelve feet high is our point of vantage, resting, like numbers of others—a cool contrast—on a carpet of beautiful herbage, consisting of heaths and the countless species of melaleuca, hovea, pimelia, bossiæa, grevillea, and boronia. The Australian rose, or boronia, is too well known in our greenhouses at home to need description or praise, but the enchantment to the eyes of a traveller through a gum-forest, who suddenly comes out upon an open piece of country carpeted with this lovely roseate star, is incapable of appreciation by any but those who have thus suffered and been rewarded. We have struck off the high road, as it is called, which trends across the mountains to "Bulli," where still grander scenery awaits us. Here solitude seems to reign

* See page 267.

supreme; frivolity is hushed, ridicule awed. One of the characteristic features of Australian mountain scenery is this same solemnity and solitude; no merry twittering of birds breaks the sense of loneness; the howl of the dingo, the unearthly screech of the parrot, or the hoot of the laughing jackass only serve by contrast to deepen the silence verging on melancholy which pervades these scenes.

Just below there, in the valley, a wreath of smoke among the trees betokens the presence of man. As we are in need of creature comforts we make for the smoke, but not by a bee-line, for we soon find ourselves forced to climb down the rocky slopes of the forest-covered hills by a zig-zag track. You could reach the house in a few minutes if you knew its whereabouts, with the option, however, of sliding down a score of feet here and there in the deepening gloom. The gleam of the twinkling light and the baying dogs welcome us to the park-keeper's "accommodation house," where we are right pleased to find ourselves, with well washed faces and hands, "accommodated" with a dish of ham and eggs, before a blazing fire, which puts the candles on the table affecting to light our lofty room to shame. After supper we pull out the beds and turn in. The night is frosty, so we keep up the fire, nominally, but actually the man on watch lets it out.

If the view was charming last night, how much more charming is it in the morning dew! After a bathe in the river which flows at the foot of the garden, the sunrise is a feast for the gods, and is followed by a feast for the grosser portion of our natures in a breakfast combining quantity and wholesomeness. The food might have been bad and ill-cooked (which it was not); we cared not, for our little waitress of sweet sixteen was the image of health and almost Madonna-like beauty, a paragon of gentle manners and good complexion, a charming copy of her mother, the park-keeper's wife. What words could those ruby lips and pearly teeth form but those of love! Any language would be rendered the sweeter by their being the means of its expression. So thought we. It had been well we had never been undeceived. Man was born to have this world rendered hollow as an "ould pill-box." One letter did all the mischief. With breathless suspense we awaited her first sweetly modest or gracefully hospitable remark, and heard—

"Please, sir, mother wants to know if you'll 'ave heggs or calves' 'ead for tea."

Who could become romantic over heggs and calves' 'ead unless he were a calf's 'ead himself? The picture lost a portion of its beauty; the world was deprived of poetical rhapsodies and sentiments, for our romantic companion rushed straightforward from the house as one possessed. More leisurely we followed.

Across the weir or up the stream by the dingy? We tried both, and it was hard to say which afforded us the most pleasure. The track is being cut right through this valley leading to Bulli, the coal depôt on the east coast, this being a shorter and far more beautiful route than the old track.

The scenery is like fairyland ought to be. By the roadway, now winding through masses of ferns of the most delicate hues of green, often tinted with exquisite pink and crimson tones, now cut round the face of some adventuresome cliff overhanging the flowing stream, itself the home of mosses, and the quaint but beautiful stag's-horn fern, shaded from the hot sun, which pierces here and there, by stately gums, fern-trees, palms, and various vines, canes, and hanging creepers, gradually we are led farther and farther up the valley, past gigantic rock-lilies rearing their flower-stalks on the hillside eight or ten feet high, outrivalling with their roseate bloom the ruddy tulip-flower itself.

This lily, which is a member of the order *Amaryllideae*, is a much nobler and more beautiful flower than its Latin name would imply. Who could imagine that *Doryanthus excelsa* is a noble plant (almost a tree), with long sword-like leaves at its base, with a head of exquisite rose-coloured blossoms, often measuring a foot to eighteen inches across? The individual blossom is as large as a full-sized Japanese lily, so that my readers will not convict me of exaggeration when I say that if these valleys of Illawarra could produce no other beautiful wonder of the vegetable kingdom, one would feel well satisfied at the time and trouble expended in a visit there.

The warratah, or tulip-flower, has received its English name

Warratah & Rock Lily

from its resemblance to the bulb of that name, but in size and stateliness, growing as it does five and six feet high, it far surpasses its prototype.

Always accompanied by the music of the river, which is fast narrowing, here and there we get glimpses of the stream, of a bright gold where the sun pierces its depths to its rocky bed, and of a deep indigo where the foliage, the banks, or the rocky boulders cast their shadows.

The poet, foiled in the morning, commences to spout Longfellow

> "Where hanging mosses shroud the pine;
> And the cedar grows, and the poisonous vine
> Is spotted like a snake."

The prosaic author assures him there may be hanging mosses, pines, or cedars, but that the poisonous thing like a snake in the log he is sitting on, is really a black snake. It's astonishing how a trifling remark of this sort takes the poetry out of our poet. He gives a whoop and jumps away in the most prosaic fashion.

Here, some miles up the valley, the roadway ends, and as we wish to penetrate farther, we strike boldly along what was once a half-brother to a footpath, but now is a still more distant relation. However, we crash boldly through, now with a crack coming down a few feet through rotten boughs, which we mistake for solid ground, now along the gravelly bed of the creek, for the river is only thirty feet across up here, now again on the lofty bank. Our glimpse of fairyland well repaid us for our three miles' scramble through the jungle, for getting into lonely and secluded parts we met with still finer scenery, where the native bamboo or cane climbs the highest trees, where the cabbage-tree palm (*Corypha Australis*) grows twenty feet high, and the fern-trees shade fallen trunks of vivid tones, ferns and foliage variegated and sparkling with a million hues in the light of the sun. Here, too, grows the flame-tree of the Illawarra (*Brachychiton acerifolium*), with scarlet blossoms lighting up the hills with such a blaze of splendour as almost to justify the sailors far out at sea telling one another that "those landlubbers have got another bush-fire." As we gaze entranced and industriously use sketch-books, a lyre-bird comes forth—a fitting representative, with its graceful tail, of this fairy glen, which we dubbed the lyre-bird's home (*see frontispiece*).

Down here the sun sets when all the rest of the world is still flooded with daylight, so we make the best of our way back, not without having lost our way, and made the timid one of our party fear a snake in every rotten log he walks on. The chance of getting "bushed" when you have a flowing stream to go by seems remote, but all things are possible to a "new chum" who tries, and so it was not long before we found that the water had either turned round and was running up-hill, or we had got on the banks of another creek. Our mistake was soon rectified, though a recent bush-fire which had charred the underwood on this stream caused the twigs to draw lines over our faces and clothes in sarcastic imitation of our artist.

Port Hackin River.

The following day we took a boat and went down the river, which below the weir is tidal. The banks were farther apart, the scenery was on a grander scale, but lost in delicacy and refinement, though our gourmet thought that a feed of oysters, which grew on all the rocks in myriads, quite compensated him for the falling off of the artistic. Thus is the ethereal weighed in the balance with the gross and found wanting. Our little nine-year-old coxswain spoke of oysters and indigestion, and all other topics of conversation, with the *blasé* air of one who had tried this world and found it hollow.

Anyone going to Sydney should not fail to go to the park.

If the same keeper is there he will find courteous attention and kindly solicitude, combined with a beautiful family and a prodigy of an infant, who at a few weeks old, ate everything from its natural food to a piece of mutton, though I will not guarantee that the infant will not have grown in the meantime. If so there may be a succeeding substitute, for the birth-rate in Australia is the highest in the world, and the park-keeper's family seems likely to flourish and increase for an indefinite period.

Having come so far from Sydney, let me advise you just to step along with me to Bulli and Wollongong, where so much butter comes from. The scenery on the way is not very enchanting after we leave these wooded gorges till we come to the vicinity of those two centres of interest, but then an excuse may be found for such an apparent lack of enterprise on the part of the residents in this district in not "running a good show" of scenery, in that they are so few. You will have either to ride or walk the whole way, unless you feel disposed to risk your insurance policy by driving along the fearful roadway which climbs these heath-grown rocky hills and dales, whose scrubby bushes and grass-tree spikes seem almost interminable. A small patch of trees—ironbarks and other gums—dubbed a forest, is intersected by the road for a few hundred yards, but beyond that *nihil et praeterea nihil*.

The distance between the National Park gates and Bulli is variable, and according to my experience, decidedly elastic. When I started I was told it was twelve miles; when I had gone six the first traveller said that there were still eleven or twelve to go; three miles farther on a couple of "swagsmen" —workmen on the look-out for work, and carrying a swag, or bundle of their household goods—assured me that Bulli was then only five miles off; yet another two miles, and my experience was that of Alice in the looking-glass, for the plaguy road had so lengthened out that I was still six miles away, according to two men and a boy who, together with a broken-down trap and horse, were a lively advertisement of the evil condition of the roads.

A few extraordinary symbols of the Australian's enterprise are visible along the roadside. See here is a wayside store in the midst of this howling wilderness, to which no habitations are nearer than six miles, except an "accommodation house" some two miles off. Where does the storekeeper get his custom? Wayside travellers are few, and he reckons that mayhap a house or two may be erected close by, and become a nucleus of a town. Besides, the new railway is coming this way, and perhaps will open up the country, though a more heaven-forsaken tract of scrub was rarely seen. Thus doth the average Australian "take time by the forelock." Here again, in the midst of a piece of bush, we come across a signpost bearing a notice, "Victoria Parade, 3 chains wide;" other signposts point off right and left, all glorified in fresh paint, "High Street, 1½ chains wide," "George Street, 1½ chains wide," and so on all along the "Parade," which at present is a cart-track through the scrub about ten feet wide, and the side "streets" are mere footpaths hewn down in the almost impenetrable jungle. This land has been surveyed for a township. Probably long ago some speculator got wind of it, and has bought up a large part of the surveyed country, taking his chance of there ever being a township erected. Government may plot out townships, but it has not yet, with all its paternal solicitude, proved capable of stocking them.

The buying and selling of township allotments makes and mars many a speculator out here, and requires considerable foresight coupled with good luck to make the occupation profitable.

The term "accommodation house" requires some explanation. A resident who wishes to turn an honest penny and does not wish to loiter about getting a license and starting an inn, if he is on a well-used track sets up an accommodation house, where a traveller may be accommodated with board and bed for the night. The accommodation is of course limited, but by no means to be sneezed at. As a rule you will find your hostess a quiet overworked woman, whom you almost feel it a sin to burden with your requirements, so many children does she seem to have and so much does she have to do. Let me assure you that in this accommodation house near the forest you will have culinary delicacies and a sitting and bedroom you never expected to see out in the bush, though it is possible you may have to share them with a "drummer"—that is, a commercial traveller—or a "swagsman."

Our road leads us close to some of the largest coalfields of the colonies. New coalfields have been lately found near the National Park which, added to those already in existence at Coalcliff and Bulli, will supply the wants of the colonies, it is calculated, for centuries to come. Victoria, Queensland, and New Zealand have all their coalfields, the last of the three being, according to New Zealanders' traditions, possessed of the finest coal and largest fields.

Coalcliff, or Clifton, itself boasts but little scenery. It is a place of use, not ornament. After we emerge from the bush which we had to walk through after leaving the rocky downs, we find ourselves on the seacoast and, skirting along over some lofty cliffs, we drop down into this coaly township, with its two or three hotels of a very rough character, and inevitable "store." A few miles farther along the coast brings us to the more pretentious town of Bulli, which leaves a strong impression on the mind as of a rather untidy and very small provincial town of England without its picturesqueness. The scenery, from Coalcliff onwards, is attractive and imposing; the seacoast is bold and rugged, the lofty scarped cliffs overhang the road and tower above with their crowns of timber; farther on they recede inland and disclose a range of thickly-wooded hills extending along the shore, leaving grassy plains varying from two or three to twenty miles in extent between themselves and the sea.

Here above Bulli is the Bulli Pass, which for scenery might rival anything in Australia. It is a climb up to the summit of the pass, and is not on our way to Wollongong, but the views both far and near are gorgeous. I went up on a fine day, disdaining the help of a quadruped, and considered that a hundredfold expenditure of muscular power and hard words would have been well repaid by the ever-changing views. The winding road takes a turn from the plains, and lands one in the midst of a fairy scene. Palms, acacias, flowering creepers, tree-ferns, bamboos and shrubs, trees and ferns, marvellous in their variety of hue and shape, grow in tropical profusion; the eye is fairly dazzled with the verdure and artistic confusion of the whole. Now the road turns again along the eastern side of the hill, and far away through the leafy network and branches of the palms the beautiful sapphire of the sea rivals the azure of the sky, the butter-growing plains of Wollongong stretch out their green carpet dotted with lowing herds to the south, and here right beneath our feet—for the road runs with a precipice on one side—are the tree-tops of gums and ferns, palms, and other timber hundreds of feet below, whereon, if tradition be true, more than one vehicle and its occupants have met with their fate. A voluble old road-mender told me that some ten years ago, before the road was well protected, it was the most dangerous in the colony, and he had known a coach full of passengers start off the brink of the precipice, all shattered to pieces as they fell with a dull thud on those innocent-looking trees below.

The rock from which the road is cut is covered with a hundred different species of fern and moss; far up on the hillside grows bush and scrub, which we soon put on a level with ourselves, for we reach the summit, and by a by-path strike to a little wooden gallery overhanging the precipice, erected by a paternal Government. The view is impressive in the extreme, though the foliage has quite changed up here. It is too high for the tropical profusion of palms and fern-trees. Here the eucalyptus takes alone all the duty of ornamentation, and naturally does not affect the beauty of its more delicate *confrères* down below.

Here the Australian "larrikin" carves his name, as he does throughout the colonies wherever he can find an opportunity, vying with his Vandal congener in the old country to perpetuate his obscure fame.

The road from Bulli to Wollongong after leaving the pass was enlivened by a circumstance showing the extreme utilitarian mind of the native. As I tramped along with sketching knapsack on shoulder, a rawboned youth came hurriedly after me on horseback with the object of asking me to show him my patterns. On being asked for an explanation of his curious request, he said he took me for a travelling tailor with pattern-books of clothing, and on being assured of the actual facts of the case, could hardly realise that there was anyone so careless of pecuniary gain as to tramp about the country sketching for pleasure. The road passes in places through a pleasing avenue of gums; the paddocks on either side speak of good rains and soil, and are not belied by the stock feeding there.

Wollongong is quite an important township. Who travelling in the colonies does not know Wollongong butter by name? Like many another article it confers its name on impostors, and consequently much more Wollongong butter is consumed than can possibly be produced in this busy little township.

The scenery much resembles rural England, except the timber in the shape of the "fig-tree,"—one of which, with a trunk scores of feet in circumference, gives its name to a hamlet,—and an occasional stately cabbage-tree palm, called so on the *lucus a non* principle.

A walk along the sea-beach should be undertaken with caution. Wishing to get a sketch far afield, I tempted the treacherous sands of a small creek which flowed over the beach to the sea, and had almost been, like the stones in the Jordan, there until this day. I subsequently heard that another adventurer, a few months before, being more pertinacious, had persevered to get through, but did not succeed, as the Insurance Company were even then searching for his body. By wandering in this way one necessarily sees a greater variety of things and places than by sticking to the beaten track.

Here and there on sandbanks pelicans squatted, staring stupidly until almost within a stone's throw of the intruder, then lazily flapping their heavy wings with a discordant and resentful croak, flew to more secluded spots. Farther up the stream milch kine, sleek and healthy, stood under the far-reaching shade of the forest trees on the banks, ruminating as is their wont, suggesting pleasant recollections of the Midland counties.

In the valleys formed by the timber-covered hills, the advance-guard of the many spurs of the great Dividing Range, are gold, iron, and coal mines of considerable value, while the inhabitants of Wollongong have the kerosene shale almost at their doors. The hills themselves stand out like regular truncated cones against the sky, curious but stiff features in the landscape.

This farming district extends some few miles farther down to Lake Illawarra, and resembles, though it does not equal, more closely than anything else in New South Wales, the rural scenery of the old country. Even the galvanised iron roofs occasionally give way to the more rustic tiles; hedges are not so rare as in other districts, and paddocks are small, comprising, like ours at home, only a few acres.

It was here I met with a distinctive piece of Australian character. While engaged in sketching a roadside scene I attracted the attention of a farmer, a great, fine, bushy-bearded Hercules, who assured me that as fine if not finer scenery lay the other side of the range, whither he himself was going.

"Come and have a shake-down with me for two or three nights, and I'll take care you see the finest views in the neighbourhood. You'll find us rough and homely, but we'll give you a hearty welcome."

The invitation, though fascinating, and seconded by a friend of his who happened to live in the same neighbourhood, who also tendered his hospitable services, could not be accepted, as time was "of the essence" of my stay in the neighbourhood; but their confidence in a stranger, a kindness of which I had some further examples later on, impressed me strongly.

When tired of the neighbourhood—for such a result sometimes occurs, rank heresy though it be in an Australian creed, and comfortable though the motherly hostess of the hotel on Wollongong beach may make you—you can easily ship back by steamer to Sydney, where after a few hours you may again parade George Street, stroll through the gardens, or have a Turkish bath at Wigzell's, a cheap and necessary luxury (if one may be paradoxical) after the dusty roads of our late campaign. Here a shaving or two taken off with the jack-plane wielded by the muscular arm of the black shampooer will fit you for fresh fields and pastures new to be seen in the next chapter.

Advertising!

CHAPTER X.

Boot-cleaning extraordinary.—Off to the Blue Mountains.—New South Welsh Civility.—"Everyone goes First Class."—Aboriginal Nomenclature.—Rolling Stock.—Penrith.—Scaling the Little Zigzag.—A Feast of Nature.—In the Ranges.—Wentworth Falls.—Katoomba.—Mount Victoria.—Mount Piddington.—Sunset from the Summit.—" Creep in after Dark."—Govett's Leap.—Mermaid's Glen without the Mermaids.—Mount York and Hartley Valley.—Nothing about the Fish River Caves.—No Inquest or Waste of Ink.—The " other side."—Paint-boxes at a Premium.—Similarity of the Scenery.—Bathurst passed through.—The Line to Dubbo.—Bribery and Corruption.—The Bitter Cry of the Overladen Coach.

ADVENTUROUS spirit! you have accompanied my erratic tongue so far to a good purpose. We will away by the morning train to the Blue Mountains. Boots not cleaned? Oh, never mind! Well, if you must pander to the vitiated trades of an effete civilisation, come along, there are plenty of shoeblacks in George Street. Great heavens! Take care not to give the man the old country copper or two; give him threepence, unless you want him to knock you down. *That* may stop his mouth until you can get safely to the corner of the next street, but sixpence would probably entitle you to a " thank you " and a whole skin. Remember the minimum standard is higher out here than at home; though many things are cheaper, labour is far dearer. Does not the shoeblack earn his bread by the labour of his hands assisted by his mouth? *Ergo*, he is a labourer in a dual capacity.

Now, then, jump into this "hansom," taking good care to

wedge yourself in with portmanteau, rugs, and such *small deer*, thus to be able to defy the jerks and bumps over the road-crossings caused by your driver's fear (?) of the white-helmeted Robert of the south. Ah, that was a shave! The tramcar missed running our vehicle down, but seems to be compensating itself by driving a hole through yonder van.

At the terminus—trains, trams, and cabs seem inextricably mixed. Eh? Did you hear that porter? He actually said "sir!" Is it possible? Would a Victorian railway official descend to such servility? Never! He goes to get checks for our luggage; this is civilisation with a vengeance! "Exchange is no robbery," say you; "but two small numbered plates of brass in exchange for two portmanteaux containing clothes, books, ammunition, and, last but not least, means for libelling nature in water-colours, hardly seems a fair exchange." Await in patient expectation the end. We shall not be troubled by having to look after our luggage till we get to our destination, and then for no charge whatever we'll re-exchange our checks for our baggage and march away with the proud consciousness of having received something for nothing, always a satisfaction to mean "humans." This system of checking luggage through is one more instance of the enterprise of the children exceeding that of their parents. Third-class? No, there is not any! We have but two classes here: the first, affording accomodation for the "bloated aristocracy," and the second, for the rest of the community. Never mind what friends tell you about "everyone travelling first." You may see extremely substantial persons going second, who though they may not be "somebodies" are decidedly a cut above "nobodies," and far from *spirituel* in appearance.

The scenery up to Paramatta has been already described in the last chapter. *Here* they cannot afford to put a new setting on the stage as we do at home, as season gives place to season. Taxation is high, but they have not yet begun to tax the resources of the climate.

Beyond Paramatta, scrub gives way to grassy plains dotted thinly with the "stable" of the country, and thickly with the primeval gum-trees, often ring-barked. We pass many railway stations for the first thirty or forty miles, all doing credit to the colony and shaming some of ours in the old country.

Now we have a breathing space to talk about the "proud independence" of the Victorian officials, as compared with his "servile" brother on these lines. Why this thusness. Report has it, that inasmuch as almost all the Victorian appointments are obtained by favour through some Government official or other, those holding, "dum bene se gesserint," these appointments, adopt that supreme contempt for and indifference to the comfort of the public not unknown in other countries. Of course you will find exceptions, but these affect the rule in the usual way. Why the so-called Radicalism of New South Wales permits such a "servile" contrast to "independent" Victoria, may be known hereafter, but is at present an awesome riddle.

Did you notice the names of some of the stations we passed through? What an odd mixture of the pleasing and discordant these native names are. Now, Wooloomooloo, a suburb on the other side of Sydney, has a sweetly poetic ring about it, apart from the prophetic anticipation of the aborigines as expressed in the first syllable. Paramatta, too, has a pleasing alliteration, but what can be advanced in favour of Warrabungles or Currangoorgong? If you have a sensitive ear at all there rankles within you a hatred for the black and all his race, which can only be satisfied by the banishment of the offending nomenclature.

What a fund of learning we in England received from the Tichborne trial! How learnedly we spoke of Wagga-Wagga, and how have we fallen from our high estate when we find that the veriest colonial infant knows better than to pronounce the word as though it rhymed with bragger! that it is sounded as though spelt war-ga, and that the name is clipped by colonials to one-half its size. Life is not long enough out here (not even infant life) to pronounce the whole of these jaw-breaking names, and notwithstanding the salubrity of the climate, the roads are not in good enough order for a pedestrian to walk from one end of the name to the other, as Mark Twain suggests anent German words.

Our carriages on this railway are by no means so commodious as they might be. "Cars" here, as in the old country, are a luxury. Victoria has led the van in considering them a necessity, but has not been widely followed in this enterprise. However, we can prevent ourselves from being suffocated or stifled, for we have Venetian shutters throughout instead of fixed windows, which we can, if on the other hand it be too cold, replace with glazed sashes.

Here we are at last at Penrith, some fifty miles from Sydney, still on the plains but with the mountain spurs right ahead of us. Do you see this river—the Nepean? This is Sydney's future water supply, a canal from which was cut some years ago when a water famine was imminent. Jupiter Pluvius will be a god to laugh at, not to stand in awe of, very soon. Poor old heathen divinity! how one's heart aches for this fresh indignity. He has been having a right merry and idle time of it inland, however, just now, playing fast and loose with the squatters.

Now our train rushes towards the mountains as though it meant to run its head against them. No such thing; when we get to their foot we turn abruptly and commence scaling the face of this first ridge by a series of zigzag movements, now to the north, now to the south, until we reach the top, whence we gaze over the plains hundreds of feet below us stretching out to Sydney and the sea.

Now that we have ascended the Little Zigzag, as this clever piece of engineering is called, which permits an ordinary engine on an ordinary narrow-gauge set of rails thus to climb the steep face of the ridge with a minimum of risk, we commence a series of curves and gradients round spur and ridge ever tending westward, bent on reaching the highest point, some four thousand six hundred feet above sea-level. Have all your eyes about you; fortunately up this gradient we cannot go quickly, so there is plenty of time to look around. The whole of these ranges are wooded—so much we can see—and wooded with timber

THE "NEW CHUM" IN AUSTRALIA. 133

chiefly eucalyptus in genus. Ah! We draw a deep breath of contentment as a break in the gums that overshadow the rails shows us a great valley of timber softening off into the distance with an extraordinarily beautiful and brilliant ultramarine.

. Very beautiful is that blue bloom which softens off all inequalities and fills up all the depths of distant shadows. It was a rainy day here yesterday, and the scenic effect has been improved and could hardly be surpassed. Another glimpse of a few seconds shows a varying scene of great scarped sandstone cliffs, rosy and golden, cutting clearly through the blue haze, and heightening its tone by contrast. See here again, this is Wentworth's Falls Station, a well-known place for sight-seers to stop at and take a short walk to see the falls, and the great gorge of timber and cliff extending miles in front. We get a glimpse of the view now. How beautiful those rosy cliffs round the face of the densely wooded mountain look! Water-colours alone will give you the requisite tone and atmosphere; do not trust the harsher oil. A peculiarity of this glorious blue haze is that it does not render the objects it covers indistinct, as we see in the atmospheric blues of the old country, the mass of blue, according to my observations, being composed of thousands of shadows in between the trees in light or shadow.

We do not see decided peaks here elevating themselves in a distinctive fashion above their fellows, consequently we do not realise, even at Mount Victoria itself, which is close to the turning-point of the railway, that we are over four thousand feet above the sea, except perhaps that the air seems brisker and blows slightly cooler.

You can stop here at Katoomba if you wish to see the Orphan Rock and another of those wonderful gorges. But you had best come along to Mount Victoria, where we shall be in the very centre of all this gorgeous scenery. You will find at the chief hotel there a most attentive host, sometime back, according to tradition, a well-known merchant skipper.

The summit of Mount Piddington, called so after a well-known member of the legislature, is just a walk behind the hotel. There are many ways of doing all things; if you care you can climb round by the gentle gradients of a built road winding through the bush, or can take a short cut and strike boldly across this little valley through the thick of the forest to the summit; but you will want a climbing talent here, and, as the positions one assumes are more monkey-like than lady-like, ladies prefer the more prosaic road.

We cross over a little abyss between massive rocks by the natural bridge of a fallen tree-trunk. If it be winter the snakes are hybernating like all well-regulated "sarpints;" if not, you had better keep a sharp look-out, as there are many poisonous vipers here. Here we strike a winding path cut roughly down the hill, and, as we are half-way down, we follow it round crag and spur, past ferns, waterfalls, and tree-ferns by the side of a little rivulet, and down to the quiet silent pool into which the water drops over these lofty rocks embosomed in the heart of an awful stillness, unbroken save by the regular splash of the stream. You find perhaps that sliding over that last tree-trunk has not improved the integrity of your habiliments. We shall have to preserve a prudent reserve and not get back to the hotel till dusk, or judiciously hold some sketches over your delinquencies. Never mind, there are no curious eyes here; not even that kangaroo we heard crashing through the scrub just now, or that rock-wallaby running down like one possessed, can see us for half a second, so dense is the jungle.

Retracing our steps, after considerable loss of breath and good language, we reach the summit, emerge from the bush, sit down on the bench a kindly paternal Government has provided here, and gaze.

The appropriate silence of keen appreciation accords in its golden qualities with the scene before us. The setting sun, illuminating the sandstone cliffs which, capped with verdure, stand up out of the sloping sides of forest, deepening in hue into the valley beneath, gilds the whole vista with its splendour. Away trends the valley, leagues upon leagues of unbroken forest gradually shut in by ridge after ridge of veritable blue.

timber. To the right a scarped cliff elevates its majestic timber-crowned head from a valley between our own rocky eminence and its rosy face, now shaded in the gathering evening from the golden beams of bright merry old Sol.

The shadows in the valley hundreds of feet below our feet all partake of that deep ultramarine hue, and with their deep melancholy tones accentuate the contrast of the glorified summits. Had not the paternal Government erected a shed and this bench we are sitting on, and were there not a notice-board from the trustees of the spot cautioning any Vandals, many a sketch had not been drawn here; but the sacrilege of libelling the beauty of the spot seems small after such commonplace conventionalism, and the sensitive conscience is set at rest.

A few miles away in an easterly direction lie the famous falls and gorge of Govett's leap. As though through a dispensation of Providence, the eight miles of road thither from Mount Victoria allow of no distant views, no peeps through the heavy timber on either side, so that all the glories of this wonderful spot burst upon you at once. The road suddenly turns a corner; you do the same, and fairly hold your breath at the sight of a gorge grander and more abrupt, longer, though narrower, than that at Mount Victoria, commencing right under your feet eight hundred or a thousand feet down, stretching away into the softer ultramarine of thirty miles distance, its walls scarped with cliffs or timber slopes, with one vast cliff nearly a thousand feet deep, to the right, almost as perpendicular as a plumb-line, over which a stream some twenty feet wide, but now only a few inches deep, precipitates itself, waving like a thin gauze veil until it is lost in the tree-tops eight hundred feet below. After heavy rains the stream becomes a torrent, and the silence at present unbroken is changed for the splashing of the distant water.

The curious may go to the top of the falls and, lying on the stone cliffs there, gaze over that awful precipice down which tradition says that Govett, a bushranger, flying from his pursuers, leapt once on a time, preferring certain death of this kind to that of a more ignominious nature. One almost envies the man this magnificent and vast mausoleum of nature.

When you have gazed sufficiently long at this stupendous scene and have all the conceit taken out of you (the remedy is a good one, and not patented) there are fresh wonders to be seen in the romantic and, for that matter, rheumatic ravine not far off, called Mermaid's Glen. After a long climb down, after

Covett's Leap, Blue Mountains

passing hosts of ferns of all sorts, including huge tree-ferns, moss-covered rocks and crags down some of which you have to slide, trusting to the insurance angel for your safety, past little waterfalls and bubbling brooks, you come to this haunt of the nymphs, a more beautiful edition of the glen at Mount Piddington. To be in keeping with the aborigines the Danaids should be black; but candour compels me to admit I never heard of even one of the white species having been seen there except an occasional nymph decked in Sydney's latest fashions, without the fascinating fishy tail.

A great feature of this neighbourhood is that even should you lose your way on your journey to a place, you will probably discover something to repay you. This happened to me again and again.

On the way to Mount York, whence one gets a broad view over Hartley Vale and the surrounding gorges, I took the wrong turning and wound down a charming wild mountain pass, meeting bullock teams with patient beasts and cracking whips, all affording a contrast to the smiling fertile plain at the bottom of the valley. When "Beauty," "Firebrand," "Dollie," and their toiling brothers and sisters, their profane drivers, and their creaking vehicles had receded into the distance, the usual "enchantment" was lent, and in the clear air the sounds were as those of some strangely sweet concordant music.

Can you tell me why an ordinary bullock-driver cannot drive his team without half a score of oaths? I know not. I knew a "bullockie" (as these men are dubbed) who had a team of twelve beasts under his command which obeyed his every word and never received a word, which a "high-born ladie" might not have listened to.

There is a story of a bullock-driver who had been cautioned not to swear, as he had a lady passenger on the tumbril, getting stuck in the mud and then coming to the occupant of his vehicle—

"Please, mum, if I mayn't call the hul lot on 'em a —— set of ——s, we'll never get out of this at all."

This story is said to be true, and characteristic of the intercommunication of thought between one *beast* and another. As a set-off to my model bullock-driver I came across one in Queensland who could "cuss" till everybody around was blue in the face, and seemed to get on about as well as the other.

From Mount Victoria you may also go to the Fish River Caves, said to be the most wonderful stalactitic and stalagmitic caverns in the world. I came across many tourists who had gone, and from their conversation should fancy that the Government had better supplement the present caretaker, or the beauties of these vast underground caverns will very soon all be in the possession of the visitors who go there. One New South Welshman, as is usually the case, assured me that it was the only place really worth seeing, and as I had not seen that I had come to Australia in vain. I may mention as a species of blood-wite or an act of compensation for his widow, that she is now open to a re-engagement. She has opened an establishment for the sale of petroleum coming from Hartley Vale, and promises to give any one having my recommendation a "warm reception." This is *founded* on fact!

As you have come so far you must i' faith come along a few miles and see the Great Zigzag, a giant brother of our friend on the eastern side of the range. By this series of steps we shall get down into the plains on the western side which stretch for hundreds of miles with barely an elevation more than a few hundred feet in height. The engineers have overcome immense difficulties and obstacles, of which the passenger might be wholly unaware were he simply to judge by the safe and easy motion of the train. He will probably, if he looks about him, however, come to the same conclusion as I, that these feats of engineering skill speak volumes for colonial enterprise.

We shall soon find that we shall be independent of the many rugs and overcoats that our partially acclimatised blood needed up in the mountains of an evening. We are lucky enough to get a sunset on our way down to the Zigzag. Was ever the roseate flush in the west more grandly contrasted than with those delicate blue shadows in the foliage. Paint boxes are at a premium along this route; colour is so brilliant that pans and tubes give unmistakable signs of being far removed from widows' cruises. Experiment proves that it is of no use to throw oil on the troubled waters, for here as elsewhere oils and water-colours are not interchangeable. The talented Miss North, whose gracious national gift of pictures deck the walls of a museum at Kew Gardens, in London, has vividly represented some such effect near the Range, Harlaxton, Queensland, almost a counterpart of the scene we are now gazing on ; but she suffered a disadvantage from the fact of her medium being oil, as water-colours alone can give these extraordinary atmospheric effects to perfection which surround us in these ranges.

Throughout the Dividing Range, the Liverpool Ranges, those of the Gippsland, Victoria, and the more northern ranges along the sea-coast of Queensland, the scenery presents, with certain climatic exceptions, the same grand wildness, the same almost monotonous blue haze.

It is well to know when to leave the mountains, otherwise one is liable to get as it were crystallised into one's own self, and begins to tire of the endless valleys and hills of gums, with their cool though vivid colouring.

As an ornamental forest-tree the gum is a failure ; I am sorry to hurt its feelings, but 'tis so, " and that 'tis so 'tis pity." Not content with presenting its worst side uppermost, namely the edge of its leaves instead of their faces, it often assumes a most inharmonious crude yellow tuft of young leaves at the end of its branches, not a lemon or citron yellow, but a hard uncompromising raw sienna tone, which may be a contrast to, but is certainly no improvement on, the grey or blue-green habit the trees usually wear. There is no such tree throughout Australia as to compare with our forest elms or oaks for intrinsic beauty. This I confidently state, even taking into consideration the casuarinas, the pines, ay, and the imported Norfolk Island pines, and the Moreton Bay figs. Vaster they grow, these mighty gums, 'tis true, but size and beauty do not, as is often the case, go hand in hand. What avails the mightiest tree, with a girth of sixty feet and a height over four hundred feet, if its head is but a few tufted bunches of leaves, as isolated as the teeth of an aboriginal gin (woman) of fifty summers.

On this side of the range, as we rattle along, we notice great changes in the forest ; it begins to lose the luxuriance of its undergrowth, and as we pass along and so over the plains we notice that ferns become rare and finally altogether absent, and grass reassumes its sway under the shadow of iron-barks, stringy-barks, bastard-box, and the like, which here and there are rendered still more unseemly by the ruthless hand of the ring-barker.

Bathurst has not in itself much to detain the ordinary visitor. A few gold-fields lie near, and some travellers make this a starting-point for the Fish River Caves, but beyond that one cannot get up much enthusiasm about the town, an important one, however, in its way, as being the largest on this side of the Blue Mountains.

The railway winds its slow way still further westward some hundred miles or so, and as the scenery is of the usual gummy pastoral character we will clear the whole line in a line, and land ourselves at the terminus, Dubbo. The obvious suitability of this name for joking gives the station-master some extra work for which Government does not pay him, for every one naturally asks why in the world the colonists dub—— then comes down the avenging official and annihilates him. It is plain that this sober official's life is not a happy one.

From here coaches and teams travel to tap the far-lying districts of New South Wales to the westward; and as we wish to get some idea of up-country life removed from the civilising influences of railways and daily posts, we must perforce trust our limbs to a real specimen of Messrs. Cobb & Co.'s coaches, reckless of the consequences. There will not be much to interest the idler here at Dubbo. It is a larger counterpart of Coonamble, described further on; the country around is pastoral and agricultural, chiefly the former, and game is scarce. A few hours suffice to shake off the effects of our ten hours' ride on the railway from Mount Victoria, and fit us to face the perils of the road.

"Take my advice and don't take up much luggage, for though you may by a judicious tickling of the official's palm get him to pass you something considerably over the fourteen pounds allowed free to each passenger, you may nevertheless have to pay stiffly for excess, and withal find your luggage a hindrance when up-country."

This was kindly advice given me, unfortunately, *ex post facto*. I speak feelingly! On that bright Australian morning when I first experienced this bitter drop in my cup, my heart was blackened with a fierce and bitter longing to assault the coach officials for not passing more than sixty pounds in excess of the proper allowance. What a poor country must that be where bribery and corruption can only command some 400 per cent. This despondent state was not much relieved when the vehicle drove up that was going to be saddled with our fortunes. I then grieved that the coach agent had not been stricter as to the fourteen pounds alone, as it seemed that such a ramshackle-looking vehicle could never stand the additional weight I was loading it with.

I felt some comfort that I had with me some packthread and court-plaister, should the state of the vehicle require such surgical assistance; and finding that other passengers were climbing in and out, to the number of six or seven, with bags and baggage and apparent nonchalance, and that sundry mail-bags were being added to our burden in a most confiding straw-on-the-back-of-a-camel fashion, I consented to carry out my portion of the contract. Accordingly the coachman took one final "nip" of raw spirit "for the future," cracked a ferocious-looking whip, and off we lumbered after our four well-groomed and spirited steeds, the most respectable portion of the whole party.

Overweight.

CHAPTER XI.

From Dubbo to Coonamble.—The way we pull up.—The Imbibing Capacity of a Driver.—The Driver's Creeds.—Pure Liquor wanted.—Bush Scenery.—A Heaven-forgotten Spot.—"Hold hard Inside."—Bad Roads and Worse Roads.—Matters of Passing Interest.—The Strong-flavoured Scents of Nature.—Australian River-bed.—Topsyturvydom.—Coaching at Night.—A Sight for an Old-Country Coachman.—'Possums.—Dawn and Differences.—Accidents by Flood and Field.—Drivers' Mistakes.—Passengers' Foolhardiness.—Our Destination.—Coonamble.—Hats of a Pattern.—The Ubiquitous Chinaman.—Stores Banks, Hotels, and Barbers.—A Good Clip.—The Silent Meals.—No Beauty in the Township.—Life in the Verandah of an Inn.—A would-be Purchaser.—"This old hors'll drink and think on it."—Epithets more Gay than Grave.—The Black fights his White "Brother."—The Blacks.

AS we started in the last chapter, did you notice how our steeds seemed to go ahead considerably before the vehicle? It seemed to jolt and bump along in an aimless fashion after them, now veering to the right, now to the left, as though hardly with any heart in the poor chase after the horses in front. From the box-seat the driver telegraphs, or telephones, to the leaders (in language replete with adjectives and adverbs not usually heard in drawing-rooms) to stop, and some good while after they have done so the wheelers think it time to pull up; and then, after another interval of greater or less duration, the coach rolls up, just in time, perhaps to prevent them all from falling into the arms of Morpheus.

The mucous membrane of a Cobb & Co's driver is, I understand, replaced by a steel lining, the consequence of which is that they can drink down most potent and fiery compounds surnamed whisky, and live like a fish, but in fire-water. Our driver guaranteed that he could put himself outside a nip of the "cratur" at every licensed house we passed, and dutifully did he fulfil his own guarantee whenever a passenger "shouted"* for him, which was the case at every house of call, whether licensed or unlicensed. At the latter house he would inquire anxiously after the "baby's health," and would emerge from the inner room wiping and smacking his lips, presumably after a kiss of the "poorty little dear." However, as he was "as hard as nails," and never let his potations affect his reins, one could but admire the phenomenal facility with which he could thus imbibe liquid fire. One other, a passenger, emulated him, and, being a hotel proprietor himself, consumed similar drinks with equal nonchalance.

Another passenger, an abstainer, tried cautiously to improve the situation after one more than ordinarily fiery drink had "left a burning sensation" in the driver's throat, but was frozen into a solid lump by the decisive views of our Jehu, who approved a "common-sense creed."

"If a man feels he can do without it, it is mere extravagance and luxury to drink it; if he feels he were better without it, it were folly to imbibe; but if he feel that it were better for him to quaff the flowing bowl, and he has a drought within him and a friend or a 'thick-un'† to stand by him, he is a poor, weak, cross-grained fool to refuse."

Such was the essence of the anti-Blue-Ribbonist's creed, though it resembled (I say it with due solemnity) another and a better-known creed, being freely interspersed with damnatory clauses.

These wayside "*hotels*," as they call themselves, in common with most up-country houses of the sort, do not seem to possess the purest cellars. Adulteration is carried on to an alarming

---

* "To shout," to stand treat.
† A coin of the realm.

extent, and a traveller passing through a place where he is unknown, and cannot feel certain of getting the "high-priced article," had much better, for the time, be an anti-alcoholist of a passive nature. The Blue Ribbon Army might make more converts than it could supply with ribbon by encouraging a pledge not to drink any but pure liquor. The coachman would have it that the potations were innocent, in which perforce one must agree, for they were indeed innocent of the usual ingredients and chemical constituents that are generally understood to form the liquors after which they are called.

You must not expect to see much scenery along the route; even though the grandest views lay alongside the road, your new chum's eyes would have enough to do in looking out for the stray branches of trees, or in dilating with horror at the state of the track. But fortunately for our unity of purpose there is no scenery; the ground is unvaryingly flat for a hundred miles, passing through stunted scrub and stalky gum-trees, and for the first eighty miles grass, except in the environs of our starting-point, is not to be seen. Here and there the track, which is some two chains wide, flanked on one side by the useful though unornamental telegraph line, passes through mallee scrub; but this is not the chief haunt of this man-defying and civilisation-retarding shrub. For the most part we are passing through an endless forest of a decidedly unpicturesque character, which the words "bush and scrub" rather significantly describe.

The track does credit to the instruments and skill of the surveyors, for it stretches out with its ruts and snags, its sinuous cart-tracks and melancholy timber walls, for miles ahead of us. The sketch in the plate gives a representation of such a "country road"—erring somewhat on the side of exaggeration of natural beauties, consequent on the absence (from the illustration) of the dull grey-greens of the foliage. That the tree-stumps have not all been grubbed up one has a forcible reminder at times from the driver calling out, "Hold hard!" an observation followed by a sudden upheaval of the conveyance. Then comes the time when the adventuresome traveller begins to think of bone-setting, or the unlucky insides of trephining, subjects not altogether removed from their thoughts, when we suddenly fall down into one of the ten- or twelve-inch ruts in this black soil, or jump a little tree-trunk obstructing our course.

At dinner, for which, having time, we pull up at a half-way house, we forget our troubles for awhile, and realise that we still are sound in wind and limb, a fact of which we are by no

Scene on a Bush Road.

means so certain farther on, when the "worse road" spoken of before exhausts at once our patience and expletives.

Few vehicles did we meet to vary the monotony of our way, beyond a team or to two going up laden with stores or coming down with wool, the chief distractions being to our noses, which had a lively time of it whenever we passed a dead horse, sheep, or other beast—the victim of dry weather, insufficient fodder, and bad roads. Sometimes we leave the track altogether, and drive in under the trees themselves, where often we find better going than on the track, and then have an exciting onslaught of boughs and branches to ward off; then we realise still more fully that nature, when attending the funeral obsequies of an "old hoss," can excite the olfactory nerves of passers-by more thoroughly than a hundred Colognes or Constantinoples. The driver took unkindly to my request to have the coach stopped so that I might sketch one of the strongest odours, which had well-nigh broken the glass lamps of our mail-coach, as he considered the colony had a copyright in such smells. The driver was a couple of sizes larger than any one else on the coach, and wont to enforce his oral with pugilistic arguments; so the point was not contested.

Towards evening we cross an Australian river. Some hundred and fifty feet wide is its sandy bed, and some ten or twelve feet deep below the banks, but never a drop of water has there been in it for months, nor may be for another series of months. When the rain falls, as it knows how to do out here, some night the dwellers on the banks will hear a great rushing and roaring, and if they have the curiosity to look out will see a turbulent stream laden with snags and logs, perhaps sheep, horses, and cattle, hurrying down so quickly that in a day or two all the water may have passed by, although there is by no means a violent fall in the land here. Water can generally be found by digging a few feet in the sandy bed; but to see dry streams and rivers is the rule this side of the Range, the larger rivers, such as the Murray, the Namoy, the Darling, or the Barwan, dwindling down often to a series of unconnected, widely-dispersed water-holes. There is scarcely anything more to be surprised at in this land of topsyturvydom, where trees are shadeless, birds sing not, and kangaroos "swallow and disgorge their young," as the Irishman said. But it *is* surprising that, notwithstanding repeated warnings and disasters, people may still be found who will camp out for the night in one of these innocent-looking river-beds, perhaps within a few hours all to be hurried to eternity without a note of alarm.

After a cosy tea with some friends I happened to meet going up country we started again for our all-night ride through the bush. We changed coaches and drivers, and found our new conveyance a copy of the first with the addition of five great flaring eyes that arched over the box seats. We started, and so would my readers have started, to see the bold, confident way that we drove into the wall of forest, and trotted along at a smart rate through a track scarcely broader than our coach. The driver had cut it himself, and, though the bush was pitch dark, and rendered still more confusing to the novice's eyes by the divergent and convergent rays of our lamps, he never missed the way, never took a wrong turning where all seemed wrong, cut round tree trunks that an old-country horse-rider would have scarcely negotiated, under branches that crushed

Coaching by Night

us flat to the coach and tried the fastenings of the lamps, and yet with scarcely a single scraze of the hub against a large tree. Sometimes if a sapling were a little in the way the driver would say, "We'll have her down," and crash the huge mass goes at the obstacle, and levels it almost without a shake. The four horses enter into the spirit, and cut here and there with a touch of the ribbons as though going along in broad daylight.

As we lumber along the economical driver rejoices, for the rising moon will soon dispense with his candles. See, what was that? We were just getting drowsy, when a black body darted into the circle of our light, dashed across and up the great gum on our left. A 'possum?

"Oh, you'll see a hul shoot of 'em as the moon gets up," says our Jehu. Sure enough they are soon cutting up and down the trees like things possessed.

"Ah, sometimes when I've been pretty early with the mails I've shot a score of them in no time. Eh, what? good to eat? No, not they, they taste too much of the gums; some whites eat them. Bill, down there at the accommodation house, buries them for a day or two and then finds most of the gum taste has evaporated. Yarn? No it isn't, not a bit of it! Ah, but their skins are worth the shot to me. 'Possum rugs down in Sydney fetch eight, ten, and fifteen quid (pounds) a piece, and though it takes a lot of possums to make a rug, you can get as many as you like for a few shillings' worth of shot and a good eye."

With such conversation, and an occasional stop at a wayside "hotel" or accommodation house to change relays of horses, all fine, strong, well-bred beasts, and to have a cup of coffee, and an occasional excitement in the shape of descending a creek bank and seeing the horses a mile or so below, or of ascending and seeing them almost falling back on you, the night passes and the wished-for dawn appears, with the usual clear rose colour of the Australian morning.

"Ah," says an Australian, "you have nothing like the perpetual Australian blue sky and sunshine in the old country."

"No," slily insinuates the Briton, "but then our seasons are fairly regular, and all you colonials have become somewhat tired of the perpetual blue sky during the late disastrous drought of 1883—4."

As the dawn gathers the plains extend in width on each side of us, and the country is evidently increasing in value and verdure. Kangaroos, bolder than the sheep, stand to gaze at us as we ride close to them, and the absence of animal life during the whole of the early part of the journey is now supplied by a plethora of birds and these beasts. As the herbage is scanty on account of the recent drought, many of these plains look like great levelled cricket-grounds studded with trees, myalls, cottonwood, whitewood, and the like, not unlike a very flat and somewhat dull park through which the telegraph poles guide our course.

All bush drives are not like this I have here described; sometimes the scenery is more—it can hardly be less—worthy of attention; sometimes excitement is provided in the shape of accidents by flood or field, turning over in a ford, or through the horses running away and trying to test the strength of the surrounding trees.

I once passed a thing which had been a coach some four hours before, then jammed up against a mighty "bastard-box" tree. The coach had caught in a tree stump in the dark and had tilted up; the spirited horses, frightened, had run away, and had, *mirabile dictu*, succeeded in dragging the vehicle through the thick scrub a hundred yards before they had jammed it up against "the almighty-powerfullest bastard-box for miles around, 'peared as though they had made a dead set on it," as the half-doubled-up driver facetiously remarked. One passenger had his leg broken and the other (there were only two) seemed "silly," though unhurt by the shock. Again, a friend of the writer driving in the Riviera by night had the misfortune to be driven by a coachman plied with spirits by an imprudent passenger. The consequence was that they lost the track, the first intimation of which to my friend was conveyed by the foremost horses going at headlong speed trying to take a flying leap over an opposing post and rail fence. They scrambled over somehow, but the wheelers and some of the passengers came to an untimely end.

Accidents in coaching are so common out here that you cannot take up the *Australasian* or the *Town and Country Journal*, two of the leading colonial papers, without seeing an account of an accident in one or another colony, terminating more or less unfavourably to the driver or passengers. As a rule the insides come off the worst, and, like the far-famed

Horace Greely, sometimes find their heads through the top, or their feet through the bottom, of the vehicle, an undignified and unnecessary posture.

I have no doubt but that the " lifting of the little finger " by the driver, as in the case above mentioned, is frequently the cause of these accidents, an opinion confirmed by colonials of wide experience, as the drivers when sober show wonderful, if not phenomenal, skill. What can you expect, when, as happened in my own experience, a wealthy squatter, going down to Sydney, was perched by his friends on the box seat, and, although already half intoxicated, provided with a couple of bottles of " Irish," wherewith he continuously plied his Jehu, regardless of his own fate or that of the other passengers? The driver himself told me that they had some narrow shaves that night of all falling down a creek bank or colliding with tree trunks, until my worthy friend, a most abstemious man usually, was carried to an inside seat, where he dozed and groaned with the incipient attacks of sea-sickness and alcoholism at the feet of the other passengers, two of whom were ladylike women!

The amenities of coaching are certainly conspicuous in their non-existence, as the jolting and heaving resemble somewhat in effect the motion of a channel steamer on a chopping sea.

As I have been chatting Phœbus' steeds mount the sky, and we find ourselves after twenty-two hours emerging through a clump of trees into the main street of our destination, a township of whose existence up to this minute we were ignorant, so far as our eyes were concerned. A great wide road hardly better than the track we have just come along except that the centre is sanded and slightly metalled, with the usual low one-storied white wooden houses, stores, and hotels, with galvanised iron roofs, and a figure or two lounging in the verandahs round the " hotels " or grouping with others at the post office awaiting the mails. Of these few are women; the men and boys are almost universally hatted in slouch felt hats, and unless mounted on horseback seem to be unhappy in their clothes.

The Chinese are in the van as usual with a Li-Hung Sy and Co., and a great odorous store where one can buy anything from a pound of shot to one of Wollongong butter, from a measure of cloth to one of bran. Enterprise is strong up here as in most Australian townships, and great hardware and other stores, such as our second-rate provincial towns hardly dream of, erect their sign-boards up and down the street. There are one or two cross roads, but they have but half a dozen houses or so in them all told, as most of the buildings can find room along this principal thoroughfare.

Banks, hotels, and barber's shops are the most conspicuous places after the stores. The first are branches of the great colonial banks established in all towns of a few scores of inhabitants; the second should come first, for they are erected before anything else, and preponderate in numbers. The word hotel hardly conveys to an English mind what these places are like. As a rule they are drinking shops where a man can get a bed and a meal if he likes, but quite as secondary concerns.

The barber-shops seem indispensable. I know not if the high-born Australian thinks it beneath him to shave himself, but these capillary operators are much patronised, shaving being commoner now than formerly. Colonial friends up country all appear to have a significantly short crop of hair, which they point to proudly as the *colonial clip*, not the mark of the convict but of the free use of reason and scissors, and nothing satisfies them but for their visitor to follow suit if he stays any time. He soon finds a use in the fashion, for his hair clipped in close to his head is thus always in trim, a matter of some slight importance when the absence of combs and brushes for days is taken into consideration; in the warm weather it also assists in keeping the head and brains below melting-point.

When going into a barber's shop up-country on one occasion to 'doff my raven locks' I was asked whether I wished a colonial clip or not. Although I had then been some time in the colonies, the matter was new and required investigation. Thinking it might be something nice, I underwent the operation, and was somewhat startled to see myself transformed into one of those members of society who frequent Her Majesty's prisons, saving only that I was minus the broad arrow. As you may perceive, there is not much in a colonial clip to tax the resources of the artist in hair. But the question naturally suggests itself, is it not imprudent to remind folks of the short hair of those early settlers whose barbers officiated at the expense of King George III. and his regal successors? It *may* naturally suggest itself, but the suggestion should be quiescent in Australian society of a class, for no man likes to have it hinted that there is any mud about him to stir up; furthermore, the average colonial biceps is developed—*verb. sap. sat.* My Irish barber turned me out of the chair with pride, in which he was confirmed by a station hand, "a broth of a bhoy," awaiting his turn, who assured me that I had "got an adverbial adjectival clip and looked quite fit."

Come whenever you may into one of these townships during the day you will see idlers in the verandahs of the inns, unless perchance the meal-bell has sounded, and they have all rushed in to bolt their silent meal. These meals are, to the wonderment of the traveller in these levelling countries, often served in two several classes of first and second, and impress the observer with a deep sense of the utilitarian Australian who when he does a thing concentrates all his powers on the action.

Once on a time, wishing to break the monotony of this awesome silence, I spake to my left-hand neighbour, and received courteous though curt replies for the first few seconds, and finally this crushing rejoinder.

"If I were you, sir, I should do as all the rest of us are doing; you'll find plenty of time to talk afterwards, and not too much for eating." The word of warning was friendly, as I soon found; everything was cleared off almost before the new chum had time to take in half a "square meal." To watch these diners return from their dinner and resume their avocations (not their vocations) of idling, drinking, and smoking, you would think they had just gone to have a look round the room and come out again.

These colonial townships are as a rule unlovely to a degree. Few of the townsfolk cultivate gardens, or timber round their houses, or climbing creepers up their verandahs, although there is land enough and to spare; nothing meets one but a monotonous glare in sunshine or wet. A few hours spent at one of these many hotels will give you an insight into certain features of colonial life not particularly elevating, but far from uninteresting.

Here, as an accompaniment to the chirrup of the grasshoppers in the bush at the back, a sharp dialogue is going on between an old "bushman" come into town for a "spree," and a young larrikin barely out of his teens who wants to buy the old man's horse. Though the buyer and his friends detract from the qualities of the steed and exalt those of the silver watch offered in exchange, by finding out that the one is spavined, winded, and broken-kneed, and the other is a timepiece "jewelled throughout with gold works," the old fellow is not so far gone as not to have an eye to his own advantage, and though willing enough to have a glass or two, which he broadly hints for at the other's expense, and gets, so as to take time to think about it, finally tires out the patience of his would-be dealer, whom he follows with the cunning leer of a half-drunken man. The language coming from the far end of the verandah is more forcible than polite; expletives, adjectives, and adverbs indiscriminately thrown in to make up weight seem unnoticed by the women of the inn and a couple of little children, who are running around and often chatting with the idlers, as though perfectly callous to these redundancies of oratory.

Here is the "boss" or landlord—we do not say mine host over here, for often the gentleman is hardly one to claim as one's own—having an argument with another maudlin, wretched-looking bushman, who came in not so long ago spruce and firm of eye and hand, troubled, however, with a cheque which he wished to "knock down" (that is, to spend on the enjoyments of the place), in which operation the boss assures him with sundry oaths he has been completely successful. There's no appeal against this law; and as the boss kindly (!) gives the poor dupe a present of a bottle to take away with him he thinks himself well out of it, but afterwards when whole and in his right mind wonders how he could have got through £50 in a few days, but yet has the remembrance of those scores of empty bottles under his bed, which the boss assures him he has emptied.

Here's a "jolly companion" coming up to ask you to "have a booze"* with him, so if you don't want to you had better make off, or he will get mightily offended.

"Eh, what you won't? Why you *adjectival substantive*, you *adverbially adjectival substantive*, you're too *adverbially* flash to drink with such as me, I suppose."

If you treat the thing as a joke you will have but little trouble, if you do not, woe betide you, you will raise the wrath of a Hercules who will thirst for your blood. See there a man who is working for yonder squatter has asked him the same question, and replied to his refusal in much the same terms. Such is the eternal fitness of things in this land of approximation to a state of nature, levelling, and unconventionality.

The knot of idlers suddenly gets excited, one of them has challenged anybody else to a fight, and finds an antagonist in a black-tracker, an aboriginal policeman who fears not the drunken fists of this poor "white trash." As even here there is a mayor and municipal council, who are responsible for the good conduct of the place, and keep rowdyism down, the assault of fists cannot take place in the open street. Round we all troop to the back of the hotel, where even the more respectable ones adjourn, as they expect more fun and frolic than

* Booze, up country, merely means a drink.

slaughter. The white man's backer has himself been sipping the cup that cheers, at any rate both are more than "jovial," and after a few rounds of a harmless description between his principal and the black, where each receives more knocks from himself than from his antagonist, and the black butts with his head, the rowdy second "thinks he'd like some himself," but at the hands of a stalwart lover of fair play standing by affords us an example of that extraordinary feat of the "ground coming up and hitting him on the back of his head."

If you want to know where to find the aborigines in a township, look for them near an inn. There's a group of two or three blacks of not unpleasing face, with their "gins" or wives (black but not Venuses), waiting around to pick up a humble coin or a drink of fire-water from some confiding and generous "loafer." Our civilisation does not always start, as Exeter Hall would have us believe, from the Church. It is too well known that among savages the white man's fire-water centralises the black's civilisation at the whisky-shop.

The women are too ill-treated to have good looks, especially if in girlhood they show any signs of comparative beauty, for they are then the object of strife amongst all their male friends and acquaintances, who frequently carry the girl off from one another by sheer violence and brutality *nolens volens*. A blow on the head from a waddy (a heavy club) makes the most refractory subject amenable to the reason of superior brute force. They purchase their wives with gum tragacanth, spears, waddies, and such other valuable considerations, when they cannot thus acquire them by force, and do not find any serious competition in the market from the whites, who are prejudiced in favour of spouses paler and not darker than soot, as are these black lubras.

The knots of idlers are again lazily excited. A buggy is seen coming up the main street. Who's that? Jones of Coonabarabin or Smith of Wangaratta? Neither; 'tis a friend to whom I have an introduction, and who carries me to his station some twelve miles off across the plains with all the *volens* and none of the *nolens*, for a stranger in an up-country township soon exhausts the pleasures (!) of a place never intended for aught but the utilitarian purpose of money-making and spending.

An Up-Country Coach

CHAPTER XII.

Station Life.—Making a Plunge.—Salt Bush in the Bush.—From Bare Earth to Gay Verdure.—Perfumes not of Barbary.—Timber.—Twenty Mile Paddocks.—Slabs *versus* Sawn Timber.—The Homestead or Station.—Its Kitchen and Cookery.—"A fast Feeder works Fast."—Mutton *et id genus omne*.—A Week's Work and Play.—Look to your "Leathers."—"That's not the way to mount a Bush Horse."—An Equestrian Pupil.—Out on the Plains.—Murder of the Innocents.—Five Hundred dead Bullocks.—A Kangaroo Hunt.—The Finish.—The Prosaic Overseer.—Capitation Fees.—Why the Kangaroos are so thin.—Paddocks baptised.—Clearing the Paddock.—The First Essay.—Breaking Back.—"There he goes prop."—A Hasty Dismount.—The Rendezvous.—Kangaroos and Emus in Sight.—The Emu's Extermination drawing near.—The Stockwhip acts unfeelingly.—The Mob in Motion.—The Wethers weathered.—Bush Riding.—Drafting the Sheep.—Counting them out.—The End of Day One.

"OOP LA, and away we go," says my friend the squatter. Consequently we fetch off with a wild plunge, and for a few minutes the whole buggy load, animate and inanimate, looks as though we had all simultaneously decided on catching crabs. "Hold on there!" No breath for thanks for the hint! We make a mad rush at a gully through which a creek runs and suddenly find ourselves 'twixt heaven and earth; a splash and a heave, and before our springs have time to break, our fresh ponies clamber up the other side and shoot across the plain to repeat the operation again when necessary.

Here we are fairly in the bush, off even the semblance of a track called the coach road, driving at a fair trot across the level ground dotted with herbage and variegated with dead sheep, cattle, horses, and kangaroos, the victims of the past drought; salt bush, a low sage-like bush, is sprinkled over the ground, one of the hardiest " feeds " there is, which has held out through the past six months' drought and has shot up verdant sprouts since the rain a fortnight since. Three weeks back even the salt bush was but a bundle of dead looking twigs, and the few tufts of herbage and blades of grass that now foreshadow the state of these paddocks in genial spring were not in existence.

Even now it is hard to believe that on these same plains grass and herbage grow to the height of three or four feet, but seeing is believing, according to the wiseacres, and within a couple of months I have seen on a piece of land where sheep had not been running marsh mallow and other herbage two to three feet high, where when I first passed scarce a blade or leaf stood out of the black hard soil. This happened in winter, so that it does not take a Jonah to swallow the oft-repeated stories told by bushmen of grass growing in summer from a few inches to a few feet in the course of four weeks. It appeared, however, in winter too cold for the grass to make much progress, and though I saw it later on assuming its usual tawny greenish tint, that was during the late spring and early summer when the temperature had risen considerably.

The black soil, or clay, and the sandy soil had suffered equally, though the stout Australian timber hardly seemed to heed the scorching and absence of rain. In the black soil we came across great fissures you could put your leg down up to the thigh, a most awkward trap for the thousands of little lambs that are now running by their mothers. The rain that came a week or so ago saved thousands of sheep, but was too late for other hundreds whose whitened bones lie around our path, picked clean by that bird of ill-omen, the Australian crow—so near akin to the raven as to merit a poem by the hand of Edgar Allan Poe all to itself.

Decomposition is quickly arrested here by the siccative

effect of the sun, which dries up the juices of the dead beasts within a few days and renders their poor skinny ribs as resonant as a drum. During those few days the sight and smell is unlovely, though for that matter a squatter I came across while up in this district assured me he had no "nose" at all, a state of evolution perhaps even now threatening the Australians up country. A smell strong enough to curl one's hair or make a disturbance in the atmosphere, or the sweetest eau de Cologne, were equally ignored by his olfactory nerves, and as eau de Cologne was less conspicuous than dead sheep he decidedly had the advantage over the rest of his normal brother squatters.

The trees here grow in belts, some of considerable size, many hundred acres in extent; in fact a new chum would describe the scenery as being a mixture of grassy plain and forest.

We are on one of the travelling sheep-routes, routes marked out all over the country by Government for the transport of these kittle cattle from one district, station, or colony to another. As there are few if any regular roads up country, these travelling routes are of course an essential means of intercommunication, and thus render localities accessible, otherwise only to be approached by the courtesy of the surrounding landholders. Over the ordinary leasehold ground a sheep-travelling route extends for half a mile on either side; but where, as here, the squatter has purchased out and out the neighbouring paddocks, he can limit the route to the width of three chains (one hundred and ninety-eight feet), which, if he be a careful man, he generally does with a fence on either side, thus forming a long broad lane. These lanes have other uses, for numbers of dead kangaroos, the victims of a recent beat or drive, lie about near one end, where a fence and gateway athwart the route have entrapped them.

Many of the paddocks we have come through are twenty square miles in extent, enclosed with post and rail, or as is usually the case now, with post and wire fencing. For a cross-country ride these wire fences offer sufficiently obnoxious obstacles to any but the foolhardy; for though Australian horses can jump right well, they cannot see the wire of the fencing when going at a great rate, and so not infrequently do themselves and their riders great damage. However, this fact will not deter run-holders from using this durable and cheap form of fencing, of which already hundreds of thousands of miles exist throughout the colonies.

Near the homestead or station the paddocks are usually

A Squatter's Home.

smaller, for the convenient working of the sheep to the "yards," and the easy catching of the horses.

The station itself, of which the plate is a fair representation, is almost universally one-storied, with galvanized iron roof and deep verandah around it. In a land where the ornamental is considered last of all (as up country is the case) one would wonder to see such a "luxury," did one not find that in summer it becomes an actual necessity to shade the walls of the house thus from the fierce baking heat of the sun. The building materials are not infrequently the timber on the run cut into slabs or sawn into planks and joists. The latter method shows a decided advance on the slab-hut, as of a frosty night there appears some disadvantage in having so much ventilation as the intervals between the slabs too often permit.

The number of wooden houses in the colonies far exceeds the brick buildings, and for homesteads the only bricks employed are as a rule in the erection of the chimneys. You see large inverted brick funnels erected on a piece of land, and you then know that the chimneys and fireplaces are ready to have the rest of the house built to fit them, a reversal of the usual course rendered necessary more perhaps by the circumstances of the case than the topsy-turvydom of the place.

The kitchen too is, as a rule, in all well-ordered stations an erection entirely separate from the rest of the house, though sometimes connected by a covered gangway. The arrangement is a good one, as the smell of cooking is banished to its own proper realms, the danger of fire to the house itself is lessened, and the servants have thereby their own quarters where they may feel at ease.

Our meals on a sheep-station are of a substantial character, not necessitating any great proficiency in the cuisine. Mutton is of course omnipresent on a sheep-station,—at breakfast in the shape of chops, at lunch in the form of cold joints, and at dinner at the end of the day as a hot leg, shoulder, or the like. One colonial friend used to have his six mutton chops as regularly as clockwork for breakfast, and then be off for a whole day, riding till sundown, when he would again line the inner man with deep intakings of shoulder or leg.

On the next station to us their menu is pretty well the same all the year round, but on this the presence of a lady and a Chinaman have created greater variety. In the train of the squatter's wife come such luxuries and delusions as pastry, puddings, and preserves, and the beneficient Chinaman employed as a gardener brings in fresh "welegables" every day from his continuously irrigated plot of garden-ground.

You would think that here, at any rate, where climate and occupation are so wholesome, dyspepsia should not raise its horrid head; but the universal bolting of his meals causes many a bushman to feel that "tightness across the chest" and many of its consequent results which assail Alderman Jones after his luxurious indigestible dinner at the club. Colonials boast of this fast feeding, and say that a slow feeder is a slow worker, and that the converse holds true. There is no doubt that a fast feeder should be a fast worker, for if he be consistent he must feel the necessity for cramming as much as possible into a life inevitably curtailed by his mode of eating. There is no doubt, too, that most colonials eat too much meat, considering the hot climate that they mostly enjoy. Were meat dearer than 2d. or 3d. a pound, fever and dysentery, nature's modes of throwing off the excess of fibrine, would be less known. But as long as you can get a joint for a shilling or so, and a good piece of beef near a cattle neighbourhood for a few pence a pound, so long will this concentrated and heating form of nutriment be favoured.

Where so many kangaroos are about, 'tis passing strange that the famous kangaroo-tail soup is not more often seen on the table. How the city gourmet would smack his lips over the thick, glutinous, opalescent liquid that this caudal appendage produces; but prejudice runs high amongst many folk out here against eating any part of such vermin, not because the beasts are bad feeders, for they feed as daintily as sheep, but in that they are "vermin."

Game and ducks abound in some places, but in common with pigeons and wild turkeys, which are considered delicacies, are not often obtainable; for, unless on a Sunday, or during the slack season after the wool crop has been gathered, no one has time to go "fooling around with a gun" after birds.

I fancy that the best way to give you an insight into the station-life as it appears to an outsider (and in this it makes but little pretence to deception) is to sketch out for you a week's occupations. If you begin with a Monday you will be able to appreciate the rest of the Sabbath at the end as much as one does in reality in the bush. 'Tis a fine clear winter morning, perhaps a slight frost on the ground, just enough to make you feel that the cold bath is more a matter of duty than pleasure, if so be that the water supply extends to such a luxury.

Breakfast over, and an unlimited number of mutton chops consumed, we wander out to the stables, a motley group, ready for the day's joys and trials. A fine set of horses stand finishing their breakfasts in the stalls. Aye, but you ought to have been here before breakfast, and have seen them being raced in from the horse-paddock, overshooting the mark, breaking back, and playing such pranks as made their respective owners, who formed a *posse comitatus* in their rear, ejaculate adjectives and adverbs.

If you are a visitor, the groom will clean down your horse and see to your saddle-girths and so on, but if you are going to stop any time you will have to take to the currycomb and brush as you did to a brush and comb in your schoolboy days, from a sense of necessity; and should the groom be a "black boy," you had best see to your saddle and girths yourself, for here a loose strap may mean serious mischief should it chance to slip at a critical moment.

It is a cheering sight to see; the squatter himself, with his cheery face and Bedford cords bestriding his steed, the pick of the lot—for what is the good of being "boss" without the perquisites?—the overseer and one or two boundary riders are receiving their final instructions for the day, surrounded by a regular mob of kangaroo-hounds and sheep or cattle-dogs, all testifying in a somewhat noisy though sincere manner their joy at the opening of another day's work.

"Now come along," says "the boss," as the station hands often call him, "we've got to clear a paddock before lunch some five miles square and ten miles off, so we must be getting along! Jump up!"

"Oh, it's very well to say 'jump up,' but the plaguy horse commences to start before ever I've got my foot in the stirrup."

"Ah, that's because you adopt the old-country style of

mounting, standing facing the animal's shoulder: turn yourself round, look over his tail, whip your foot in the stirrup, and his very start will get you seated. Ah! there you are! Why are the horses in such a hurry to get off? Well, riders over here haven't got time, they think, to teach their horses to stand still while being mounted, and are accustomed to jog off into a canter even before they have firmly fixed themselves in the saddle."

"Firmly fixed! you say; I should just think I am."

"Well, your pommel is higher here than in the old country, and the saddle is more hollow in the centre, so are the knee-pads much larger, but you'll soon find out a reason for these changes in the old-pattern saddle."

"As you're a new chum, you may be glad to hear that your steed is a fairly quiet one, as it is not at all an uncommon trick for the new chum to be mounted on a buck-jumper, a term you will find to have a painful meaning further on." We canter away, with the sun's slanting rays already warming where they fall on us.

"Can I get a trot out of him?"

"No, few horses are taught to trot here in the bush. Cantering is easier, both for horse and rider, particularly if it is much prolonged; and though trotting looks better, you'll soon find that looks count for nothing out here."

Are you a raw recruit in the ranks of equestrianism? Fear nothing; you will not be told, as you would be by experienced riders in the old country, to tuck your elbows in, hold your head up, put your hands down, turn your toes in, and so on, and thus soon fancy yourself verging on the brink of drivelling idiotcy. A much more liberal and open-handed method of teaching awaits you here. Your friendly tutor tells you to jam your feet well down into the stirrups, feel yourself well fixed in the saddle, lean back as far as you like, and above all things stick on. The consequence of this judicious method of tuition is that your humility and modesty will give place to a pleasing self-confidence, and you will soon find that this great quality gives you a "seat" to which you may add "style" at your leisure, whereas under the old-country tuition you would have paid so much attention to toes, elbows, and the rest, that you would not have acquired a third of the confidence or "seat" in the same time.

Losing sight of the homestead shortly after passing through some of the many belts of timber, we see before us a plain some miles in extent, dotted plenteously with white wool, principally alive, though here and there a dead beast reminds the squatter that he must send the wool-gatherer around to pick up the "dead-wool," worth sometimes more than the live sheep without the wool would be. Just see how frightened the sheep seem; we have but just emerged from the timber, and yet they are away half a mile or so, running together as though we were demons, as fearful of our band as the kangaroos we see hopping amongst them here and there.

"Whoa, come back, Cæsar; no, you don't, my good dog, not here, at any rate; you'll frighten the sheep too much, and they aren't over strong just yet after this drought, if you give chase to the bounding marsupials here. There'll be plenty of opportunity farther on for you to whet your canines."

Mushrooms dot the plain here, but we cannot stop behind for them, or we shall never catch up our friends ahead.

"What is that crowd of crows collected for over there?" Let's go ahead. You might have guessed what it was. "Where the vultures gather," &c. A poor weak lamb dropping for a few yards behind its mother has fallen a victim to the relentless iron beak of this vulture of the Australias. There they go croaking at our arrival. The poor little fleecy animal, deprived of its eyes and eviscerated, for crows have their tit-bits like emperors, is a forcible example by antithesis of the survival of the fittest. For had it been strong enough it could have kept up with its mother, and would have thus saved its life; but the maternal instincts are at a low ebb just now, when food is so scarce, and body and soul can only be kept together by scraping, without having a dependent family, and so perhaps 'tis best that it should have spared its mother further exhaustion, whereby it might have endangered its dam's life, and after all perhaps have fallen a victim to the trials of rain or summer heat. Ah! in the drought you would have seen worse sights than these. See here by this creek side, where the clay soil has been so kneaded by thousands of cloven hoofs. Do you see the skeletons here and there, or even the still fresher carcasses, hard and resonant? These are they who came down to cool their parched tongues only a few weeks back, but were so starved and weak that they got "bogged," and there, perhaps within a stride of the tantalising water, sinking deeper in the yielding mire, were attacked and blinded while still living by these bloodthirsty scavengers, the crows. What a silent tragedy was enacted here!

We have raised a regular hurricane of yarns by our sympathy. Every one of the party can tell of hundreds of sheep and cattle being killed in these same water-holes every dry year. Within twenty miles of where we are now riding there are five hundred carcasses of bullocks piled up around one water-hole or pond, who only a few weeks since were, if not enjoying, at any rate possessed of, a living, breathing frame. Their drover, unable to restrain them and the other hundreds he was driving up country in search of better feed from this mad rush to the water, had to stand by and see his charges trampling each other to death if only they might moisten their swollen and cracked tongues in the slimy-looking fluid called water. Decomposition being much slower in this comparatively damp and shaded spot, the surrounding air is poisoned.

We soon espy another mob of the long-eared marsupials ahead. "Let the dogs go, and put your horses to a gallop." Before even the gaunt, long-striding kangaroo-hounds have made half a dozen bounds, the mob has caught sight of us, though half a mile or so away. See the tremendous leaps they take, not hurriedly, but seemingly to a slow and dignified air, their great tails keeping time, and striking the ground with a balancing thump at every giant stride! They hardly seem to feel that it is a matter of life and death to them; not yet, but as we near them and the dogs lay themselves into their work, they too see it is more serious than they expected, and accelerate their speed, though by the side of the rapid movements of the dogs' and horses' feet their own seem still to affect the slow and sure movements of security. The dogs have singled out one from the mob, aye, and that a big one too. 'Tis a long race, as is always a stern chase, but it will soon be over, for we are approaching the wire-fencing at a terrific rate. The foremost kangaroo, fortunately for the rest of the mob, sees it and gathers up his strength, clears it easily, and is followed by all—no, not all, for the dogs are pressing this big brown fellow hard. He felt their breath on his tail that last time it came down; his wind is failing; in his fright he doesn't see the fencing; the dogs in the excitement take no heed either, and just as they close in, one on each side, to grapple with him, the whole of them, the hunted and the hunters, come with a terrific crash against the wire.

The quarry serves fortunately as a buffer to the dogs, but one of them has got a great scrape off his coat where that jagged end of wire-joint caught him. Undaunted by the sudden stoppage *in transitu*, the hounds tackle his throat, but 'tis almost needless. The poor brute's head and ribs are crushed in by the fencing, and the *coup de grâce* was practically given to a dead kangaroo. The others have made the best of their escape, and are far away in yonder belt of scrub, there meditating perhaps on the absence of the big brown father who will never come to them.

There is something rather pathetic in the hunting of one's first kangaroo, for the poor brutes seem to have so few chances beyond their speed, so few of them know the value of those terrific hind-toes as weapons of defence and offence, that to have assisted in the hunting of the quarry at first gives one a mean idea of oneself. The overseer doesn't see it, however, in this light, for he laughs, and jumping down from his panting horse, whips out a jack-knife, cuts off the scalp from ear to ear, including those appendages, makes a circular hole in one of the long hare-like ears, and strings it on his belt like a veritable Indian scalp-hunter. Why this mysterious and bloodthirsty proceeding? Know, most sympathetic and romantic new chum, that the presentation of this scalp to the Government officials will mean sixpence to the happy possessor, as there is a reward on the head of every kangaroo in the district, nay, in every part of the colony, where they are numerous and destructive.

Destructive? I should think so. Why, some of these big ones will each eat as much as three sheep! The kangaroo is a gross feeder, and nothing comes of it after all, for his flesh is never eaten but by the station dogs and the occasional aborigines; and he is almost always thin and wiry.

The overseer has cut him up to show us what Banting system he adopts, notwithstanding his healthy appetite. See yon crowd of little white filaments in his stomach, a species of worms like threads of cotton, but yet so many that he does not get half a chance to "show a double chin," as the bushmen say. "Send the dogs away," says the squatter. "They're not unlikely to get diseased themselves if they eat too carelessly of the carcass, and they're thin enough already, heaven knows! these grey and staghounds" (for kangaroo-hounds are but little else). You may, however, occasionally see kangaroos after a great feast of newly-grown grass during a rainy summer, so fat and unwieldy that they hardly care to clear out of the way for the dogs, and then are so demoralised that soon losing heart they will face their inevitable fate; but such cases do not so often occur as our friend the squatter would like, for more reasons than this alone.

Fortunately for our chance of sharing the kangaroo-hunt, the course he ran is well in our way. Along the fence and through the gate, we are now in another paddock, rejoicing in some such name as Carmel, Balligolong, or Warrambool, for all the paddocks share the privilege of christening prevailing in Christendom.

We have now arrived on the scene of action; this is the paddock we have, in bush phraseology, to "clean" or "muster." There are some five or six thousand sheep here, which we have to collect together without, if possible, missing one of them—a feat not so easy as it sounds, when it is taken into consideration that we are five all told, and that the paddock embraces some sixteen to eighteen square miles, half of which are covered with close-growing timber. Curtly giving his instructions to his "hands," the squatter sends one along to one side, another to another, and so on, all with instructions to meet at a certain spot, which our good friend vaguely tells us is "over there somewhere, near by a pocket with a few box trees growing close around."

Now, if you are willing to help, your services will be accepted though not asked, and "as you're a new chum supposing you come along with me, and we'll take good care not to be bushed, and if we are we shall be fellows in affliction, if that's any consolation." In half a minute we have all lost sight of one another, so thick is the scrub here, and as we have to bear down the middle we will just notice how the sun lies and steer by his genial rays. Did you notice how those old station hands rode away at a steady canter through the bush, thick as it is, where we can barely walk our horses without scraping a knee or a toe, or being obstructed by a bough? You will see some finer riding than that very soon, and have to learn yourself to take less of the bark off the gum-tree—or your shin—if you want to do any good.

Did you hear that "Cooee?" How clearly it sounds! Then a crack of the stockwhip each stockman carries, and a dog's bark. Bark of dog, voice of man, and crack of whip all clear in this glorious air, though distant. Some one has sighted a mob, and is getting them together. Here we are, out of darkness into sunshine; not a bit too soon either, for the sheep on the plain ahead, startled by the whip on our left, have made for the bush ahead on the right.

"Now, then, old Banker, put your best leg foremost. Rise to it, old fellow. Clear the fallen logs! Away we go!"

No time for words now. Did you ever fancy sheep could

go so fast? The foremost have got to the scrub; a few seconds more and we shall lose the lot. "Now, cram it on, old horse! Let's give them a good yell. Ah, just in time! You're circumvented this time, my woollen beauties." As they are winded with their scamper over the plain, we give them a few moments to recover breath.

"Drive them gently, and you'll do twice as well and quickly as though you drove them fast. They'll break back, and all over the place, too, if you go too sharp. Ah, I told you so. Now you'll have to cut back to the left and bring those stragglers making off. They're like the swine possessed of the devils. You're on an old stock-horse, so you'd better take care of his turning sharply!"

How quickly the trusty steed heads those backsliders! Prop he goes, turning almost like a circus horse on his hind feet, for he sees, long before his rider, such is his experience, that he has headed them, and that if he does not get back to the other side, those plaguy stubborn wethers will have made a flank movement. There he goes, prop again! this time a little too soon for his rider, who consequently gets a "hasty dismount," much to the amusement and astonishment of the horse, who looks on (fortunately) at his fallen friend.

"Hallo! you're not hurt, are you? It's a good thing you were not riding amongst timber. A fall on the ground won't damage you much, and you'll get up to join in the laugh against you if you're wise. You didn't see anything to make the horse 'prop,' you say? Ah, but the clever beast did: he saw that young 'wild' sheep just turning his head for a run, and his prop probably saved you another canter after half the mob."

Now, then, we have to drive our mob through this dense scrub ahead. We separate, and keep them going slowly through. If we had a well-trained sheep-dog we might light our pipes and walk behind inactive. Carefully does it: quarter of a mile of scrub, then another wide open plain, with a few mobs of white-coats grazing around. "That looks like the rendezvous over there." "Yes, there's a dip in the 'lie of the land,' and there are a few box trees close by. Well, as we've had the easiest part of the job, we'll just put our mob into the middle of the plain, rounding the others into it as we go, and make a few excursions into the scrub to see if we have unconsciously passed any open spaces, and thus perhaps missed some sheep."

Away on the plain are a few herds of kangaroos of all sizes; the does whinny for their little ones, and anxiously expecting some evil, bid them jump into their pouches ready for an excursion from the destroying human.

Farther still we see a mob of emus, gallant birds, running, although we are more than a mile away, as though for dear life— a semblance still more realistic from the fact that you think it proper to carry a revolver at your belt, and that we have the misfortune to belong to the same race who hunt and are fast exterminating them. Not that they are destructive to the sheep, directly or indirectly; the emu being a strict vegetarian, has never cultivated a taste for live mutton, nor do they consume much grass, but their skins with feathers sell for a round sum in Sydney and Melbourne, and their eggs make such an omelette as would cause Epicurus himself to smack his lips.

"Did you hear that 'Cooee' again—and again?" Now the whips resound like musketry, and the bark of dogs comes nearer and nearer, with all that intense resonance and clearness that a dry atmosphere alone permits. From the scrub on each side sheep are pouring by twos and threes, the forerunners of the larger mobs each stockman is driving before him. Soon we are all together, only awaiting the arrival of the squatter himself, who was going to take the most difficult part of the paddock. So the stockmen sit down in their saddles, let their horses browse the herbage, and pull out the inevitable pipe and plug of twist.

While we're waiting one of the stockmen shows us how to crack a stockwhip. "Eh, nothing easier? Well, here you are. What's wrong? What have you got it twisted all round your body for? Oh, only a preliminary flourish! Why, you've given a secondary flourish now that has left a livid line upon your cheek and narrowly missed your eye! Never mind, try again, but crack it. Eh, what? a tertiary flourish! Not? Well, then, why is the pesky thing walking down your back? Why, the very sheep are getting interested!" It's no use; the new chum had better go in some quiet paddock, with his head in a galvanised iron bucket, and try the art for a few days, and then perhaps he will be able to get a crack out of the fourteen-foot thong, which now seems like a serpent incarnate coiling around him.

The kangaroos the other side of the plain are bestirring themselves; the "boss" is surely coming along through the scrub. Yes; for in another second a few white specks come out, followed in one long running stream by a thousand or so. No time now for yarns and pipes; we must look alive. The stream pours into our big mob and rather disturbs their serenity. "Now then," the boss says, as he canters up, "we'll away with this mob to the yards, and as we go collect any stragglers we may see. Ah, my good sir, you don't want to come out of the shade; find the sun too hot in the middle of the day, eh? What will you think of the summer heat when it comes along, if you make a fuss over this!" Yet if truth be told, 'tis warmer now than on an average summer's day in London. We do not study etiquette here, so we throw open our coats and waistcoats, and put a handkerchief under our caps if we do not wear the shady steeple-crown.

The strongest of the mob soon get in front and the weaklings straggle back here; but the van must not lead so far ahead, or we shall be minus an odd hundred or so very soon.

"Hallo ahead there! Look where those evil-minded wethers are trotting; they're in the scrub, and if we don't head them will give us trouble."

Away goes our trusty stockman, galloping across the plain, aye, and right into the scrub too. He turns and twists about, riding at headlong speed, reckless of life and limb, and yet this dare-devil is not insured; is it possible that he can retain his integrity very long if he tempts Providence at such a reckles pace through the scrub, where you would even have to walk your horse carefully to prevent a grazed knee or bruised head? No, his knee-pads protect his knees, and, that his eye acts on the alert for the rest of his body, you could tell as he dodged that great bough just now, which would have unseated him and crushed in his ribs or broken his head had he not just eluded it in the nick of time.

Such wonderful celerity of eye and hand come only through constant practice of man and horse, combined with a fair share of pluck and dare-devilry in the former. The horse, obedient animal, would often crush his own and his master's head out if he were guided that way, but if you let the reins fall on an old bush-horse's neck you soon find that he will take good care not to scrape his own sides, though his civilisation has not yet progressed so far as to permit of his calculating for *your* head or knees.

If there is any sight of all others to make a new chum feel his own nothingness and the vacuity theretofore of his education, it is the contemplation of a stockman carrying his life in his hand in his mad everyday rush through the bush. Not often have I ventured *desipere in loco* so far as to join in one of these mad, harebrained rushes, and then as a rule the motive was not my own, for my steed being of a playful and gregarious nature would not be left behind in the "run." Once I deemed myself lucky only to have lost my hat, which an envious bough, baulked of its natural prey, my head, swept off, and on finding it some time afterwards by pure chance, I felt thankful that, to use an Hibernianism, I was not contemplating my head on the ground by its side.

The bushman sometimes becomes an evolutionary Absalom, and is suspended, by the bough of a tree, from any further interest in life, although the shortness of his cropped hair * gives

* If the bushman be far from a township he may be an Absalom, in very fact; as he must, and does perforce, let his hair and beard grow in a most dishevelled manner.

the suspension a different form. I have heard of men having their skulls and their ribs crushed in, themselves unseated, their legs and other limbs broken, and occasionally their usual tight hold on life unclasped by the rude arm of a native oak, a myall, or a gum.

While I have been speaking of riding, "Jim" the stockman has brought the errant mob together. A few more miles, and after astonishing a few kangaroos and collecting a few hundred stragglers, we find ourselves, on emerging from a patch of scrub, following our bleating thousands close up against the yards—great fenced-in portions of the plain opening one into another, the largest, covering a few acres, converging into smaller and smaller pens, which finally permit only one sheep abreast to pass up the narrow lane at the top of which stands a swing gate and two series of pens distinct from one another.

We find other station hands awaiting us here, as we have a long job before us, to get all these sheep to pass up and be divided off into the two distinct bands they are to henceforth run in—wethers and ewes. These are last year's lambs, which have been mingling up to now in the sweet unconsciousness of innocence and the bliss of ignorance; now the ladies and their brothers will part, perhaps never to meet again in this land of squatters and sheep-dealers until perchance they hang side by side in some butcher's shop or the abbatoirs of Sydney.

Our work now commences in earnest. Tying up our horses or hobbling them, as our tastes and possessions severally incline us, a wild babel of men and dogs—a chorus more animal than human—commences, a palpitation of thousands of hearts inside their woolly coats, and a determination at first of the owners not to trust themselves within any of the yards. After much persuasion of a forcible character, they are driven within the fenced yards, the slip-rails are dropped, the gates shut, and the squatter himself, taking the post of honour at the gate, *magis honorosus quam onerosus*, guides now a ewe to the left, a wether to the right, and so on, according to the order that they come up this narrow fenced-in lane, urged on by the stinging words and actions of the station hands, all yelling, prodding, and perspiring with the energy the Anglo-Saxon displays in a clearer climate than his own.

The work goes on without much variation till the decline of the sun and the last score or so, always more difficult to get through than their predecessors, warn us that the day's light and work are coming to a close. As the squatter wishes, David-like, to number his subjects, he sets open the gate of one of the great pens, where the ewes watch with half-reassured gaze his actions, and counts them as they rush out into the open paddock in twos and threes, as though Burns's Maggie in her "cutty sark," with all her wizard train, were after them. As a "hundred" is called, one of us calls out "tally" and cuts one notch in a stick, pencils and paper being accounted the unknown accompaniments of an effete civilisation for such purposes. As every hundred goes through, the same process is carried on, until, if the stick be small and the sheep be many, the "tally-keeper" has to tax his ingenuity to find room for all the notches.

See yon mischievous stockman throws down a twig before the exit gate, and the next sheep bounds up into the air as though emulating a chamois; the next, and the next, and so on, perhaps for scores, do the same, not because they see any cause of danger, but because they think they must act as their sisters ahead. Are there not some other members of the animal kingdom with only two legs who often act sheep-like in imitation without reason?—the "masher" or the "dude" for instance.

The sheep when counted out have got to be "rousted" out of the way, for though the majority of them make straight for the scrub, some hundreds straggle about and may be confused with these wethers we have now separated, which we also have to count and drive through into an empty paddock some mile or so off. No sooner said than done; cracking their bloodthirsty stockwhips, with blood-curdling yells, a couple of stockmen jump on their refreshed horses and chase the ewes expeditiously out of the way.

Now that we have numbered the wethers, counted them out, and taken them through the paddock to their temporary abode, we light pipes and jog homewards with the glorious roseate hues of sunset such as are peculiar to Australia to warm our way, now fast becoming cool again.

After a sharp canter we are not half sorry to be welcomed by the twinkling lights of the homestead and deep bark of the kangaroo-hounds. After seeing to our horses' wants and our own lavatory needs, the evening meal, a yarn or two, the inevitable pipe, and perhaps a glass of the liquid with which they dilute the water in Scotland, combine to make us feel somehow as though sleep were not altogether a mistaken institution, and a bed, even though hard, when thus earned a couch of roses.

Stockwhip.

CHAPTER XIII.

Another Day's Work and Play.—Out after Scrubbers.—Blue Sky *versus* Clouds and Fogs.—Praying and Whistling.—Jim's Yarn of the "Parsons."—The Visitation of the Clergy.—The Scrubbers smelt and sighted.—Well done, Jim!—The Squatter Ejaculates.—The Bull-fight barring the Saxpences.—The Execution.—Don't dress Tripe. —An Old Scotchman and the Drink Question.—A Squatter's Farewell.—A Cure for Snoring.—The Third Day.—The Scrub-cutter and the Rams.—The Ants' Lesson to the Sluggard.—Ants of all Colours and Sizes.—The Danger of Attitudinising.—Another Kangaroo-hunt. —The "Old Man" shows Fight.—Pathos and Sentiment cut short. —The Tank-sinkers' Camp.—Their Board and Lodging.—The work of sinking a Tank.—The pleasures of getting Bushed.—A True Story.—A Bushman's Memory.—Sundowners.—"Old hands" and "Roustabouts."—Rain at Last.—Spirits Within and Water Without.

"TUMBLE out there," says my friend the squatter, "if you want to see some fun. We're going to run in some 'scrubbers' to-day."

"Impossible!" quoth I. "What have these poor innocent folk been scrubbing that they should merit running in?"

"Good heavens!" says the storekeeper, who pokes his nose in and surveys the bed and its drowsy occupant, and joins the squatter in a great guffaw. "What is the fellow dreaming of? Why, you know by this time that 'scrubbers' are nothing much else than wild cattle."

"Well, my dear sir, my first remark is equally apt, changing the folk to cattle."

"Why," says the squatter, "it isn't what they've merited

but what they're useful for, and that is summed up in a word —'wittles.'"

So off we all start after breakfast for selves and our horses, who seem none the worse for yesterday's work, to a remote paddock of the run where we are to see our friends the scrubbers and bring them to civilisation. An incautious remark as to the serenity of the weather gives the squatter a chance to expatiate on the superiority of the climate of Australia to that of England.

"See," says he, "this lovely blue sky. What chance here for a man to get the megrims? Drink in the champagne of the air, and then say if a man could become a cynic or a misanthrope."

"Ah," says the opener of the debate, "what's the good of talking of blue skies and sunshine when you are all praying for a drop of rain? What's the use of all your geniality of climate, your champagne-like air, if all your herbage is withered and you have to forsake your run, as Nicholls of Wangaratta and Johnson of Billabung have had to this last drought?"

"Ah well," returns my friend, "every life has its disadvantages, and here the rule holds as elsewhere, but these droughts don't come every year; and as to praying for rain, no, my dear sir, not I! Last drought we had, in '78, the parsons throughout New South Wales exhorted us to pray for rain, and we had special services on pretty well every run, but do you think the rain came any the quicker? No, my good friend, not a bit. It came just when it usually does, at the end of the droughts and the beginning of winter, and I can't say I think the Ruler of the Universe would have watered my run or Johnson's over the way any the sooner because we lifted our little voices and made our little requirements known by word of mouth. I guess His actions have a good deal wider scope than that would indicate. The parsons told us that we had the drought sent because of our sins. Do you believe that anyone gifted with human capacity for mercy would punish a man for a fault by killing off hundreds of poor sheep by a most lingering and painful death, which man himself has never equalled in all his cruelty? And how much less could the Divinity! No, my friend, I guess that won't wash. Why, if we had been such blazing big sinners we might have had an epidemic of small-pox, or every married one of us had his mother-in-law locate herself upon him; but I calculate you'll find less sin up in the bush by a great way than you will down in the towns. No, I calculate we laid our heads together and decided that it was because it *was*, and there wasn't any use fighting and jabbering about it. So when this last drought came the parsons found that we'd taken more to whistling than praying for rain, and though a few of them sort of represented our needs and assumed our repentance for sins we'd never committed, as it were by deputy, the plaguy drought just stopped as long as it liked, and we didn't have the rain till the usual time; and by the way, I won't be sorry to have a drop or two more."

"Ah," says Jim, trotting up behind, "did you hear how they served Parson Turner down there at Ballymaradine last time he stayed there? Well, you see he was travelling from one station to another for Sundays, and finding it rather slow work at Wooloomara, where old Jones only has mutton, spuds (potatoes), and damper, he moved on one Tuesday to Robinson's place, where there was a Mrs. Robinson, and he calculated on getting some 'soft tack.' Sure enough he got his soft tack the first evening, and went to bed chuckling that he had fallen into a good 'billet.' But when the boss heard in the morning he was going to stop over the next Sunday, and heard him grumbling that his boots hadn't been cleaned, and wanted to know why his horse hadn't been groomed, he went right away, got a big wood-axe, and up and told the parson that it was the custom for the cook on that station to make all 'sundowners' work for their grub, and that he couldn't see why a fine stout man like the parson should break a well-established rule; and the cook wanted some firewood, so would the parson mind and cut down a myall-tree close by the creek. The parson of course couldn't well excuse himself, so he tackled to rather gamely at first, though greatly disgusted and went for that myall. By lunch time the myall didn't seem much nearer coming down, though the bark looked from the ground for about three feet up as though a kangaroo had been gnawing it. When dinner-time came the tree was cut through, but the parson said he'd have to knock off as he had a blister on each hand as big as an emu's egg. Next day they went out after sheep, and by a curious coincidence the parson was mounted on a young fresh-broken horse instead of his own horse, whose legs he wanted to save, which made a bolt for every bit of scrub it could go for, and twice or thrice tried to jump the fences. When the parson came home in the evening he didn't say much, but sat down with a smothered shriek, and started up again as though he'd sat on an ants' nest. Next day he wasn't over particular about his boots, but seemed to prefer standing around and looking at his hands, and as he rode off with a grim face he told the boss he thought he wanted too muscular a Christian to officiate at his station, and although he could give a good character for soft tack there was too much hard tack mixed with it. The squatter told him he needn't fear he'd lost much by the bargain, for what he had lost in weight the horse, which had swelled visibly, had gained, so he couldn't say he'd sent him off any lighter than he'd come."

When we have done smiling at Parson Turner's misfortunes the squatter says, "You musn't suppose all parsons are like Jim's friend. Some of them are right merry good fellows, who fall in with station life as they ought to, and who really do one a power of pleasure to see. I'm not what is called a parson's man myself, but I always give the men a chance of hearing Parson J—, or the Wesleyan Parson C—, when either come around, and, as a rule, the men appreciate it. Once a rather rowdy chap we had amongst the shearers struck up a comic song, but he was promptly squashed by a big mate, who told him in pretty plain language he needn't be so fond of showing off his (adjectival) voice; when they wanted him to sing they'd (adverbially) quick tell him. One great thing is we don't often get them more than about once in three months up here, and so they come along as a novelty, and if they make themselves pleasant are treated like any other guest."

Jim the stockman is a leveller of caste, and without any feeling of disrespect for his employer, trots now by his side, now talks to one or the other, regardless of all conventionality in this levelling land of the Southern Cross. The squatter is not so long-winded as to give us all his wise saws and philosophical remarks above quoted in one harangue. The pipe which he smokes, according to usual custom, prevents any unnatural tendency to speechifying, and render· a cross-examination by his audience necessary to elicit the whole discourse.

After such essentially bush chat we arrive at the paddock, and commence searching for the scrubbers, which were last seen here some months ago, during the drought. After some time we scent a member of the herd, as he too has fallen a victim of the drought close by this mud-hole, and is "pretty considerably high;" another and another, until we fancy the whole band must have been gathered in by the reaper Death, and thus have frustrated our efforts.

But no. See, as we emerge on this plain, a mob, some thirty strong, is cropping the welcome herbage the rain has brought. Ah, they mean to give us some trouble! Do you see how the bulls run in on the mob?

"Now scatter around along that side, ride for dear life, and don't let them get into the scrub."

Away goes the loquacious Jim, and only just heads them in time. For some time man and horse are neck and neck with the tail of the herd. He creeps up their flank, and gradually forges ahead; now with lightning speed the old stock-horse turns sharp to the left, and guides the whole herd away from the dangerous spot. Jim sits through the fearful "prop" as though he were a part of the beast he bestrides. A new chum would have been hurled a dozen yards by centrifugal force. Jim does not know so much of the theory of centrifugal forces and the *vis inertiæ* as a new chum may, but he does understand how to meet and neutralise them. It is a pity that he cannot withstand the centripetal force of the whisky-bottle when he gets into the township close by.

Pines & Wattle

Now we have pretty plain sailing, until we strike the sand-ridge, when the denser undergrowth of the blooming wattle and the small pine, the trunks of the native oak, and the bastard box and gum-trees, make it necessary to ride up close with the little herd.

The squatter rides too close to a savage old cow with a calf by her side. She makes a rush at him, and tries to dig his horse. In a trice the horse turns and jumps aside, but brings himself dead up against that great oak, with the squatter's leg as a buffer. Fortunately, the squatter's limbs are firmly put together, and encased in leggings; but his face gathers up into one vast pucker, his lips groan forth a sound, drowning the angry bellows of our charges ahead, and shape themselves to utter—no, can it be? yet it is—a great big D! At home they say that if there is one thing to justify a man in using this capital letter *in extenso* it is to have hit his finger instead of the nail he is aiming at, but here *autres pays autres mœurs*.

After passing through sundry gates, each of which one of us rides ahead to open, and at each of which an exciting sort of amateur bull-fight takes place before the cattle make up their minds, which they do of a sudden, and then rush through, we arrive at the homestead, and turn most of the beasts into one paddock, while we select one for immediate killing, a couple or so to join the bullocks in the team and be broken in to labour, and a cow or two as a milker, if perchance the old groom can persuade her to give of her plentiful supply to any but her offspring.

We cannot drive our intended victim into the shambles without the presence of a few others, so we cut out half a dozen and rush them towards the great stockade, where the "gallows" stretch aloft their weird windlass, and herald their presence by sundry clean-picked skulls and feet lying around. Now they are in. We jump down; one of us pops up the slip-rails—the common colonial substitute for a gate—and the more venturesome spirits climb over, and urge the beasts to the far end of the yard, where a narrower pen or yard, roofed over with timber like a square birdcage, forms the place where the murder has to be committed.

Now comes all the excitement of the bull-fight without the payment of the bawbees. The cattle enclosed in the yard rush round as though thirsting for blood. The stockmen have to be nimble with their hands and feet to jump up the stockade before the enraged mob catch them in the rear. One fellow actually does get a hoist; but he politely thanks the animal for giving him a "lift on his way."

"Ah, now's your chance! they're near the far end! Rush them in!" With one great yell we advance in skirmishing order, and, more by our threats than actions, close them in the inner pen. Bang goes the gate. They're frantic with fright in their narrow pen, with scarce moving room. A stockman stands cautiously above the gate, knocks it open, and lets one or two out, then, dexterously engaging the attention of the others with his pole, he gives an opportunity for another of us to jump down and close the gate again.

"Now then, shall we *peth* it or shoot it?" says our butcher *pro tem*.

"Show us your skill, Tom, and peth it," says one of our hands. So up jumps Tom on the bar overhead with a long pething-pole, like an abnormally long and heavy Alpenstock in his hand;* he selects the beast to be killed, stands over it in breathless but seemingly careless silence, adjusts his point over the centre of the verterbra, and with one plunge sends the cruel point with unerring aim into the spinal cord. The massacred innocent drops as dead as the traditional door-nail. Its living and lively companions are let out, wondering what it all means, and the station is the poorer by one live beast.

The butcher does his work with the knife, to which, with usual inconsistency, he does not apply the adjective so often at other times in his mouth. Perhaps it is because the knife itself takes the place of the epithet. The windlass-like gallows are revolved by means of long ropes, and what was but a short time since a living, breathing creature is now hoisted up only a substance or material of a chemically compound nature, partaking of phosphates, fibrine, and the like, fit to grace any London butcher's shop, for our butcher understands his work, and skins his beast and cuts it up with skill and nicety. Stranger, pause here awhile, and take my advice; if you ever attend one of these "judicial murders," and are desirous of

* See sketch at the end of this chapter.

lending a hand, whatever you do never take to tripe-dressing, for, though the results may be satisfactory to the station cook, yet they can never compensate you for the painful interviews you will have had ever since with soap and hot water.

As we are sitting around the sparkling fire after dinner, having our "two draws" apiece, a visitor taps at the door.

"It's William Thompson, a boundary-rider, commonly known as Old Bill, who has come back to work to-day, after having been for a fortnight's holiday down in Sydney."

Is this the fresh-faced, clear-voiced, bright-eyed man who left a fortnight ago in the pride of health? It is; but it is hard to recognise him in the sallow, grey-looking, blear-eyed, thick-utteranced fellow who now stands, bent and shaking, with unsteady hand and wandering eye, in the doorway, asking the "boss" if he can give him a little nip to keep off the "blue devils." It's the fashion here, as sometimes at home, to "let a man who has been on the spree down gently," as it is called—that is, not to make him abstain straightway, but just to reduce the alcohol by degrees. This fashion is condemned by many medical men here as at home, but finds favour with the settlers, a few of whom are themselves at times in need of the same gentle treatment.

This man went to Sydney with about £50 in his pocket, the earnings of nine or ten months, and has come back minus the whole lot, and plus an incipient attack of "delicious trembles," as Mrs. Partington said, or as he calls it, the "blue devils." The "boss" "lets him down," but *does not* improve the occasion with mention of the blue ribbon. I have heard squatters defending the system of a man's squandering his earnings in this way, "because," said they, "otherwise their 'hands' would get too much money together and leave them, which they" (the squatters) "could ill afford, as it was generally their best workers who acted in this style."

The cause of these insensate "sprees" is apparent to anyone going up country. For months, nay, years together, the stockman works, perhaps in utter isolation, a dull routine of labour. What to him are the beauties of nature—the blue skies, the flora and the fauna? He has long got tired of them—if ever he appreciated their artistic qualities. As with a sailor after his voyage, when he comes amidst temptation he falls an easy victim, for he really derives satisfaction afterwards from his conduct, in throwing about his money like water, even at the expense of his stomach and liver. Has not he cut a dash? Has not he got something lively to think over? So he goes back to his daily routine, and through the extraordinarily good climate and healthy conditions of life probably regains his former robust state of health.

It would be difficult for some squatters to deprecate this custom of "breaking out," for they occasionally indulge likewise; that is, the gay and festive bachelors do, and though their "spree" may be conducted on a grander scale, it is in many cases none the less debasing to the sentiments and destructive, even though temporarily, to the health, and it would hardly be fitting for them to pose as preachers.

I have carefully avoided generalising, for there are many squatters, as also a minority of their hands, who are long-headed enough to avoid a course which has sent many a "good fellow" to the dogs, and impaired the progress of many another. It is not at all an uncommon thing for one man to say of another, "Oh, he'll get along well enough if he doesn't take to drink;" the impression formed by a stranger being that not so long ago it was the exception to find a man, more particularly a young man, who did not " grease " his esophagus too liberally when he had the chance.

The ghostly stillness of the night is disturbed after we have turned in by the undue snoring of one of the sleepers, which resounds with such awful distinctness through the timber partitions of the homestead that it wakes up all but the wretched perpetrator, whose first knowledge of the fact arrives with a shower of boots thrown upon him through his open door. Then the thunder ceases, and the alarm of the new chum, lest an earthquake or cyclone were coming along, is appeased.

Our third morning is a replica of the other two, but our scenes of action are to be diverse.

"Now," says the squatter, "if you are not accustomed to be without a midday meal you'd better put something in your pocket, for we shall be out pretty well till sundown, and not see a soul, except, perhaps, a bird or two or a kangaroo."

First we are off to the ram-paddock, a great enclose of a few square miles, where five or six hundred rams are running. As we near it, we hear the sound of axes rising in the still, clear air. We soon learn their meaning. The paddock has not been favoured with herbage during the drought; the rams are eating the grass up as soon as it grows, and to let it make a little headway, a few station hands are lopping down branches of the trees, thus to give the poor brutes a few mouthfuls. See how they follow the sound of yon woodman! Hunger has indeed tamed them; as he stands up in the fork of the tree they gather around the base in thick numbers and catch the falling boughs, regardless of hard knocks if they can only get a mouthful. Before the woodman can descend, the boughs are well-nigh stripped, and as he moves on to the next tree he has a retinue behind him worthy of a prince of the first water, in fact, he receives a perfect *ovation*.

They do not seem to have much preference, so that they get something to fill out their woollen coats, though if asked they would probably give the vote for the foliage of the myall. It takes a sheep to say what pleasant qualities may lurk in that most astringent and drug-like leaf, whose bitter flavour would almost out-vie quassia. It seems like giving a man a glass of bitters and nothing at all to follow.

See close by here a curious though tragical instance of the intensity of the last drought, when eleven million innocents are calculated to have been massacred in New South Wales alone, irrespectively of Queensland, Victoria, or South Australia. A sheep, striving to get to the lower-growing boughs of this tree, has slipped and fallen so that its head was caught in the fork, and without the power, if it had the sense, to extricate itself, there hangs its bleached bag of bones, a warning to all other imprudent foragers.

Now then, here we go by the margin of a dammed-up lakelet, where parrots, soldier-birds, and the "twelve apostles" chatter in the surrounding trees.

"We haven't got much water at this dam; but we hadn't any a few weeks back; so we'd best be thankful for small contributions," says the squatter.

The dam has been erected with sweeping arms on a slight depression of the ground, along what is in wet weather a creek, but is now only a succession of shallow water-holes.

These dams were but a few years ago the only means employed on large runs to save water. As the deepest water-holes formed by these dams were never deeper than a few feet, the evaporation of a long dry summer soon exposed the mud at the bottom. In fact the country was, to use a colonial joke, only dammed. Quite within the memory of man these natural watercourses were deepened just before the dam, the earth excavated serving the purpose of an embankment; in colonial jocular phraseology, the country was said to be cursed or coursed as well as dammed. Finally—and the youngest squatters remember this evolution—great tanks have begun to be dug over the plains to catch the surface water, so that after the country has been doubly vituperated, it is at last, as a Dutchman might say, "tanked."

Have you noticed these great ant-hills all around, some two to three feet high and ten or twelve feet in diameter, built of sand and stones as it were concreted together? Beat the hill and see the busy omnivora rushing forth. Here you may see them an inch long—great, hairy, soldier or bulldog ants, that, could you but train them, might come in as beasts of draught. As it is, the only drawing they seem to do is that of blood-drawing. The truth of the old adage, "Go to the ant, thou sluggard," was forcibly pointed the other day, when that great fat Sundowner, who rested from earning his "tucker" by sitting down, with axe in hand, on one of these mounds, afforded very soon a *tableau vivant*. Yes, "go to the ant, thou sluggard,"—to the Australian black ant—by all means, for it will teach thee energy, will put that *vis vitæ* into thy movements and thy voice for which now one looks vainly, and if thou carest not to exchange a large portion of thy carcass for a hundred thousand poisoned wounds, thou wilt soon learn the use of thy legs, and wilt change the venerable copy-book maxim, to "Go from the ant, thou sluggard—in double-quick time."

It may be a question for ethnologists in time-to-come to decide whether the push and energy of the Australian is not in some measure due to those qualities respectively existing in the many species of ants which dwell in the land. You never seem to be quite safe from them. If you lean up against a tree there may be a great ant's nest of mud and twigs hanging in the branches above you, and you may be regarded as a foreign body by the army going up and coming down, or perhaps a regular New Guinea to be annexed. You may be attitudinising by the verandah; the same fate will perhaps greet you, for there may be an ants' nest in the roof; you may be reclining on a sandy patch without knowing that the bulldog is in muster down below, until you find yourself gripped.

Brown ants, black ants, red ants, and white ants, winged and unwinged ants, seem to vie with one another in the warm welcome they give the stranger, and it is doubtful, where all do so well, to whom to give the palm. Had Dr. Watts ever seen the swarms that will get into your stores, that will swarm around your verandah before a wet night, and that will take every opportunity to show you their energy, he might have left suffering humanity a balsam something in the style of his ode to the bees. It is but charity to assume that their activity *is* industry, however misapplied it may seem when you find a soldier-ant fixing those fierce mandibles of his into your finger.

"Look out, we are in luck's way to-day! We've sprung upon another mob of kangaroos out here on the plain." The new chum, so pathetically tearful the day before yesterday over the fate of his first kangaroo, now reproaches the dogs for their stupidity in not having caught sight of them before, and thus giving them a start, for they are making off at a smart pace already. Jump as they may, the lithe thin kangaroo-hounds gain on them, the horses enter into the spirit, and one and all race along, now jumping a little creek, now clearing a fallen log, now narrowly shaving a tree-trunk; all is excitement, spiced with an element of danger which always adds zest to the dish. The hounds have singled out a great brown fellow; you can tell he is an "old man kangaroo" by his size and pluck, but we are bound to have him down. Helter skelter over the plain, everyone choosing his best road, frightening that quartette of native companions, sending a whole flock of galars screeching and fluttering heavenwards, ever nearing the scrub, in the thick of which lies a great snake fence. Here we go, all swept in, careless of the life insurance offices, into the dense scrub close on the dogs' track.

One young hound has pulled down a doe to the side there. "Never mind, we'll come back to see about her afterwards." The excitement lies in front, the older dogs know that their quarry is the noble buck ahead.

Ah! there we can see the fence close ahead; surely the kangaroo will jump it, as probably his comrades have done in their hasty flight, though lost to sight in the scrub. No; the dogs press him too closely. He swerves and doubles up the fence, hoping perhaps to find an opening which the boundary rider has overlooked. Not a chance; the station hand has done his duty, there is nothing for it, the dogs are close on you, your fate is sealed, "old man." Not a bit of it! With the speed of lightning he turns with his back to a tree-trunk, pulls himself up to his full height, and stands at bay, determined to fight it out, a six-foot monster, with a toe-nail like a razor.

We pull up around him, the dogs bark sharply, and the youngest and least experienced makes a great jump for his throat; quick as lightning one of those hind legs, worked by the massive tendons and muscles, strikes out; the hind claw cuts the dog a fearful gash in his side; he has begun the fight in sober earnest. While thus assailed another dog steers to one side, tries the same dodge, and though he makes his teeth felt for a second in the fur of the quarry, he may deem himself lucky that he has not got his death blow like his colleague, but has only "got a scratch," to use colonial parlance, in his thigh. The scratch happens to be a cut three or four inches long and half an inch deep, and will take many weeks to heal even in this healthy winter-time. The other dogs feel more shy now, and keep at a respectful distance, merely barking and yelping. So one of our stockmen jumps down, and picking up a bit of a fallen branch, with more courage than discretion approaches the brave buck. The squatter calls him back, tells him one of us happens to have a revolver, and will settle the animal's fate with less risk, but the adventurer knows that a blow from the stick will crush in the brute's skull, so thin is the cranium, and values his life as do many of his brethren, at a low price.

He advances within a couple of yards of the beast, but no farther; with a great spring the animal bounds forward, and taking his foe by surprise, strikes him a nasty wound in his leg, which makes him sick and faint, and he "gives the kangaroo best." The dogs rush in again, but are again discomfited, and one of their number again "scratched."

"Here," says the squatter, "can anyone fire a revolver straight? Our friend here has got one in his belt in true bushranger style; we must put an end to this slaughter."

"Wal," says old Jim, "I reckon I used to know once, when I was a marine on the *Inflexible;* I'll try again."

He dismounts, throws his reins to his mate, advances within a few yards of the animal, raises the weapon, and it is all over. A re-echoing "ping," sounding like an ice-crack in the clear air, only tells the tale of the messenger of death; the wound is in the heart, and with a tribute to the pluckiness of the "old beggar," Jim cuts off the scalp with his jack-knife, and counts the death another sixpence in his pocket.

One of us canters back to see after the doe the young hound

pulled down, and finds her wanting no *coup de grâce*. The cub, true to his instinct, has killed her outright. But she is not alone; that movement in the pouch betokens a young kangaroo there. "Ah, but it's a shame," says our pathetic friend, "to destroy such a pretty befurred little thing." Well, 'tis true some folk up country make pets of them and tame them, but they are always in trouble with the station-dogs, who get demoralised in consequence.

In the middle of the protest up rides the overseer. "Eh?" says he, "a pity to kill the little Joey? Not a bit of it; don't you see, two birds at a stone: the Joey's scalp is worth three-pence under the rules for the extermination of the vermin, and his mother's sixpence. There's a clear sweep at one transaction." Somehow one doesn't quite see the force of the argument, and lets the overseer assume the unenviable attitude of Herod for the occasion, which he does with the greatest nonchalance, seeing only the practical benefit he is doing the station by clearing it of one more "pest."

Here we go, on again through this sand-ridge which anyone less practical than a colonial would call a sweet-smelling pine forest, glorified with the golden balls of the flowering acacia, through one or two paddocks, until we reach a far-off paddock where a tank is being sunk.

Here, in the middle of the plain, just where it dips slightly, showing a watercourse, a camp of tank-sinkers is located. Their little tents and a big fire in front of the cooking-tent, all testify to the fact that they have left civilisation for awhile. Their beds are made by driving four stakes into the ground, and stretching a piece of sacking across from each corner. These are the couches of the luxurious, who care not to bivouac on the ground, or fear that a rainy day may water their bedding unduly. The men's dining-room has a slab on two posts for a table, with forms made of undressed boughs of trees nailed to stakes driven in the ground. No effete luxury here, no lengthy sitting over wine when you have no wine to sit over, but a three-inch snag sticking into your back. The tent of the foreman has a few more conveniencies on account of his wife's presence, who cooks for the gang of her husband's workmen. But she has to put up with makeshifts and inconveniences which would break many a charwoman's heart at home. See those two buckets suspended over the fire blazing out there: one is half-full of tea, and the other is just on the boil and going to be turned into that beverage by the liberal application of a packet of tea-leaves. Dark coloured? I should think it is, and just taste it! Eh? strong enough to knock you down at forty yards? Well, not quite; but then you see if these pick-and-shovel men didn't have "summat to bite," they'd grumble that they were not well enough provided for.

"Mrs. Jones sees you tasting her tea, and wants you to have a bit of cake." Eh, what, cake?

Is it possible? Quite! She makes "browney," a sort of sweet currant cake, for her customers, who, notwithstanding their beards and brawny muscles, still have the sweet tooth of their childhood. She is rather proud of her catering. She shows us the joints, the bread, the puddings, and the cake she's going to give them for dinner, all cooking as comfortably over this gipsy fire as though she were in a well-appointed kitchen; and if you come along at tea-time, you'd see preserves and marmalade, and perhaps tinned fish adding their luxurious presence to the heavier and more humble victuals.

Truly these tank-sinkers are said to live like fighting-cocks. They have a cup of tea and cake when they start at six, they have a substantial breakfast, such as would satisfy three of us, at eight, they have a lunch at ten, dinner at twelve, afternoon tea about four, and supper or meat tea at six or seven, when they knock off. They do not waste much time on feeding, however, as you may see if you care to wait for their dinner-hour. They are soon out at work again, and we can see for ourselves what work that is.

The ground here is stiff black soil, and requires a deal of labour to excavate a yard—labour which under the mid-day sun is not to be sneezed at. The foreman or contractor himself has the handle of the plough, driving a strong team of bullocks. The share cuts off a slice of the surface, which is now in the centre six feet below the level of the plain, and this is dragged up in a scoop by another team, or shovelled away into carts.

The scene is very animated, the bullocks and their driver exchanging remarks according to their respective natures; the running up and down of the horse-scoops, and the continual hurrying to and fro of carts. Now you will be able to understand how it is that these tank-sinkers can do such justice to their many meals. "But six meals a day! Well, it does seem pretty close fitting, doesn't it?" "Just come down here a week," says the foreman, "and if you don't get up in the middle of the night to attack the tucker,* I'm a Dutchman." "You'd better look out," says the squatter, "and defend your camp and tank from floods; the glass is going down, and we may have rain in a day or so." "Thanks for the hint," says the contractor, "but we've done so; we've only left the small receiving tank outside unprotected, and we'll be very glad to get that filled, as we have to fetch water a mile and a half, and then it isn't very clean, inclined to be green, and smacks of tadpoles."

We have to ride to another paddock now to measure out a tank for these tank-sinkers to dig after they have finished here. They are going to carry this about twelve feet down in the centre, with regular sloping sides called "batters" to prevent it from silting up quickly.

At one time folk thought a depth of six feet was enough, but old Father Sol thought differently, and made the bottom look very foolish after a spell of dry weather. This tank will be over sixty yards long, and fifty wide at the top, and will cost about £250 from first to last. A bibulous sheep can "stand" a brother toper a good many "drinks" out of this when full up.

* Tucker, food.

The contractor and one of his men have their horses out, and accompany us to choose the spot. After a few hours' riding the knowing ones settle on a "pocket," where they reckon a watercourse flows in wet weather, and here "in the lone wilderness," we measure out the ground and drive in pegs to mark where the main and the receiving tanks shall be. How ever the tank-sinkers will find the spot again, where every open piece of ground looks a counterpart of the other, and we are enclosed in thick scrub with the fences a couple of miles away at the nearest, would astonish anyone but a bushman. As a matter of fact, bushmen are so accustomed to taking sights of things and places that they can almost always tell where they are if they have been there before, and will find out their way without compass even on a dull clouded day. The new arrival up country is bewildered by the numbers of plains and patches of scrub, the sand-ridges and the gum forests; every one seems so like the other, and if the sun does not help him, he is not at all unlikely to get into that ridiculous though unpleasant predicament of being " bushed " in a fenced-in paddock.

Once after I had been thus lost for an hour or so, and had by a slice of luck regained my comrades, the topic turned on men being lost in the bush. Almost every one had undergone some such experience, or had helped to extricate a bushed man from his predicament, but under more dangerous circumstances. Where the country is not fenced in, and therefore probably is very thinly populated, to be "bushed" very often means death.

To give an instance which actually happened, and is but one example of hundreds of cases which terminate even more sadly, will take but a few words. One day it was rumoured on a station on the outskirts of civilisation that Harry Jenkins had got bushed somewhere in the mallee scrub.

This mallee scrub is one of the worst features of Australian scenery, as it often indicates a poor soil and grows about ten or twelve feet high, without a break for miles, or an opportunity to scan the surrounding country.

Harry was the hand of an adjoining station, but the interest was a common one; the kindly offices were reciprocal, or in anticipation of reciprocity, and so as many as thirty men turned out to search the scrub. For days they searched; at last the black trackers—aborigines with a scent as keen as that of a hound—were brought up, and after an entire lapse of seven days found the poor lost man a helpless imbecile, a mere bag of bones, *naked* and apparently dying.

They took him back and revived him; he recovered his senses after awhile, and when stronger gave them an account of what had happened. He had gone into the scrub to look for some sheep, and, although he noticed the sun, somehow he lost his bearings. He ran along as well as he could and then got frantic, tore off his boots because they seemed to impede him, ran along in stockinged feet, and from day to day divested himself of his garments, deeming that they only hindered his chance of again finding his way. His fearful thirst he described as infinitely more terrible than his hunger; he never saw a drop of water once, nor came across any of the trees whose roots sometimes hold a little of that precious beverage. His tongue swelled up and filled his mouth like a ball of leather; his mind was subject to hallucinations; he would think he saw the homestead in the scrub; he would think he heard the "cooees" of his comrades, but ever as he ran forward and answered the illusion would vanish. After the third day a merciful blank fell on him, but his subsequent history was a matter of circumstantial evidence produced by the clever black trackers. They showed that he had gone round and round, describing a circuit of fifteen to twenty miles a day at first, decreasing as he grew weaker; every evening he would return to within half a mile or so of the spot where he had first lost himself; in fact the six "camps" he made were within a radius of a mile from this spot. It appeared that the plan of throwing off boots and clothes is very frequently practised by a lost man, particularly in warm climates; and bushmen have assured me that the track of a stockinged foot is to them a startling tale " that some poor beggar has lost himself." The reason of a man always when thus lost travelling in a circle is a mystery. Reasons in legion have been given, such as following the sun, a weaker leg, a cant to one side, and so on. But no two bushmen seem to agree on the practical reason, and they have thrown cold water on a theory that they are the mere examples of the centripetal force that governs the position of the globe, gravitation, *et cetera scientifica*. As far as the sun is concerned, that bright-faced impostor may not be able to shine on account of the clouds, yet none the less, nay, rather the more, does the lost one describe this great circle.

The faculty that bushmen have of taking their bearings of places relates also to things and persons. They seldom forget a man, and never a horse they have once seen. I have heard a bushman asked if he ever remembered seeing a light-bay colt with a white spot on its fore-leg, and he answered, "Aye, indeed, and it had ⊓ over **A** inverted on the off shoulder, hadn't it? Aye, I saw it on the stock-route to Bathurst only about eighteen months back led by a chap with a bent nose and a lisp in his talk." In a land where one man may so easily run off with another's cattle, sheep, or horses without his being much the wiser for months, or perhaps years to come, this bush-dwellers' system of keeping their eyes open materially prevents theft and assists detectives.

That it is an easy thing for a man to lose a number of cattle and never know about it for a long period, I am in a position to confidently assert, for I know of a large run-holder in Queensland who not so long ago had five hundred head of horned cattle stolen from him, but never was cognisant of the fact until eighteen months later a "sundowner" casually remarked that he had noticed about a year ago a mob of cattle marked like those on the run being sold in Adelaide, South Australia (two thousand miles away), and wanted to know why the squatter sent them down so far. He instituted an inquiry, and found he was minus five hundred head of cattle, which had long ago probably gone to the abattoirs in Adelaide. I have spoken of "sundowners" before now. To those who have had no experience of what is becoming a nuisance in some parts of the colonies I should explain. The article is of the animal kingdom, genus *homo*, and generally tramps along during the day from station to station seeking work, timing his way so that he may reach a station about "sundown," in time for tea and bed. He has been described by a M.L.C. of New South Wales as a man going through the country seeking for work hoping that he may find none. He is thus a degenerate specimen of the "swagsman" proper, or tramp, who carries his "swag" from one homestead to another with a view to obtain employment. As a rule there are very few swagsmen who have to go far for work, but the species sundowner is looked on by master and man with some amount of disfavour, for he comes in too late, as a rule, to "earn his tucker" by helping the men's cook, and is only in the way, as the accomodation is rarely too large for the regular station-hands.

While on the topic of names, I would suggest that no one address such a mistaken compliment to an Australian as to say that "you see he's an old hand at it." The expression "old hand" is synonymous with "lag," or convict, and is still a sore point in a country where not so many years ago the very customs officials were ticket-of-leave men.

Another term of doubtful value in a visitor's eyes is that of "roustabout." It is synonymous with "handy man," *i.e.* a man who can put his hand to almost anything, a most necessary *employé* on a station far, as it may be, from civilisation. The term roustabout, though lacking the dignity and the consistency of "handy man," is nevertheless often selected by those to whom the two are applicable, though for what reason I may not say; perhaps because here we are in topsyturvydom, certainly for no very rational cause.

As we are sitting over our pipes after dinner the squatter suddenly jumps up as though shot. "By all that is damp and moist," says he, "there's the patter of rain on the galvanized roof." Out we all rush, and find the rain has come in verity;

those clouds that have been banking up all the afternoon, and have hidden the moon and stars, are at last pouring down of their plenty.

"Rig up the rain-gauge; we'll see what Jupiter Pluvius sends us."

Steadily does it come at first, then in fearful gusts; great bucketfuls, as though the heavens were indeed opened, dash down on our resounding roof, and make sleep at first an impossibility, and afterwards a series of noisy dreams.

I have known clouds to come up day after day for weeks together, and go away in the morning without parting with a drop of their precious contents.

The generally accepted theory is, that the vast current of hot air which must ascend from the sandy plains of the interior every day keeps the vapour at a point far above condensation, and unless the clouds can fall below the current the parched earth will continue unmoistened. The worst of such a state of things is that even the dew may not form on a cloudy night, as the clouds reflect back the radiated heat of the earth and prevent the temperature from falling to the dew-point. The Australian climate must be taught hygrometry before it can be deemed perfectly satisfactory.

The squatter mixes an extra stiff glass for the imbibers of our party to drink success to the rain before we turn in, as it is indeed a red-letter night, and the first rain for many months is, of course, a harbinger of better times.

Pulling a Bullock.

CHAPTER XIV.

Fourth Day.—The Tanks and the Rain.—A Buck-jumper.—The Reality precedes the Romance.—Mustering, Drafting, and Examining.—"Culls."—Hair *versus* Wool.—Supper and Nightmare to follow.—Honesty a poor Bedfellow.—The Fifth Day in and out.—The Sleepers rudely awakened.—Rain and Work.—Swimming a Creek.—Retransformation from Dry to Wet.—Science fails at the Gateway.—Words heavy and Language of the Ornate Character.—Women-kind in the Bush.—Sport.—Ducks, Swans, and Teal.—Pelicans.—Native Companions lead off the Ball.—A long Shot at a Kangaroo.—The Pigeon brings its Fate on its own Head.—"Scalps."—The Dingo, his Tail and his Tale.—Wild Pigs.—Travelling Sheep.—The Drover's Camp.—Drover's Artifice.—The Kangaroo Drive.—Emus.—Natural History at a Discount.—Kangaroo Shooters.—Bushmen's Hospitality.—Their Occupations.—"Hatters."—A Bower Bird.—Wild Horse riding.—Horse-breakers.—Hydrophobia and Hydatids.

THIS fourth morning opens gloomily. The welkin lowers near the earth, and still pours down its contents though with diminished energy. The effects of the rain on the parched ground are already visible. The creek is running gently in a few spots. Some of the lower grounds are flooded with a few inches of water, while many of the yawning cracks and fissures we saw yesterday have become great water drains, flowing sluggishly. It is a dreary outlook, but work has to be done to-day as on any other day. You have seen the more agreeable features of bush life, now learn some of its disadvantages. After a strong fortification in the shape of breakfast, we all sally forth to see, as usual, to our horses.

"You'd better take care how you get up this morning. As soon as you're in the saddle make up your mind to stop there, for when the weather is 'soft' your steed may 'buck.'"

However, we all mount without any casualty, and set off in the well-nigh blinding rain to a distant part of the run, where we have yet to clear a paddock.

We pass the tank-sinkers' camp which we visited yesterday, and find that they have had to "knock off" for the day, as the clay soil is as tenacious as glue. Now we understand why the squatter suggested the protection of the "camp" and the tank. The soil which was grubbed up has been set in a sort of rampart all around the "camp" and the large tank, to prevent the water from flooding them out. Balked of its prey, the flood has filled the little receiving tank to overflowing, and we understand now why they dig a smaller tank to receive the water before passing it on to the great tank, for the wash of the flowing water cuts away great gutters wherever the fall in the ground is considerable. I have seen dozens of cartloads of soil thus washed off the sides and carried down into the tank by a small rainfall where the slope or "batter" was too abrupt, and the large tank not properly hedged round with a rampart a precaution not only unnecessary but virtually useless for the small receiving-tank which can be easily cleaned out. I have seen a camp of tank-sinkers who had not taken this precaution covered in a night with eight or ten inches of water, the half-finished tank swamped, and work for weeks to come rendered impossible.

As we ride slowly along, one or the other attempting an antidote to the slush of the rain with a rippling song, the store-keeper's horse takes it into his head to shy at a fallen tree, and acknowledges the receipt of whip and spur energetically applied by commencing to buck. With almost solemn deliberation he plants his head between his forelegs, curves his back, and with one vast simultaneous leap off his four feet jumps into the air perpendicularly, with the intention of unseating his rider. Our friend jams his knees into his knee-pads and tightens his reins, and with a firm, grim look on his face determines to ride it out. Down come man and steed together, the one a trifle after the other. Without a second's hesitation Rosinante repeats the dose with the same want of success a second and a third time, squealing the while most inharmoniously. The saddle-girth is slipping ominously backwards; one more great buck and the girths give way, saddle and rider are hurled half a dozen yards, fortunately just clear of a tree, and as the triumphant beast bolts off it gives a vicious parting kick at its late rider, fortunately without damaging anything but the saddle. One of us hurries after the runaway, while the others assist our poor friend, stunned and unconscious, to a more natural position than that of being rolled up like a ball. We bring him to his senses with the help of a handful of water, and find that no bones are broken, but that his face is fearfully seamed and scarred in the gravel, and that he has got a "kink in his back." He refuses to return to the homestead, pluckily resolving to ride his "warp" out, but, being rather nervous and shaken, accepts the kindly offer of the overseer, who exchanges steeds with him. As though resting on his once-gained laurels, the refractory buck-jumper does not perform again, though for that matter the overseer gives him no chance, as he makes him carry his head well up, a position in which no horse can buck.

For months together this horse may never repeat the operation, then one day he may take it again into his head to treat his rider for the nonce to a piece of his mind after the same fashion as I have just described, with perhaps worse results to his bestrider. One rather rough way to cure a buck-jumper, if the rider possesses the presence of mind necessary and has a heavy-handled whip in hand, consists in hitting the horse a heavy blow between the ears as it thus attempts to throw him. One horse I knew—a fine blood mare—though rendered almost senseless by such treatment, never suffered from any after effects, and proved a living advertisement of the efficacy of the remedy, which old colonials widely advocate.

This is the reality of buck-jumping; the romance is sometimes told in a humorous story, where a man who mounted a buck-jumper afterwards described his sensations. First he felt himself soaring high above his comrades in the air, and came down plump into the saddle, only again to be shot up like a rocket. The second time he came down rather abaft the saddle, and was again elevated, with the result, however, as he said, that he somehow missed saddle and horse altogether on coming down, for he found himself seated on the hard ground, with his steed a mile or so away. As he said, his game of cup and ball was played by an inexperienced player, and resulted in a miss.

Accidents with these buck-jumpers are too frequent to be pleasant, more especially when the beast begins his dance of death in the close forest, where contact with a gum is not unlikely to perform an undesirable disarticulation of the cranium. I knew a new chum who was given a buck-jumper for his first "mount," and on the third day had the misfortune to break three ribs in "missing his saddle," a fact which gains in solemnity when the reader is told that the nearest doctor was about two hundred and fifty miles away. Others that I have come across, have broken their limbs and lost some of their lives (a veteran bushman has more than a cat), and some have got into that predicament known in the game of pool as "having to star."

The rain clears up before we reach our destination, a small log hut kept by a boundary-rider and his Irish wife, standing twelve miles distant from any other dwelling in the solitary bush. After leaving the storekeeper behind, in the tender cares of the good Irish Biddy, we start off to clear the paddock, and succeed in mustering the four thousand sheep back at the yards long before dusk. Work now begins in earnest, still in the drizzling rain. The sheep are separated into three sets by the swinging gate as on the first day, a process not of course adopted by the steaming mob for the mere asking, and strong is the language and many are the home-thrusts launched at their heads and saturated coats.

After they have been thus divided up, a portion of the sheep —the ewes—are treated with still greater indignity. Caught one by one in the pens, they are brought to an improvised form, where two of us sit astraddle a yard apart facing each other; they are then delivered over head and legs into our charge, and passed under the careful scrutiny of the "boss" himself. He grows his sheep for wool, not for food, and takes the precaution of weeding out the inferior-coated animals thus brought under his notice. The inferior sheep are "culled"— ear-marked in a peculiar fashion—and turned away from the rest, who go to swell the ranks of his stock-ewes. The order "cull" sounds too often this year of drought and famine; 'tis a wonder that the proportions of the skinny degenerate one-year olds are not greater.

The wool of some shows unmistakable signs of getting hairy, a curious instance of nature's adaptation of the beast to its surroundings. Here in the heated interior the woollen coat is very often more of a burden than a protection, thus nature is slowly thinning it out and replacing it by the cooler hair. Up further north in Queensland, where the summer is hotter and longer, the matter is continually before the squatters, who, if they wish to maintain the breed of their stock, often have, after ten years, to import a fresh stock entirely from the cooler climes of Victoria, Tasmania, or New Zealand.

The "hands" laugh loudly at the two seated ones, as some more determined candidate for examination gives vigorous kicks or butts, though the laugh is not altogether on their side, as the chasing or catching of the wet-coated sheep in the muddy yards does not tend to promote either the integrity or the cleanliness of their garments. Dusk comes on apace, the laughing jackass laughs his erie cachination from a neighbouring tree-top, and we ride back to the hut in the roseate glow of the sunset sky. Those of us who belong to the upper ten are royally entertained by our host and hostess, who persist in thinking that the true essence of hospitality consists in making their guests emulate

the fat boy who "busted hisself rather than waste mum."
Should a loin of mutton come along, and there are four of us,
'tis divided in four great pieces, and the other victuals having
been served in the same way, are expected to vanish like the
magician's penny. *That* goes up his sleeve; would that for
the sake of a dreamless sleep it were within the province of
policy to make a large portion of the viands follow in the same
way! The squatter himself could make three or four mutton-
chops look foolish, but when huge chunks of "plum duff" and
browney followed, even he began during the small hours of
the night to act Lady Macbeth with variations.

There happened, fortunately, to be two rooms in the hut,
both of which had been well papered inside with illustrated
papers, wherein lay a certain pathetic contrast—that of town
and country, the old and the new. Our fireplace was like a
small room, so large was it, built of slabs, but puddled for
some feet up with clay, so before the blazing fire we all lay down,
with saddles for pillows, our handkerchiefs and honesty as a
mattress and covering respectively. In one or two cases the
sleepers complain of being lightly covered, not warm enough,
and so on. The squatter does not; *ergo* he's an honest man. As
the night goes on the logs die out, and the squatter finds out
also that this world is hollow and human honesty a poor
blanket.

Next day, Friday, is a repetition of yesterday. Although,
for my reader's sake, I would like to proceed to fresh fields and
pastures new, in justice to the sheep waiting to be drafted,
examined, and "culled," I could not leave them thus, for otherwise the eternal fitness of things would have been wanting
had I managed to muster, draft, examine, and cull (on paper)
four or five thousand sheep in an afternoon. That next
night, as we lay each testifying to the solidity of supper by a
special and particular note of the snoring type, a drop of water
falls on somebody's face. It works in with his dreams till
another and another, then a little rivulet coming down his face
finds a weak point by his collar. Hey, presto, now he's alive!

Why, what can it be? The rain again, surely? Go out and see. Yes, the ruddy sunset of a few hours ago and the prophecy of the laughing jackass were true. It is coming down, and pitilessly. In the early morning, before even chaste Aurora has disturbed Erebus from his sable bed, we are all astir searching for our horses in the small paddock. "Here's your horse, Mr. Jones." "Ah, so it is; here's yours, Jim," and so on. Though how in the world anybody can tell in the blinding rain and darkness one horse from another would make you wonder, if you did not remember in your heart of hearts that escapade of the storekeeper's house the other wet morning, and that precludes all such small amazement and fills your mind with anticipation of evil.

There are a thousand culled sheep to take out of the yards away some dozen miles, and if we do not start immediately we shall never get them across the creeks. After a hasty snack each man takes to his saddle. One old horse takes it into his head to clear his back, but succeeds only in getting a stunning blow from his rider's stock-whip handle. "That's the only way to cure him," says the bearded Hercules as he canters by. "Try it yourselves if your horses buck." The first creek we have to cross was yesterday a dry sandy watercourse; now the sheep are swimming a muddy, angry torrent. Some patience and skill has to be exhibited to cause them to "tempt the briny," but these qualities combined, achieve their deserved success. For eight miles the wet-bedraggled mob are driven by a wet-bedraggled crew, sometimes through swollen creeks, again over plains, yesterday as dry as an Australian barman's throat, now standing inches deep in water. Such are the extremes of Australia—drought one week, floods the next. The last creek our horses themselves have to swim; this creek, where the day before yesterday you could have walked across in dancing shoes, is now a swollen stream some thirty feet broad, overflowing all the dams, boiling and seething in its course along the plains as though it were in a desperate hurry to reach its grandmother the sea.

At the last gate we try a new dodge of getting our charges through. A mob of sheep in front of an open gate is like the audience of the street showman when the hat goes round; each seems to think that this cannot be meant for him. The process adopted when there is a party of drovers and their dogs is to run them up in closer and closer order until the rear ranks push the vanguard through; but here the advice of an old colonial comes to my memory, and I determine, being alone for a time, to try it. "Let them have a good look at the open gateway first," said he, "and then they'll walk through like *lambs.*" It were well for the hitherto uninterrupted harmony existing between myself and that old colonial that I should never meet him again.

After a quarter of an hour of patiently forming a rain-water butt I observed part of the mob stealing off into the scrub on one side, part on the other, but not a single one through the gate. A few touches of the reins and the stock-horse crowds them up again, but a few more minutes of watching and being washed is attended by the same results. After successive repetitions of this farce, and the despatch of a telegraphic message to the squatter to take up my bones if he finds them at some distant date when the sheep are all through, a big D has the desired effect of bringing up another "hand," and of getting the refractory ones through. The question naturally suggests itself whether the same object could have been attained without that word that "Sir Joseph Porter" never used. The station hand avers, "An adverbially adjectival word or two is all powerful with the brute kind." Opinions differ hereon. I have referred to the bullock-driver in Chapter X. who never, not even hardly ever, used that word.

The senseless use of the dissyllable corrupted from By-our-ladie prevails in the colonies as at home. Swearing is proverbial in Queensland, say the New South Welsh. The Queenslanders return the compliment with interest; and I do not think an unprejudiced critic would find any very serious difference in the merit of the two colonies. Victoria certainly is more genteel, though why so she knows not. Gold-fields and rowdyism generally are found together, and Victoria has had her share of both.

When a lady at home tries to fasten a nail and hits her own finger, as she inevitably does, she says, "Bother!" When the bushman sends an adze through his boot and foot or gets a horse's hoof on his pet corn, he builds his language after a more ornate and florid style, but it means the same. But even when he does not have occasion to relieve his feelings in this way he vulgarises this architecture of words by too free a use, and then the moralist may well step in. The bushman has not that nice sense of discrimination that sees the advantage of storing up a string of these epithets and exclamations for a really useful occasion; though one pleasing feature concerned with this custom is that the bushman's wife does not copy her spouse. I should add that as a rule the bushman has no wife, which perhaps accounts for this pleasing feature. Women are indeed *raræ aves* up country, and rather put on airs, as though it were due to some virtuous act of their own that they *were* of the gentler sex. There are at any rate but few inducements to a woman to immure herself in the solitude of a stockman's hut or a boundary-rider's cabin; not even the melancholy satisfaction of criticising another woman's apparel remains to her. The squatter may have a wife, but unless she be young and given to riding about the run the occupants of the outlying huts do not often see her shadow across their doorstep. Occasionally one sees a lady of that colour affected by our base coinage, some lubra's daughter, who on the strength of the tinge of white blood in her veins carries her nose a long way above her darker-skinned sisters whose blood has none of this aristocratic blue. She often thinks herself too good to mate with a brother half-breed, and in a place where the dearth of her sex is a chronic complaint has some "method in her madness."

As we cannot do any more sheep-work to-day, the squatter proposes to his guests that they should take his guns and try at a few ducks. He himself and his "hands" have to see after the tanks and dams, which are probably full by this time, and may want some repairing. But where are the ducks to be shot at? naturally inquires the "new chum," who has not seen until a few days back enough water even for the lady ducks to do their back hair before. "Oh, you'll find plenty of ducks, pelicans, and native companions about the tanks and the dams now, and perhaps on one or two of the swamps!" Eh, what's that?—swamps? Why, there can't be any swamps

At the Dam.

on a place that a few days back looked, like King Alfred cakes, a good deal overbaked.

We take a good pair of boots, clothes that will not spoil, and a shot-gun. Here we are near the dam, and have to pick our way carefully; the waters are running all round the end and cutting channels on their own account. Silence is as golden now as ever it can be; the birds will get away in half a second if they scent, see, or hear us. "Now lie flat on the damp greasy clay of the dam, wriggle your way upwards, and let your head appear above the top as gradually as doth the sun appear above the horizon when, as in a London fog, he's a bit sleepy. Fortunately that young gum sapling hides your head." A goodly

P

sight of ducks, black and grey, and a whole mob of black swans meets our view. "Where did they come from? Never mind now; pay more attention to their going into our bag. Get your gun over quietly!—sight it! Now take careful aim to let your shot scatter amongst those teal." We can get a larger bag of them than of the black ducks, which are larger but much further apart; and as for the swans, their only use seems to be in their skins, unless the larder be very empty, when if the hunter buries his swan for three or four days and then disinter it, and recks not for a somewhat high flavour, it may be said to be palatable. "Give them both barrels. Bang, bang! There go the mobs; the teal one way, the black ducks another, both wheeling round as is their wont, and off go the swans making a bee line to some other piece of water where the murderous iron barrel ceases from troubling and the powder is at rest. Load up again, and take another shot at the whirling mob overhead. Ah! that wasn't very successful. You may fire upwards for half a century and not hit one if you haven't the knack." We retrieve our bag, and that quickly, for a wounded teal makes for the land, and lies so dark, hiding behind bushes and rushes, that it conjures up a reciprocal sombreness on the brow of the dogless hunter. Seven teal at one shot (as we lay them out on the bank) are a pecuniary recompense for the expenditure of two cartridges. I have known even a greater massacre of the innocents where they were very thick, seven falling to one barrel, four to the other. Our bag will give the squatter a change from mutton and beef such as he has not had for six months. On our way to another paddock to search for the marsh we find walking to be a repetition of John Gilpin's excursion through merry Edmonton. You can hardly realise that all this dried-up earth has been unable to suck up the rain.

"Now, then, you wanted to know where the ducks and swans come from so soon after the rain. From the pools left in the half-dried-up Murray, which runs hundreds of miles away to the west, and from the few pools and running streams in this side of the dividing range some three hundred miles to the east. They scent the water from afar, and like the vulture rushing to the carrion, so they carry on their mid-air career only very often to fall a prey to, instead of praying a fall of, some human being armed like ourselves."

We find the marsh snugly esconced in a patch of "scrub," and have to stalk the quarry, if there is any here. "Dodge from tree to tree, taking care where to tread. Eh? what? that sounded rather like 'confound that kangaroo.' Don't mind; the birds are used to seeing them about. Now can you see through the trees those moving masses of white? Pelicans they are though not of the wilderness, rejoicing in their stalk through the marsh. See, again, those long-legged stork-like birds, they're the native companions, an awkward bird to shoot, for if they turn edgewise you lose sight of them, and when broadside on their mass of feathers covers about six cubic inches of body more or less."

If you want to have a good laugh watch the native companion for a minute or so. He is a tame, sociable sort of bird who has seen better circumstances, as he soon shows us by bowing most assiduously to his wife, who with equal politeness returns the courtesy. Then he leads her out into a quadrille, inviting two others who have just come up to join their party. *Vis-a-vis* they place themselves, bowing and scraping just like those other companions called human, now jumping up successively or all together, bending their long necks, kicking out their legs, and flapping their wings, they go through a series of evolutions and contortions that immediately show any student of Darwin that dancing is not an inherent virtue of man, but is evolved from these purer-coated and minded fellow-creatures, who furthermore carry out the maxim that people do more harm with their tongues than their toes by maintaining a grave deportment and silence until the end, when with a slight croak from each, apparently intended for an acknowledgment of the courtesy of the others in gracing the ball, they separate, the ladies probably to muse on the get-up of each other, the gentlemen to hunt around for another luscious worm or beetle. The size of our "bag" depends on our silence, so we have to smother our laughter, though you may at times approach within fifty yards of these Australian storks.

The pelican and the native companion are of little value beyond their skins, few bushmen having tasted either, and fewer still liking the flesh, which is strong flavoured; and the black ducks, are, as we have found out, very shy. Another and careful sight, two bangs, a puff of smoke, and amidst the consternation of screeching native companions and quack of duck and flapping of pelicans, a couple more birds fall to our "bag" for the day. After whirling around in ever-increasing circles, the survivors make in a bee-line for some other waterhole. Then as darkness is not a pleasant accompaniment to a wet walk through the bush, and sunset is close at hand, as the decreased glare on the tree-tops tells us, we retrace our steps.

"Wait a bit, don't hurry out of the scrub, there's a fine mob of kangaroos ahead; we shan't get near enough to use a shot. gun, we'll try the old buck with this Winchester. Look out! he's seen us; now for it, aim at his retreating form." He jumps leisurely at first, and waits for half a second between each leap. A suspense of a second that seems like an hour, a loud report, and the kangaroo falls. "No, he's up again. Ah, poor brute, give him his *coup de grâce*." When we come up to him we find him a fine fellow, some eight feet long from tip of nose to end of tail. His skin is well worth preserving, being of a lovely red colour that melts away into grey and white in front.

Skinning sounds easy enough when the object is a potato, but 'tis a task of some difficulty to a new chum to peel the quarry of its coat of fur or feathers. Somehow when first skinning an animal one's knife is too short or blunt, too round or square, too long or short, that is all that's in fault. "It's easy enough to cut the skin off!" There you make a mistake, oh Nimrod *in posse*, you don't have to cut the skin off, you must make your incisions and then use your hands, carefully prising and pulling it off. Slit up the tail on the under side, and pull the skin from the kangaroo. Great heavens! that must have looked funny to those two pigeons on the myall yonder. We pull too hard, and each of us feels the ground suddenly come up and hit us. One consolation we have as we laughingly rub our bruises is that the animal is skinned. We have *come* and *conquered*, and the pigeons have done the *seeing*. Their hilarious laughter at our proceedings must be avenged, besides which the cook will thank us, as pigeons make a capital pie, much better than parrots, which are somewhat full flavoured. Bang goes the shooting iron, down come the fluttering birds, two birds at a stone in very truth. The whirr of others flying away in the gathering dusk sounds like a small thunderstorm on a provincial stage.

The pigeon is a pretty bird, with its buff plumage and its little top-knot, and were it not so excellent a substitute for its European brother in a good crust, there might be some qualms of conscience attending its destruction. We tie up the kangaroo skin in a bundle, fling it in our bag with the birds, and make for home, where the cheering lights of the house remind us of the Christy song, and the baying of the dogs warns us to look well after our booty. The squatter hails our return with delight.

"'Tis not often at this time of the year, with shearing so close on, that we get a change in our diet," says he; "and as for the kangaroo, its a good job he's off the run, why he'd eat as much as three sheep. We've killed over twenty-three thousand on our run during three years. Come and see the bonfire of scalps we are going to make out here by the wood heap. A brother assessor rode over this afternoon, and we have been counting out the returns off this run for three months. There are fifteen hundred scalps altogether, and we know that the last drought has killed off many a jumper besides these. Burn them? I should think so, otherwise the men would be bringing in the same old scalps again, and then we'd be in a nice hole."

"Hallo! what's this long tawny piece of skin with scalp and tail at opposite ends?" "A dingo's or wild dog's! may the children be fatherless and the wife a widow of everyone in the counthry! shure!" says the other assessor, whose run adjoins this.

The dingo is a thief and a coward. Perhaps the squatter might be inclined to respect his enemy were he a brave robber, a sort of Dick Turpin of the bush. A third count against him is that he injures more than he eats. He will worry a dozen sheep out of a flock and only kill one outright, but the rest will rarely recover if they have been much bitten. His saliva is like virus, it poisons the whole system, and his poor worried victims pine away slowly and die. What is the dingo? ask the naturalists; and the dingo can give no satisfactory explanation of himself. Is he the degenerate son of a tame dog, brought over by the early inhabitants or some of their visitors from the adjacent Asiatic islands or continent? or is he an aboriginal himself? The wretched dingo is torn hither and thither; say that he is a piece of native industry, and scores will tell you that he was unknown in the earliest traditions of his aboriginal human brethren; express the opinion that he is an import, and scores will ask you how he lived before the sheep came, and that he has got hair like the *canis domesticus*.

The fact is it does not very much matter how he sprung, whether like the three-headed dog at the gates of Hades from the loins of Typhaon and Echidna, or, like Faust's black dog, from the imagination of an evil spirit, he is a very Hades in himself, so at least the squatters of affected districts say, using a word less rhythmic than Hades. Would you shoot a dingo you must be very wary and cute. "Throw yourself on the ground immediately you see one," said an old stockman; "I have done it, and almost always the cowardly brute has come sniffing around me thinking I'm dead, when with a lucky shot I've bowled him over, and pocketed a sovereign."

The squatter has another enemy in the shape of wild pigs, the progeny of those long ago introduced by the early settlers, who often change their diet of dead mutton to live lamb. Great big tuskers run amongst them, affording sometimes "elegant sport" were there only a few pig-stickers about. The animal may get dangerous at close quarters, when the six-shooter comes in handy. In some parts of New Zealand, where the pigs increased after the arrival of the whites last century to an astonishing amount, it is the custom to have a battue, often exciting and not unaccompanied by danger; but here time does not often permit of such luxuries as pig-sticking. "Why does not the squatter kill them for food?" Well, there are some objections in a warm climate to eating pork which has been nourished by semi-decomposed kangaroos, sheep, horses, and the like. I knew a kangaroo-shooter who employed himself occasionally in killing and salting hams from wild pigs; he found a ready market for the pork in the townships, but he took good care both by *suppressio veri* and *suggestio falsi* to conceal its source.

During dinner a stranger rides up, and shouts out at the front gate that he wants to see the squatter. It appears he is a forerunner of a mob of sheep which are coming up the lane; though he ought to have been here hours before this, so as to give the squatter timely notice that the mob would pass over the run and let him have time to get his own out of the way, and thus prevent *mistakes* and confusion which will happen, and which sometimes result in a drover driving *more* sheep off the run than he brought on at the other end. This horseman's master, the drover, happens to be a friend of the squatters, so the breach of regulations is forgiven.

The bleating from three thousand throats sounds clear and soft on the night breeze, and very soon the quivering and leaping fire out yonder in the dark shows that the drover has pitched his camp for the night. He has not managed well or he is short-handed. He ought to have got his sheep over their regulation minimum of six miles long before dusk, and have sent on his cook ahead to get the camp ready.

After dinner we walk out and smoke a pipe with him. Two

or three canvas tents are pitched on the bare earth, still far from dry, around a blazing fire, such as a bushman knows so well how to make, even out of damp wood, and feels the need of these clear, cold nights. The master drover himself, whose interest it is to get as many of his sheep through their long journey alive and well as he can, tells us he cannot drive his poor charges along quickly, as they are exhausted and weak, not having had a "square feed" for six weeks prior to his starting them down country a se'nnight since.

In that time he has travelled them over fifty miles, but has to do it by very easy stages. He is a tough, wiry, tawny-looking man, and has to have his wits about him, but if he's careful generally makes a pretty penny out of the transaction. His hardships are many. For weeks together, at one time or another, he has had to content himself with water of an opaque and slimy character charged heavily with organic matter, bread and mutton his fare, the earth wet or dry his bed. He seems jolly enough to-night as he refuses the squatter's invitation to sleep in a civilised bed, excusing himself that his men are tired and want looking after as well as the sheep, and to cover his retreat he roars out an old ditty about Betty and Susan and a snatch of "How we beat the Favourite," or some other colonial rhyme, occasionally taking a pull at the great pannikin of tea by his side. His men in the other tents see no use in losing valuable time, and, except those on watch to prevent their charges wandering into the scrub, are digesting their well-earned supper in sound sleep.

A kangaroo-hunter rides down shortly after, and tells the squatter that he is "going to *drive* the kangaroos in a paddock on the morrow, which is to be first cleared of its sheep, and would anybody care to come and help him;" so pipes are laid aside for a bit, and shooting irons of all sorts and sizes got out and cleaned ready for the morrow.

Next morning sees us setting out like a band of irregulars, with every conceivable species of bush fire-arm on saddle, back, or belt. We soon come up with our friend the drover, who is travelling slowly across the run in order to let his sheep crop the luscious herbage for which their mouths have watered so long.

"Hallo, Jones," says the squatter with a smile, "I guess those mobs of yours to the right are a good half-mile off the stock-route."

"Ah," says the drover with a quiet twinkle, "the fact is, you see, that chap that's driving them has got his eyes somehow mixed; they get sorter crossed when he's driving, and his right eye tells him he's only a quarter of a mile from the route while the left one can't see the route at all. Mighty convenient chap to have, for his left eye always seems to catch sight of the greenest patches."

We help him to put them through the boundary gate of the run on to the next one, a matter of some three miles from his starting-point in the morning, and watch with amusement his delight at the great clumps of marsh mallow, trefoil, wild carrot, and the like that the new route discloses.*

"Ah," says he with a grateful sigh to his foreman, "you can leave them around here, Tom. I'm sure Old Brown wants them weeds kept down; and I'll ride in and report that we expect to be on his run first thing to-morrow. If a boundary rider don't come along and spoil it all Brown 'll never find it out."

"*O tempora! O mores!*" cries out a classical Nimrod, but only challenges the reply that should he wish for more ease he'd have better stopped in the hammock in the verandah, as classics are at a discount in the bush.

After a good canter we come to the scene of our future exploits, past great tanks overflowing with water, their channels and ditches still flowing sluggishly; past flocks of ducks, swans, and pelicans; past sweet-smelling pine-scrub and the gilded balls of the acacia-trees, pulling up at last when we hear in

* It must not be thought that this wealth of verdure was the product of a few days' after rain; as a matter of fact the change from bare hard earth to lush and tall herbage occupied about five weeks.

the thicket close by a whispering caution not to make a noise, but to jump down from our horses and post ourselves in the bush, for the kangaroos are coming. With bated breath we exchange a few whispers, tether our horses in the scrub, look to our guns, and post ourselves in the points of vantage shown to us by our quiet informant, the kangaroo-shooter himself. We are at the narrow end of a converging lane formed by the paddock fence on one side and strings threaded with paper like the tail of a kite on the other. The wild beasts of the field are supposed to recognise that the elongated kite-tails * are merely reproductions of the wire-fencing, which they know by painful experience to be tough subjects to crack.

My first kangaroo drive, as is usually the case, was fraught with some excitement to me, but after the second or third, one grows as hardened as Pharaoh and as cool as iced lemonade. Every second a kangaroo may come at headlong speed out of the thick scrub ahead and pass safely by in a few jumps if you are not ready and quick.

Hark! the beaters or drivers are not far off; hear the cracking of their whips; now look out. A miss-fire now and you might as well have stopped behind. Hear the crashing of the boughs! "They're coming," cries the old shooter under his breath. Before any one can tell how it happens the whole of the patch of ground between us and the bush seems alive with the leaping marsupials, young and old, buck and doe. Bang! bang! on all sides, shot and shell do their work. Then comes a lull. The old chums commence reloading, and advise their guests to do the like. The whips sound again, a "cooee" comes along the breeze, another mob of kangaroos breaks cover, and receives decimation from our united ambuscade. Without a second's delay another great rushing comes nearer. "By Jove! a mob of emus," says the old hunter. "Shoot at the breast, and don't aim too low. Before he has got his words out the emus break cover fifty yards off. A noble sight indeed! fifteen great birds running up to our ambush with a speed that

* Called wings.

almost equals that of the kangaroos. At our first discharge the whole mob gets utterly distracted, and on seeing three of their number lying helpless on the ground or jumping in the air in their death agony, stare wildly around for half a second and then turn tail and make for the scrub. There they are turned back again, and finally free themselves by bursting the *wings* of the lane.

The great destruction to the feathers of the wounded birds through their repeated bouncing off the ground, and the desire to put them out of their misery (the motives are placed in correct order, *verb. sap.*) impel one of our number to give the *quietus* to his quarry—a course that calls down an economical lecture from the old hunter, who wants to know " what in the name of fortune he *wasted* that cartridge for?"

The drivers soon appear, and help us to skin or scalp our game according to the predilections of each one of us. The emus in winter get covered with a layer of yellow fat, which makes the process of flaying an unpleasantly greasy one, and somewhat prevents the skin from being cleansed before curing; but fortunately for amateur curers, this fat, if once dried, will act as a sure preventive of insects, &c., as no mortal animal, not even the omnivorous flea, can stand a dinner of emu oil. It has a use beyond this : in the stockman's pharmacopœia it has a prominent place, being supposed to be a specific for neuralgia and rheumatism.

Our hunting ended for the day, various old chums have an unpleasant way of recalling drives when they had a dozen kangaroos falling to each gun, and thought nothing of it. Now there are only six a piece. What degeneration ! Quite enough to make a pretty considerable perfume in a few day unless the sun acts as a siccative.

The squatter opens up a fierce dispute *apropos* of that young unformed kangaroo that Jim the kangaroo-shooter just now drew out of its dead mother's pouch, an example of the awful mystery shrouding the first moments of life. The poor little thing had no independent existence, and yet it was in the pouch. The squatter affirms, taking his cue from many others, that the young kangaroo is born, and then immediately transferred to the pouch by its mother, where it still leads a dependent existence, continually nourished with its mother's milk. Old Jim takes the contrary opinion, that the Joey takes its rise in the pouch and draws its nourishment from its very commencement from its mother's milk. He says he has found them thus attached when only a few weeks old, before even they had much else than rudimentary limbs. Colonials have split somewhat on this question and have not settled it yet. Pompey and Cæsar very much alike, specially Pompey.

The young kangaroo is tied to his mother's apron-strings long after he is capable of leading an independent existence. He has not the sense of shame that comes to an old-fashioned animal of the old world when its mother tries coddling it. I don't think he voluntarily abandons his mother's pouch until he outgrows the accommodation, elastic though it may be, of his mother's apron.

The kangaroo-shooter often spoken of is one of a class of men who, like lawyers, make capital out of other men's ills. So much per scalp is paid them by the squatter for clearing his paddocks of these pests, and were there not the pests heaven only knows what they would do. Perhaps there might be some who would start a kangaroo farm, like a rascal did in Victoria for dingoes. For some time this defrauder of the revenue made a great profit by breeding dingoes in an enclosure, killing them at maturity, and pocketing the Government reward of a pound per head. When found out, on the approach of the police he threatened (and subsequently performed his threat) to turn out the whole mob into the scrub. The consequence was that for months afterwards the squatters far and near had a regular epidemic of wild dogs.

Our old kangaroo-shooter suggests a ride to his hut for a " bit of tucker and a cup of tea," and the guileless ones of our party are taken in and literally done for. The squatter suddenly manifests an earnest desire to eat his lunch *al fresco* while the others enter. When once inside they are attacked and almost put an end to by an immense army of fleas, who give their master moral as well as physical support by affording his guests a very warm welcome. Bushmen have so little society that they think these little companions rather an advantage than otherwise; indeed, I heard of an old shepherd who had taken the trouble to train his rank and file to come at call, eat off his hand, and perform such-like innocent tricks.

The noun flea suggests to a new chum the similar-sounding verb, but unless the visitor wishes to offend his would-be host let him take care how he puts the suggestion into practical force. A bushman's hospitality is proverbial; in fact, if it be rejected, or even if when passing an acquaintance fail to drop into the hut, and fail either to be helped or help himself to the food he finds hanging up in the bags from the roof (a larder intended to circumvent the ants, though not always successful), he will not improbably give his would-be host much offence.

The stockman is, notwithstanding his rough life, rather sensitive on the score of fancied slights, and this refusal, active or passive, to partake, is in his opinion but the expression on the part of the inchoate guest of superiority, a quality which the levelling colonial admits in very few mortals. If you find the stockman away from home the orthodox custom is to go in, hand out the meat and bread, put the "billy" (a tin quart saucepan) on the fire smouldering in the big chimney, throw in a *quant. suff.* of tea and then take your fill, always remembering to rake the ashes back again over the blazing logs, and to place the viands back in their proper places. Should you wish to enjoy these "surprise" picnics you must not look too closely into the *menage*. Each one dips the tin mug or pannikin he is drinking out of into the billy, each one carves the meat and bread probably with his own knife and fork: neither pannikins, knives, forks, nor plates boast that scrupulous cleanliness which English housewives move heaven and earth to produce. This, however, is a general statement; I have lunched with an old boundary-rider who would have put some of our kitchenmaids to shame with his spotless table, bright pannikins, plates, &c.; but he was an exception, and strange to say, his cleanliness never received much appreciation from his mates who might drop in, who used to call him an "old woman" for taking so much care of the outside of the platter. His bedroom, a portion of the slab-hut partitioned off at the end and papered with illustrated home and colonial papers, with its sleeping-bunk half hidden in blankets and kangaroo rugs, its books (for he was a reading man), stockwhips, and general stock paraphernalia, was as picturesque a scene of disorder as you could well find. He lived alone, but would gallop into the homestead once or twice a week to report progress or to get provisions, generally the latter, for the work of a boundary-rider is tolerably mechanical and lacks a large portion of the small excitement the shepherd of the olden days might have.

What chance of getting himself or his charges lost or speared by aborignes, is there to the boundary-rider in his fenced paddocks before which the black has steadily retreated? His greatest excitement a gap in the fence found on his riding round his boundaries, whereby sheep may have strayed into a land whither they should not. In all weathers he has to do his twenty or thirty miles riding, varied perhaps in floods by the necessity of getting his sheep over to a dry sand-ridge where they may feed in security. Kangaroo or emu-shooting to him lacks much of its first excitement; the former is perhaps a mode of increasing his wages, the latter rarely, as he does not usually take the trouble to take off the skins and send them down to the markets in Sydney, Melbourne, or Brisbane, where a good emu-skin will fetch a "yellow-boy."

Many of the "hands" on the station have seen very stirring times. Old Crimeans are sometimes, Anglo-Indian soldiers often, met with; sailors, mechanics from the old country, and not seldom the sons of English gentry help to swell the ranks of these solitary ones. Sometimes by great solitude a man gets eccentric, sometimes "goes off his head" altogether. One or two cases I came across were of the milder class, merely cases of the want of a tile or a screw; many others I heard of through colonial doctors, who often have these solitary men to cure of their madness, an end generally achieved in the course of a few months by change of scene, and more especially by prescribing society of some sort or other. A man may thus sometimes get the reputation of being what is called a "hatter," and none but the boldest will spend a night in his hut; the expression, *as mad as a hatter*, seems to have something to do with this perversion of the trade-name of a most useful and industrious class of tradesmen, though who is responsible for this simile colonials may not say.

On leaving the kangaroo-shooter's hut with our trophies tied to our saddles we strike across country to try and find the tracks of certain wild horses which are reported to be "rampaging around on the run, breaking fences and doing other damage." These degenerate scions of the Rosinantes of the early settlers do much damage to the wire fences; they see not, or care not to see the wire, and in their mad rushes often break big gaps which the sheep are not slow to take advantage of.

We pass the bower of a bower-bird, that curious little alley built by this bird-architect in which to play at ball with his wife, where he stores up countless treasures, such as pieces of bright cloth, stone, and metal.

Many are the stories in colonial fireside-talk where the bower-bird comes in. He seems to be partial to the coinage of the realm, not relying on its useful so much as its ornamental qualities. Perhaps it is so, that if the parson-bird—a black bird with a white choker—were to come along pressing him to subscribe to a bazaar or some mission to the benighted soldier-birds, he might drop a coin in the outstretched palm of his interlocutor. To him more than once has been fairly ascribed the finding of gold. Attracted by the glitter of a nugget or a streak of the shining metal in a lump of glittering quartz, he has added it to his heap ignorant that his fatal curiosity might cause the destroying "human" to render his native haunts hateful with the resonant blows of the pick or the wild thunder of the blasting gunpowder. Bushmen say that these birds often build their bowers a mile or so away from their nest, probably so that the gentleman bird may have an excuse at times for leaving his wife to her household and nursery cares, and of going away out of hearing to his club.

We come across traces of the wild horses clear and plain in the recently trodden soil, so we know that some of them at any rate are here. The squatter means if possible to drive them down this time, as they have escaped him before. So we scatter over the paddock with instructions to bear down to a certain gate, far away hidden in the scrub, and if possible run then home to the yards, there to deal with them as his pleasure directs. Hark! there goes a cooee and the familiar crack of the stockwhip; somebody has sighted them. Thud, thud! look out, they're coming this way! Yes, there they come racing down to get into this scrub, with two of our party striving hard to head them. Dashing out at full speed we strive to work round their noses, and having the start and a clear field we ought to do it. This is life indeed! The old stock-horse takes a malicious interest in it all; gallantly he cuts along, now rising to clear some heap of fallen brushwood, now to jump a little mud-hole treacherous and slippery. Stumble, crack! over the two of us go; rider and horse are mixed up for some time, pitched fortunately into soft ground. The spirited beast picks himself together and we're off again, but the wild horses—a mob of half a dozen, with a couple of foals—have got the advantage of us and we must ride well and carefully alongside to prevent their entering the scrub. That last stumble seems to have made our nag rather ashamed; he pulls himself together and goes at a tremendous pace, over log and under branch; the logs and trees now being much closer together, he never makes a miss, and finally and triumphantly heads off the mob, whose want of training and discipline far outweigh any advantage they may derive from being unburdened. The mob is winded and tired, one of us gallops on to open the gate, and with a great rush the whole of us pass through. Had an unprejudiced bystander been called upon to judge, he would have said that wild and ridden horses seemed neck and neck, the latter perhaps *leading by a trifle!* We repeat our tactics through the next paddock, avoiding the thick scrub by throwing wings off our main body to protect the flanks of the wild mob, and after having thoroughly tired the wild and our own steeds, with a sigh of satisfaction the great yard gates are closed on the "brumbies" and their doom sealed.

The best will be kept and trained, the others shot. It is sad to see how in-breeding and improper treatment has brought down the high-stepping, arched-necked, straight-backed trotter, to a shuffling, ewe-necked, hollow-backed "thing *like* a horse." These would be useless to train and dangerous to ride. The better specimens may be equally dangerous, but they can be and will be trained in some sort or other.

Of horse-breakers the colonies boast a motley assembly. Some there are who, as though by the magic of gentle but firm handling, dominate their charges in a few hours, a result achieved by others, and with perhaps less permanency, in a harder and more painful manner. There are many blacks and half-breeds as well as whites who will ride anything with four legs, and though they may sometimes really take care and time over breaking a horse in, station horses are not infrequently said to be in this desirable state when they will let a man get on their back without kicking out at him more than half a dozen times, and without skying him like a rocket immediately he is mounted. Many new chums are said to learn a painful experience by their adventures on the backs of such partially broken-in horses. I heard an old horse-breaker say that patience and firmness would achieve far better and more trustworthy results than cruelty and harshness. "Teach a horse," said he, "to feel that if it does what is right it gets approbation and a kind word, a fact it will very soon appreciate, and at the same time make it fear disobedience firmly but not cruelly, and you will turn out good reliable steeds who will scarcely ever buck thereafter. Payshienshia does it, as my old schoolmaster used to say."

Over our pipes in the evening we have a learned disquisition on hydrophobia. Many a time and oft has it been said that this terrible disease does not prevail south of the line. A case or two have been reported, however, as occurring in South Australia, although this colony, in common with all the others except Tasmania, imposes a severe quarantine on imported dogs. I do not know if the anomaly still exists, but in 1884 a man could bring a dog into Australia *via* Tasmania, and thus introduce him without the vexation of any quarantine whatsoever into any Australian colony. A case occurred within my own knowledge, and I was informed that it was but one of many.

Says the squatter, "I myself have never seen or hitherto heard of a case of hydrophobia in Australia, which I ascribe to the fact that dogs are said to perspire here through their skins, not only through their tongues as in the old country. But the promiscuous feeding of our station dogs gives them the terrible disease of hydatids, communicable to men by their saliva on a sore or cut, or by drinking or eating where a dog may have drunk or eaten before."

Says an old wool-sorter who dropped in for dinner and bed on his way up north: "Ah, I knew of a man who got these hydatids in his leg, a painful and objectionable burden to carry about, you bet—a lump of parasites as big as a child's fist; and he cured himself by eating an enormous quantity of tomatoes for six months. The cyst dried up and went away, his legs took the same sized stocking again, and he never got ill again." As tomatoes grow here like weeds, when irrigated, the cure should be at everybody's door, a fact which cannot too widely be known where such a disease is unhappily too prevalent. The consequence of the conversation just before going to bed is that one of us has nightmare, where the frisky hydatid alternates with the hydrophobiac dog in making us ride a wild horse over Sydney cathedral. *Ex uno disce omnes!* At least any one might do so from the noises that resound in the stillness of night from every room in the homestead.

Laughing-Jackass and Snake

CHAPTER XV.

Sunday.—How to Dress.—Various occupations.—The Mail-man and his news.—Soldier-birds and their fate.—Botany by a non-botanist.—Gums, Pines, Wattle, and Scrub.—Mallee.—Foliage and how it grows.—Galars.—Native Companions and how to shoot them.—Emus, how not to catch them.—The Sun's power.—Sheep-shearing.—Horseracing.—"Inglis bail good."—Treating a Pocketful of Apples.—Back to Sydney.

"HALLO! Macdonald, what are you making all that noise for in the middle of the night?" said one of the colonial-experience men in the next room. "Don't you know it's the Sawbath, and that there's an hour's extra blanket-drill for all so disposed? Go and hum your hymn tunes somewhere not so close to my head." Toilet operations and conversations in a homestead up country require some circumspection for their harmonious fulfilment. It is not that the walls have ears so much as that they record and conduct all sound almost as truly as the violin string-board.

Sunday morning "get-up" varies according to circumstances. Should there be a lady on the station, respectability and broadcloth assert themselves; failing this charm to society the weather decides whether the occupants of the homestead shall assume warm and clean garments or shall have breakfast parade in *deshabille*. This latter fashion is one of the most delightful signs of Sunday's presence, so as it is a warm day, and there is not a lady, we sit down to a protracted and somewhat dissipated morning meal in unconventional attire.

Next come the writing of letters, reading of newspapers and last mail news, and perhaps, if the mail comes on a Sunday, the advent of the mail-man. This is the great event of Sunday on our station. We look down with scarce disguised contempt on a station that cannot boast this luxury. There he comes jogging along, his horse probably having cantered the larger portion of the twelve miles from the township; he hangs his bridle on the palings or puts his cob in the stalls, and gives us loungers in the verandah the latest bits of township news and gossip. He has a sort of olla podrida in his mental store, and up country the absence of ordinary sources of news makes the bearded sex as curious to hear gossip as are their wives. He tells us that the river has been running ten feet deep, that Briggs of Wooloomahalla has lost five hundred sheep through a freshet, that the wife of Wilkins of Boolamaragong has had another son, that it's generally supposed that young Jake Walker of Baradine has made a match of it with Betsy, the fair-haired flirting barmaid of the Creek Hotel, and finally that the horse-races which are to come off next week have brought a few bookmakers up through the mud and rain to try and fleece the innocent and guileless (?) bushmen.

"Ah," says the squatter to us, "if you haven't seen up-country races you ought to go; you're sure to have fun." So we make an affidavit in bush fashion to do the same.

We are on the point of dismissing our worthy gossip to the appreciative and expectant audience in the kitchen and the men's hut, when he tells us he forgot to remark that Jim Baker had got the "blue devils" (delirium tremens) at the Republican Hotel and used his "six-shooter" so freely that Bob Williams and Tim O'Flannagan had been gathered to the majority, a piece of news at once startling and reassuring, as we reckon Jim will now see the folly of his ways and avoid such unseemly accidents in the future, especially if helped to that frame of mind by the Government executioner.

After discussing the pros and cons of home and foreign news contained in the latest Sydney papers only some four days old, a couple of the party ride away to visit our neighbour to the east, some fifteen miles off; a couple more, including the squatter, write up business matters and otherwise "break the Sawbath;" and the balance *virtuously* refrain themselves from such worldly pleasures and take a gun apiece to bring down some parrots. With these I might wish to lead the more adventurous spirits, while for those who countenance not such pursuits, even when scientifically and ornithologically pursued, the verandah and a book, for the station has a mixed library, sacred and profane, grave and gay (generally gay) afford a fitting way of putting in an hour or so.

The science of orinthology is conducted in Australia under various and varying fortunes. As we wander through the bush looking for a bush-turkey, one of those luscious rivals of our friend of that ilk at home, the little soldier-bird—not much bigger than our thrush at home—sets up a most ear-piercing twittering, warning all good and righteous birds and beasts to clear out of the way of these destroyers. One of our party balked thereby of a good shot at a white cockatoo, which has taken his little friend's well-meant advice and is screeching aloft on the top of yon gum-tree (as though he were imitating Xantippe or running for the legislature), impatient of his little enemy, puts a charge of No. 4 into him, somewhat discomposing his poor little voice and reducing him to permanent silence.

Punishment for the rash and unconsidered act quickly follows. In a moment the whole scrub is alive: cockatoos, parrots, and parrakeets screeching, pigeons whirring, bowerbirds and "twelve apostles" chattering, parson-birds exhorting, and the wretched little soldier-bird's boon companions indignantly denouncing the murderer in tones more forcible than polite. With a grim face the man of the stained conscience replaces his spent cartridge and patiently bears the abuse of his comrades, who find the scrub for some distance around cleared of its occupants. Unable to study natural history, we turn our attention for the nonce to botany.

Of ground-flowers there are few, and what there are even in warm rainy weather up here on the plains are small and almost unnoticeable. Grass is usually of the tawny hue like that long grass that an unmowed meadow on sandy soil displays during a hot summer. Trees then are our next consideration, and these in their diversity affords us much discussion as we walk amongst them. Gums growing sixty or seventy feet high, with ragged bark and strongly scented leaves, with occasionally a hole wherein a possum lies concealed or a snake hybernates, gnarled and boled as though with gigantic warts, are the largest objects of interest. Their wood is of immense use and varied application. The iron-bark has a hardness which will turn any but a good tool, the red gum almost equals it; from the stringy-bark those "oak" palings round the garden are split and the shingles for the roof of the stables; the blue gum, with its straight grain gave the roof-tree, while the bastard box is giving us our fuel day out and in.

The graceful pines rear their pinnule-crowned heads close by, suggesting the beautiful grain their wood affords, beautiful but rather productive of strong language from the carpenter, who finds it warp, twist, and crack in many directions if not nicely handled. Put a pine-log on the fire and hear it puff and blow; as it enters into the spirit of the thing it cracks its jokes and hurls its witty sparks far up the chimney, and, like great wits very often exceeds bounds of discretion, by setting the shingle roof on fire. What the aboriginal did before the white man introduced the wooden tile which he called shingle we know but fear to copy. Branches and mud may make a cosy roof, but with tropical rains are rather liable to prove the bruised reeds they are.

Under the pine grows the acacia, known to the unromantic bushman as "wattle." Wattle, by the way, applies to many distinct species of acacia, not to one as is commonly thought. The sight of this golden-flowered tree under the blue pines with the red sand at their feet, affords a charming and instructive lesson in harmony of colour. The equivalents of colour are just about in the right proportion, and the effect, though commonly before a bushman's eyes, is unnoticed and unappreciated, yet extremely soft and beautiful.

The colonial oak, or casuarina, with its pine-like sombre foliage, speaks rather for use than ornament. Its wood is hard and durable, close-grained and permanent when worked, and from its colour is called beefwood. Besides these trees there are scores of species of gum in Australia whose woods have all the lovely colours of, can take the polish of, and are in some respects superior to, our chestnut, walnut, sycamore, mahogany, and rosewood. A church in Melbourne (I only instance one, there are scores throughout the country) is decorated with the *eucalyptus rostrata*, a wood much like our mahogany. If iron ever gives out, as scientists say it must, the Western Australians have got a eucalyptus that will hold its own with teak, will put English oak to the blush, and build as many "wooden walls" as the future navy of Australia may require. I refer to the jarrah, or *eucalyptus marginata*, which covers vast tracts of that Crown colony.

Of scrub, that is small trees not more than twenty or thirty feet high, there are hundreds of species; the wattle which I have mentioned numbers over three hundred species. The mallee scrub, which I have referred to in Chapter XIII., is a thorn in the side of colonists in more ways than one; a man, unless a botanist, should avoid it like poison. It has the awful capacity of making you lose yourself; it grows so densely that if your broad acres are cast in those parts you had better lose all your money than try to reclaim mallee land, at the present state of land prices; and thirdly, in rabbit-infested districts it affords a home whence these pests may continually assail in enormously increased numbers the lands of all, both far and near. The myall has had a mention; its delicate-toned foliage helps more than its pipe-making wood to make it stand out from the thousand and one other species of scrub trees, burra burra, whitewood, cottonwood, and so on, and its sheep-feeding properties give it a practical value in the eyes of the squatter. The curragong, also known as a very good feed for sheep in dry seasons, drives the myall hard for first place, which many squatters are loth to deny it, and is of a similar type but with an additional wealth of blossom.

The quandong that grows hard by is of a species that boasts the largest fruit in the colonies. The jam that an up-country cook can make from this fruit would make a Westminster boy's heart leap within him, more especially as the kernels or quandong-stones are in great requisition for necklaces and other ornaments.

Up in the interior, beyond the dividing range, you will rarely if ever meet with a tree which has its foliage shaped or hanging like the foliage of the British trees, say the elm, beech, &c. Everybody knows the shape of the foliage of the young blue gum, the *eucalyptus globulus*, which has become so fashionable of late years in greenhouses, but everybody does not know that when it is a couple of years or so of age it cuts its teeth, drops its oblate and horizontal leaves, and commences to put its teeth on edge and shapes them like a scimitar. Look up through a gum-tree of the densest foliage; the branches stand out with great distinctness against the sky, although there are leaves in plenty which would, if they only grew in the orthodox fashion, form a dense shade. The character of the scrub foliage also is rather of the pinnate or misletoe shape. I am not speaking as a botanist but merely as a humble observer of nature, and trust that I have sufficiently vituperated the up-country foliage in my readers' eyes to make them perceive that you might as well try to drink soup with a fork as seek protection from Jupiter Pluvius under a gum or myall *et id genus omne*. These remarks, however, in no way detract from my former panegyrics on the coast foliage of the continent.

While speaking of the flora of these parts we have debouched on to a plain where not far off a large flock of the rose-crested galar—a grey and rose parrot, well known by bird-fanciers—is feeding. Our destructive would-be taxidermist aims point-blank and knocks one over, to the consternation of the flock, which hovers around the stricken one with harsh cries, uncertain what has caused his sudden fall. Were not the murderer's hand stayed by a suggestion that they were having church, he might go on and knock over the whole flock, the survivors each time contenting themselves with discussing in loud tones the fate of their lost brethren, rather than remedying the evil or preventing further disasters by flying away. A sarcastic new chum, who has not altogether forgotten the ways of legislative and other human bodies, singular and plural, suggests that herein is another proof of Darwinism. "*Verba non facta ago*," says he, " is undoubtedly a maxim handed down from our winged ancestors of the parrot type."

Farther on, a long shot at a cockatoo brings down the doomed bird, who, with canary-coloured crest and breast, and spotless feathers and wings of snowy white, is now, as I write, supervising with glassy eyes these remarks.

A couple of native companions are waltzing about for worms and such small deer a few hundred yards away, but both glide away on outstretched flapping wings, unscathed by the whistling shot. I am convinced, from long study of the matter under congenial circumstances, that the proper way to shoot a native companion is to apply Æsop's fable of the bull and the frog. Flatter it up until it develops its skinny frame to an abnormal size, get it to open its long beak, into which place the barrels of the gun, and, with steady and slow movement empty the contents down the " critter's " neck. Some people, who have been hitherto unsuccessful in the pursuit of our bony friend, complain that this recipe is not sufficiently practical. It is not my fault, for, if after following it out they have yet missed their object they must be to blame themselves. You cannot expect the native companion to lie down and die so as to fulfil the recipe.

Even the recipe of the proverbial pinch of salt on the tail of the bird does not succeed when the fingers are unmoved by healthy and sane volitions, but because some men are not gifted with brains, is a principle of such consummate worth to be pooh-poohed! If so, then go and attack the aboriginal method of hunting emus. As is tolerably well known, the emu has a mind of an inquiring nature, and the wily savage is said —in books of natural history and the like—by lying down flat on his back and kicking his heels in the air, to attract the attention and the presence of any emu within visible range. I never came across a savage who had played this off on the cast-iron-legged bird, but a "new chum" I once met, told me, with melancholy face, how but the day before he had lain for half an hour on the ground, adopting this undignified pose, but the "pesky creatures only ran away the more." The idea of my friend, generally so energetic, forcing himself thus to repose almost within shot-range of his quarry, frightening these very birds away in his frantic efforts to draw them to him, was too much for the risibility of the bystanders, and, if I mistake not, the young "new chum" is still seeking for the blood of his audience.

Thus passes the Sunday, not too quickly nor too slowly. Work is a pleasure, and much pleasure a labour, in a climate where three-fourths of daylight is sunshine. When the sunshine gets too hot for work, as it sometimes though rarely does, then also it gets too hot to enjoy a pleasurable existence. The wicked soldier of San Francisco would make a fortune in retailing his blankets to colonists who have passed through a baking heat of 98° for days together. The epidermis seems to be an unnecessary burden, and hair a hollow fraud. Then even the hammock under the verandah may afford no relief, and the thin-blooded up-country man may wish that he could turn himself inside out to give his interior a chance of being equally cooked with his exterior. *Then*, if you expect blue in the sky, you will often see but a bright glare, abounding in warm tones; if you look for relief in the foliage you will see but the reflected glare of the sky and sun, blurred by the tremulous motion in the atmosphere of the upward-moving mass of heated air. *Then* you will know why sheep hold a meeting and move resolutions to dispense with their woollen coats, why horses are occasionally being born without hair at all, and why the leaves oppose but their thin edge to the zenith. *Then* you will wonder how old bushmen can manage to eat so many mutton chops and yet be unfevered, and will sigh for the flesh-pots of Colombo, the banana and rice, or a plate of nothing washed down with iced water. *Then* you will marvel that the iron roof of the house, with its concentrated heat, does not set the woodwork alight. *Then* you will probably see some of those gigantic bush-fires, which light up the sky for miles at night, which obscure the sun by day with their smoke, which

Woolshed & Wool-Room.

devastate almost annually hundreds of square miles of property.

A description of an up-country life minus sheep-shearing and horseraces would be like a plum-pudding minus its life and soul, namely, plums. Sheep-shearing as it is done in the old country is hardly known here. A man will do his hundred and eighty and more a day. I saw a shearer once who boasted he could shear two hundred and thirty, and have heard of those who could shear over two hundred and fifty between morning and nightfall.

The shearing and wool-sheds of the station are great wooden erections, built either under one roof or side by side, often connected by a little tram-road. At one end are the pens, capable of holding thousands of sheep, and all down the shed on each side are separate pens, where sits a shearer, who with miraculous speed will clean his charge of his coat and dismiss it into a separate pen behind, whence he may be "counted out" at the end of the day. No waiting to catch the sheep: they are all crowded up the middle aisle of the shed so close together that he only has to reach over, catch a victim, pull him over the fence, and operate straight away. If in his express speed he, as not seldom occurs, nips a bit of the cuticle too, a cry of "Tar" calls up the small boy with a brush and pot, who dabs a little of the antiseptic on the cut part, to the no small edification and parti-colouring of the living canvas. The wool is straightway gathered up by the other boys, carried to the wool-sorter, who, with his assistants, with incredible speed and almost invariable judgment sorts the different fleeces according to quality, and the different parts of each fleece according to its nature, those from the back to one bin, from the legs to another, and so on. Carried to bins, it is thence packed into huge bales, which by means of tremendous crank and lever action are compressed until you could scarce get a pin into them.

The old custom of sheep-washing is going out of vogue in many parts of the colonies; it costs an enormous lot of trouble and labour, which are not appreciated by the manufacturers, who prefer to wash it once for all themselves. The poor sheep may think himself lucky thus to have been the unconscious object of what turns out to be an act of kindness. I wonder if Jones, as he pulls on his Melton overcoat, or Mrs. Jones, as she adjusts her woollen comforter, ever thinks of the cuts and nips, the half-drownings and noxious washings, the poor sheep have had who gave them of their store. Possibly not, or if so, Jones and his wife would retaliate by asking one of us how many cochineal insects were annihilated to die our silk necktie, how many silkworms parboiled to make it, or how many fur-bearing animals have been cruelly trapped to furnish our wife's jacket, or the rugs about the room. I'faith 'tis true! every one of us would unconsciously be throwing a stone at a neighbour's conservatory with a greenhouse of our own tempting retaliation.

Next the horse-races. Few townships of any size, *i.e.* of more than one street, situated in a fitting locality in the Australian colonies but will possess a racecourse. Here is one taken from life. A small grand stand, with the orthodox judge's box, and trainers' notices at the foot, the orthodox railings alongside the course just by the stand, with a few stalls where cakes, sweets, and fruit tempt the lesser lights, and stronger viands and "long drinks" their seniors; a few drunken stockmen sleeping off their excessive potations, to be ready, presumably, for another insane bout. Here a couple of aborigines are trying to understand what the poor, half-drunken white trash is saying. One of them refers to me to know whether "um white fellow speak um Inglis all well?" The thick utterance of their white friend so disguises his speech that, with all fairness, I could not give judgment in his favour, but with as much gravity as possible I have to reply that "Um fire-water got in um white fellow's mouth, so make um white fellow bail (not) speak um right like this white fellow." At which, their honour being vindicated—as the besotted man and brother has been jeering them for their want of understanding —they fall into panegyrics on the good sense of the "Daniel come to judgment." One old station hand runs up against me, and, with a sickly leer from his soaked eyes, puts it to me whether I can refuse to stand him treat. I question whether a hardened wine-bibber could have "treated" this poor wreck of his former self (he had been at it for three days). Not being a hardened wine-bibber, I substitute some Tasmanian apples for a drink, to show no falling off in British generosity, and raise a laugh among the bystanders to see his vacant, helpless smile at his bulging pockets, as he fetches a tack to get back to the rails.

Friends and acquaintances, these latter including the very station hands, greet one on all sides; the clerk of the course, with his red coat unworn since last year, gallops up and down trying to make himself believe he is no sinecure; the bookmakers with their dissonant calls of "I'll bet, I'll bet, I'll bet," and their "two to one bar one," announce that matters are coming to a climax, and about three-quarters of an hour after the announced time the flag falls and a fair show of horses with amateur jockeys, the sons of local tradesmen, hotel proprietors, and others, in silks too big or too little for them, run a quiet and rather unenthusiastic race in the orthodox fashion. The smallest "jock" is at home on horseback; an Australian boy up country would sooner perish than be a "duffer," and the skillful sitting-out of a tremendous series of "bucks" from yonder filly has no more effect on her rider, than it would were he a part of her in very fact.

As the afternoon goes on the number of inebriates increases and the mounted troopers become more useful than ornamental. In one drunken brawl close by a man falls and breaks his leg— a most iniquitous proceeding on his part, as he thereby upsets all the preconceived notions that a drunken man comes to no hurt. Hereupon arises an occasion on which the brotherly good-fellowship of up-country men shows itself. One good fellow, a station hand himself, pulls out a sovereign, gives it to a man with a cart close by and bids him drive the poor wounded man away to the hospital. Another starts a subscription which in a few minutes reaches £7 or £8 and is presented to his friends. He is taken away and no one thinks anything more about it except the big boundary-rider who struck him down, and who, sobered by the misadventure cannot help recollecting how the wounded man swore a terrible oath as he went away that he would "clean him out" for this. So the afternoon goes on, the last race is run, the spectators dawdle about to chat and "take nips" or help their friends "overcome with the heat, you know," into the two or three conveyances that are doing omnibus service to and from the township. The sun goes to bed and is followed in due course by those upon whom he has shone.

These past few chapters have detailed much of the work and life of a sheep station, but the experiences contained in them are condensed from a few months ' life ' and would speak fairly well if multiplied for a few years. On a sheep station all this excitement is not crowded in together; there is a great deal of monotony when you have once settled down to it, and I should not wish any one to run away with the idea that it is all "beer and skittles." To any one fond of roughing it and of leading a free open-air existence, with ambition for the time at rest, there can be few more suitable places than a position on a sheep or cattle run; but to the delicately nurtured and the ambitious man alike such a life were a mistake; his refinement and delicacy would have a hard trial in the one case, his patience in the other.

I do not mean to weary my readers by repeating my journey to Sydney, which was in most respects a fac-simile of that up from Sydney which they were so kind as to share with me. Suffice it that after the usual hand-shakings and crossings (with coinage), after the usual trophies of an up-country visit had been packed and safely despatched, after a hundred and one matters had been disposed of, after some perils on the coast journey by road, akin in their effects on the gastric centres to the perils of the sea, had been passed, I once more found myself in Sydney Harbour steaming for the Heads en route to Brisbane.

CHAPTER XVI.

Colonial Steamboats.—" Heave to, and he hev."—Meal-time.—Coasting to Brisbane.—Fishing Question.—Brisbane River.—A Running Commentary.—Government House.—Law Courts.—Flowers and Trees.—Botanical Gardens.—Suburbs.—One-tree Hill.—The View of the Notice Board.—The Principles of Scenery.—A Sanguinary Conflict.—The Mosquito and the Sand-fly.—Cockroaches and their uses.—Complexions.—Boots!—British-India Steamships a Stroke of Policy.—Wanted, a Free Library.—The Theatre and its Uses.—The Missionary Question and some of its Results.—King Billy.—Ventilation!—Drafting Cattle under Difficulties.—The Cattle have burst the Rails.—An Aboriginal's Civilisation.—Is that a Black or a Kangaroo.

ON board a colonial steamboat one soon finds that a good deal of the science of sea-travelling acquired by passages in the large liners has to be learnt over again. To begin with, the size of the boat and the large number of passengers it ordinarily holds, particularly if it be one of the favourite A. S. N. Co.'s large fleet, precludes the possibility of having that elbow room which one has been accustomed to. Again, as the trips are small, if you do not make acquaintance with the captain and officers the first day you will probably not do so at all. Your steward, too, addresses you as a man and a brother, not as a possible aspirant to the strings of your purse. The people you meet, too, are of that varied type which is always pleasing. Young " drummers," as the Yankees misname commercial travellers, generally full of fun and good-fellowship, squatters going to or from their runs or their town residences. A stray M.L.A. going northwards perhaps to have a look at the labour traffic, or southward to inquire into the existence of coal-mines, speculators in stores, hotel keepers who show themselves brave, cool-headed followers of Bacchus, young professional men and others hopefully seeking openings, or returning with disappointment from closings, if one may say so, one or two ladies, very few, and a very small sprinkling of people travelling for pleasure.

The average Australian, always busy, with a store of nerve energy never expended, has a secret contempt for the man of leisure who can find time to look about him, and has not to consider everything he says, does, and thinks in the light of £ s. d. I remember once when on a sketching trip in New South Wales being asked what I expected to make out of "that there painting." My self-attached interviewer on hearing my reply that I was working for love, not dross, replied, "Look ye here, mister, ye may say so, but du ye think I take ye to be such a fule as that? Eh, ye must be a deep 'un, but ye can't catch I." Over and over again, in different forms and from different mouths, generally male, and often from persons of good standing, have I received similar answers, couched in more courteous and grammatical form, so that in order to avoid being taken for a consummate liar I had to invent a formula of a crushing though courteous nature so as to place the impress of *truth* on my remarks. Accustomed only to travel on matters of business, the average Australian does not quite "fit in with" board-ship arrangements; the sad sea waves make him feel sadder, and when the captain calls out from the bridge, "Heave to," without any delay he complies, though with a great deal of unnecessary groaning and anathematizing of his dire lot. The more recent of these A. S. N. boats, as the Australian Steam Navigation Company's fleet is called, are decorated and fitted up in good style, and afford very fair accommodation, berthing, and tables; but the smaller and earlier boats which are still running, boats many of them under 800 tons register, create a good deal of confusion amongst delicate livers, and when sailing with ports closed and cabins full, there is as close a resemblance to the black hole of Calcutta as a first-class saloon might be.

The celerity with which meals are despatched is another enlightenment to an ocean traveller. He, accustomed to see these important duties of ship life protracted *pour passer le temps*, finds himself mastering his second mouthful when all others are ready to have a second helping, or have moved on to the next course, so that if he persists in his more moderate pace he will find himself perhaps tackling an entrée when the rest are already leaving their dessert. The correct thing at meal-time is to notice the average rate of speed indulged in by the feeders (excluding the ladies, who eat more gracefully and slowly), for in this a man finds his guiding star, his standard wherewith to measure his own pace, and thereafter and until the end of the meal to notice nobody and nothing else, except the clearing of his plate as soon as the first is whipped away by the express-speed stewards. If you notice or look up, you will find yourself alone in this eccentricity. Perhaps you may be a little breathless, a little winded, when you arise, but never mind, you have the satisfaction of having taken a further step towards casting away the reproach of new-chumism and acquiring the *toga virilis*.

A useful suggestion I once heard given to one who had not thus graduated was, "Never take a seat opposite a joint." The joints, entrees, &c., are placed all down the centre of the saloon tables, and every unlucky wight who is thus "subtended" by a dish is bound to do two things at once, to satisfy other people's and his own hunger. This he may do if to the manner born, but otherwise it were better for him that he had the joint and its dish hung round his neck and he were cast into the sea, for the unskilful combination of these two results often breeds dissatisfaction around and indigestion within. The readiness and ingenuity with which a man placed opposite a dish will relieve himself of his responsibilities by handing the carving implements to his *vis-a-vis* with a remark that he does not know how to carve, but his friend opposite probably does, is only equalled by the indignation of the latter at being thus entrapped, and the farce requires to be seen to be appreciated.

The forty-eight hours which are spent in the boat from Sydney to Brisbane are not fraught with much incident as a rule, nor are the land and sea scapes of a marvellous character. The shore, or what can be seen of it, consists of a long series of low bush-covered hills, cleared here and there, which sweep down at the rivers' mouths to the very sea margined with the bright green mangrove. The mouth of the Hawkesbury and the other rivers which pour out their waters along this coast would never of themselves foreshadow the beauties to be seen by boating up their bush-lined reaches.

Newcastle, whence comes so much of the coal for Sydney and Melbourne, is a busy coal depot, not a place for the globe-trotter to frequent. On the other hand, the Hunter district, called by some New England, is quiet in its scenery, and boasts the most wonderful fertility of Australia, which is saying a good deal, for in this land of extremes the most heaven-forsaken, sterile, sandy deserts of the interior rub shoulder with the most fertile spots under the sun. An old New England farmer told me that year after year he could and did grow and cut six crops of lucerne per annum; not an exposition perhaps so much of economic farming as of generosity of soil and climate, for the rich alluvial flats are watered by an average rainfall of some fifty inches, and the mean temperature is most genial; frosty nights however are not unknown, and play havoc with the plantations of those who attempt the cultivation of the sugar-cane in these cooler latitudes.

Here grows another of those many anomalies of Australia— a nettle which, if it have reached its teens, will require climbing, if you are ambitious to be stung by it. As it grows some eighty and a hundred feet high, one would think that there is no great need to fear its presence, but unfortunately it rains an army of children all around who while striplings manage to make their presence appreciated. On the few secluded spots of these rivers the jabiru, a flamingo-like bird, though of quieter hues, may still be seen, though its safety against total destruction probably lies in the slimness of its body and its capacity of turning itself edgewise to its antagonist.

One is astonished to find along the shores of Australia, comparatively speaking, so few fishing townships. Of isolated stations there are a small muster, but the amount of capital and labour employed is by no means commensurate with the possible proceeds to be obtained from these fish-haunted waters. In all Australian townships fish is a great rarity, and even in the markets of the capitals the demand so often exceeds the supply that the price to be paid for the same is often prohibitively high. Oysters may be had for the knocking of them off the rocks, where they grow and shoulder one another for room; yet good oysters are not over plentiful or cheap in Melbourne or Brisbane. Cod, schnapper, whiting, flathead, flounders, and many other species of fish are prolific, and might be supplied in large numbers, but at present they are conspicuous by their repeated absence from the tables of all but the well-to-do. The fishing for the *beche-de-mer* or sea-slug, of which the Chinese are very fond, has attracted more attention than most of the other branches of fishing; but these great gelatinous creatures, which you may often see about the mouths of the Queensland rivers, well earning their repellent name from their appearance, are but lukewarmly patronised by Australians. The great stinging-ray is a frequent and feared inhabitant of these waters, its wound causing great temporary pain and inconvenience to its victim. Bathers and fishers have to take great care, and the former are not free from the risk of being indirectly killed by these creatures, as the sting will often paralyse a limb. A man I knew well, whilst fishing with a seine net, and reaching over to secure a great schnapper caught in the meshes, received a sting in the arm which paralysed it for three months, and never allowed him the free and full use of it for many years. The pain was, he said, intense, but momentary, and immediately his arm fell down powerless, while his friends had to prime him with the inevitable whisky-flask in order to keep him conscious: a sure proof of the potent effect of the sting, otherwise he would I am sure have helped himself.

Connected with the fishing industry are the important trades of pearl and sponge collecting, which are now attracting some attention on the north shore of the continent. These pearls are harder to come across than sponges, of which vast numbers of great diversity bestrew the shores of Australia, where in half an hour I have picked up fifteen different and distinct species, though the majority were unfit for the purposes of the bath.

The approach to Brisbane lacks in dignity. A lighthouse or two; a broad winding river with many beacons to indicate its shallows, margined with mangroves and bush; then as it narrows a few clearings, where the bright vivid green of a cane-field, or the ragged leaves of the wind-torn bananas are silhouetted against the scrub-covered hills in the distance; a sugar-mill or so; some more beacons; and finally two very sharp curves which our steamboat negotiates slowly but skilfully, open up the wharves and city of Brisbane, stretching away to the northward up a slight eminence, with cliffs overhanging the water. A straggling town you will say, when you learn that it covers an area the size of Birmingham, and has about thirty thousand inhabitants. And you will confirm your statement when you hear that the thirsty stranger wants at least three long drinks of some sort or other on his way to the ordinarily remote suburbs; nay, that he may require more should the weather be dry and windy, for then heat and dust change his garments and temper to a white colour (the temper referred to is a white heat). Not that its Botanical Gardens and reserves take up so much of its space; I think with advantage they might be supplemented, for this city is bound to increase in size and wealth out of all proportion to the present breathing-spaces it possesses.

The streets accommodate themselves now to the natural conformation of the place, now to the parallelogramic plan, combining much of the usefulness of Melbourne and the comparative intricacy of Sydney. Comparative this quality certainly is, for no one but a sucking-babe need be lost in the township of Brisbane. Broad are its walks, and not legion its streets.

Its buildings are, as to many good, as to many execrable, so far as architecture goes. The Government offices, including the Governor's residence and the Houses of Legislature, which, in geometrical phraseology, subtend the Botanical Gardens close by the river, some of the banks, a hospital, and the bridge are worthy of notice, and certainly speak in loud strains for the push and enterprise of the inhabitants of the capital of a youthful colony, for it is only sixty years ago that the colony was born, then as a penal settlement, and but twenty-six years since she broke away from the apron strings of her New South Welsh mamma.

The Supreme Court is a dazzling white building, standing amid a few borders of semi-tropical flowers and shrubs; its great feature, a long corridor and roomy courts, its offices being on the *multum in parvo* principle. The library contains books! Don't laugh, it is not every library that does. Both in her Law Courts and House of Legislature Brisbane leads ahead of her mother colony (with her dingy buildings), and boasts the finest residence for the representative of her Majesty in the colonies. But few of the private residences boast that elegance and beauty conspicuous in the villas surrounding Sydney and Melbourne; yet those few that have affected high art or horticulture show how successfully these can be applied in the shape of deeply verandahed bungalows, surrounded by winterless gardens, and shrouded in exquisite jasmines, plumbago, clematis, and other creepers of various species. The way the azaleas, poinsettias, and abutilons flower in the Botanical and private gardens would make an English gardener's heart to ache with envy, and were I to describe the mass of bloom *in extenso* I should be likened to a sailor spinning a long yarn. These Botanical Gardens are neither so old nor so well cared for as their counterparts in the southern towns, but the bamboo walk—a shady avenue of these gigantic canes—forms quite a distinctive feature of the Brisbane gardens which the southerners cannot show.

Scene on Brisbane River.

The scenery around—that is, the natural scenery—is for the most part quiet and unobtrusive; it has not the variety of Sydney, with its harbour, sea-coast, and river views, but it has many natural charms unknown to Melbourne. From many points on the banks of the winding river views may be had both above and below the town worth undergoing the slight danger of miasma in summer and greater danger of things that do both fly and walk by night and day all the year round. A few red-tiled, rustic-looking houses, already fast changing colour with the rain and sun, give that appearance of picturesque old age to certain points which are lacking from the villa-crowned heights of Sydney Harbour, or the bungalow-covered plains around Melbourne. Again, within easy reach of the town by road or rail is a hill called by way of a " goak " One-tree Hill, from which there is a truly Australian view. The fact that its sides are covered with dense scrub and bush, and that the scenery comprises in almost all directions a wide expanse of gum forest, seems to have suggested to some past humorous colonist the aptitude of the name. A paternal government has erected a board laying down the ten commandments concerning the use and abuse of the place, and when you have done reading it you may perhaps feel justified after your climb in looking at the distinctive scenery.

Before you read what follows, I should like to know if you have a Brisbaner looking over your shoulder? No? Well then you have away to the south the silver river cutting a sharply defined line amongst heavy masses of blue and green foliage, to the east the city of Brisbane silhouetted against the shining blue sea in the distance, to the north and the west the wide expanse of a dark, quiet, noiseless, motionless sea of gums stretching far away melting into the vivid Australian blues of the timber-clad spurs of the Dividing Range, whose scenery in many respects resembles that of the Blue Mountains and, in a greater or less degree, all Australian mountain scenery. That is all well and good, but look closer in. No varied tints of spring, summer, or autumn meet the eye, no delicate tracery or shapely masses of foliage. What can be done with the gum foliage for scenic effects Dame Nature has done. I give her credit for that; but even she, non-plussed at a point a very short distance from where she commenced, sickened with her want of success, has glided away and left her creatures weeping at her absence with pendant leaves, dull of hue through their unhealthy sorrowing, and gawky of limb through premature straining heavenwards. Now you know why I whispered asking after Brisbane folk.

One friend, after undertaking the personal guidance of my ungrateful self around the suburbs to see the *prettiest sights*, gave the matter up in despair, shrouding his grief in the observation that " It takes a matter of twenty years to educate a man up to Australian scenery." Perhaps so; a guinea pig's eyes will drop out if you hold it up by its tail, but then this little rodent, as is well known, has no tail, and I very much fear a "new chum" would not have a sufficient tale of years to live out a twenty-years' *continued stare* at gum-trees.

All honour to Australian colonists for the progress they have made in opening up jungle and forest to agriculture and grazing, in building cities and establishing industries, but why attempt to create beauty where it is not, why exaggerate natural advantages tenfold, if it cannot serve to give a stimulus to colonial advancement? Exaggeration when applied to an object the qualities and nature of which are readily ascertainable as are those of scenery, prevents the would-be enthusiast from raving, and the sober-minded lover of beauty from appreciating, the scene at its true worth, and makes the dyspeptic Bombastes growl all the more.

I am afraid that I am going to get into hot water with Brisbane folk, although they are notably hospitable and friendly, and, considering the numerous letters of introduction they receive, really do put themselves out for their self-invited guests to a most admirable extent.

The very first night I was in Brisbane I was murderously assaulted. "Ah!" says some one, "that was an exceptional case." Not so, my friend, scores of people suffer likewise throughout the year, and the worst is that the police have as yet taken no measures to put down this fearful state of bloodshed. My case also, though personally brought before the notice of an inspector of police, only served to elicit abusive laughter and gross hilarity. While wandering around at night I had been somewhat startled to see gigantic cockroaches as big as a *branch of a tree*; but undaunted, and having routed this enemy, I did hope that the hours of slumber would be undisturbed. Fate ruled otherwise, however, for at the dead of night, with low mutterings and indistinct murmurs, the bloodthirsty assailant crept near my bed, unsheathed his dagger, and without any more ado plunged it into my defenceless neck. To add insult to injury, my gory foe sat on the end of the bed and shook it with his laughter, while I glared, powerless to attack the "skeeter."

I had forgotten my mosquito nets, which are more a necessity than a luxury to the syrup-blooded arrival from more temperate climes. I cannot conceive anything greater than the sense of satisfaction at hearing the imp of darkness buzzing with disappointed trumpet outside, except it be the sense of disgust at finding that by some means or other the enemy has forced your defence works and is perhaps attacking you in front, rear, and flank simultaneously.

I fear the mosquito in the stillness of night as much as, if not more than, the Poet Laureate does "the villainous centre-bit," but in many parts of Australia the midge, or evolutionary sand-fly, wins the race of devilry by many a lap. *He* confines not his actions to the night time; nay, he is more active, as an honest man should be, during daylight, when the warm sun causes the rich blood of thousands of his victims to course with delicious flavour through their veins and *his* throat. But his honesty is only a blind. Don't believe in it. The mosquito at any rate lets you know when he's coming; the sand-fly sweeps up so gently and so softly, and fans your hand so deliciously with his tiny wings the while he draws out your life-blood, that, like the vampire's victim, you know it not—at the time. Wait a few minutes; up rises a small lump no bigger than a man's nail; wait again a few minutes, the small lump has increased, and feels like ten thousand red-hot needles, and if you had the patience (which few folk possess) to wait the whole time allowed according to the cookery—I mean the quackery—books, you would find that instead of your carrying about a lump on your arm, finger, or face, as the case may be, a lump had monopolised you, was walking you around, sitting upon you, making you as broad as you are long, in short, had reduced your individual identity to that of Tom, Jack, or Harry likewise bitten. The bushman's remedy—a big D—does not seem materially to affect the position or size of the lump. I am only speaking approximately; I have never used a micrometer in this research. In the words of the great Longfellow slightly altered—

> "Beware all insects on the wing,
> But most beware the sand-fly's sting,
> Your feet, if scathless you would bring,
>   Accelerate."

With the utilitarian view that Australians take of all things, certain fiends in men's clothing have suggested that the cockroaches are a valuable adjunct to local manufactures. That beautiful syrupy black-currant jam——but there! I've not the heart or the imperturbability to go on with the tale. I would much more readily believe from the animals' size that other story that they are trained as watch-dogs, and are led about like puppies by strings by the children of Brisbane; at least I could had I seen them thus domesticated. I do like to be able to believe a story when I hear it, but to have to swallow that jam story would require as much fortitude as to swallow the jam itself after such a libel had been spoken against it.

The children of Brisbane do not look as though they did much of the *leading about*, and certainly appear from their pallor to swallow too much meat, probably, not jam. Melbourne, Sydney, and Brisbane complexions are in a progressive ratio from bright, clear, and rosy to sallow. Not that it is purely a matter of latitude, for on the plains the other side of the Dividing Range, where the air is drier, in the same latitude folk look much healthier.

To have to ride on a warm day in a public conveyance, car, or omnibus, with a complement of sad-faced looking children, is a delirious enjoyment the excess of which cannot fail to lead to evil consequences. This amusement may be obtained all the year round at Brisbane for the sum of a few pence, and as the roads some short distance out are not as smooth as asphalt, the "inside" passenger may thus combine the motion of the ocean with all its interior results and the exterior abrasions consequent on jolting.

Means of conveyance suggests boots! The chain of thought

is obvious! Does not every one remember the ingenious reply of the husband to his large-footed wife on her displaying her new bottines. "Look for all the world like a pair of ferry boats, my dear." "Ferry boats, sir; what do you mean?" indignantly answered the lady. "You misunderstood me, my dear; I said fairy boots, not ferry boats."

When you are in Brisbane you do not require to have boots *suggested* to you—they suggest themselves in a most conspicuous fashion. Tens of thousands of ready-made boots are for sale in great stores devoted to nothing else, and a wholesale boot vendor told me with some chagrin there were thousands turned out weekly by the local manufacturers. What in the world do folk want so many boots for the "new chum" naturally wonders, considering the population of the whole of Queensland is only 250,000, and Sydney and Melbourne have their own supply, local and imported. The fact is that when a colonial wears out a part of a boot—starts a seam, or the like—he doesn't seem to think of getting a cobbler to convert him, *i.e.* to repair his sole, but straightway invests in a new pair. I have often heard such economical actions as boot-mending referred to contemptuously as "a new chum's tricks." It struck me that the sooner the "old chums" copy the new ones in this respect the better for their pockets.

Stores and shops in this capital are gay and well provided. The British India boats come direct from English docks to the wharves in the river *via* the Torres Straits, a stroke of policy attributed with some justice to Sir Thomas McIlwraith. The effect on the forwarding trade of Sydney and the freights of the coasting steamers since this happy idea of Queenslanders of exporting and importing without the intervention of middlemen has been most marked. The subsidy to the steamship line would be gladly paid even though it did not commercially "pay," as it gives Queensland an extra and quick mail service, but the lowering of freights and the cheapening of imports has long ago established the policy as being on a sound financial footing, though succeeding ministries have thrown cold water on the scheme.

A want of Brisbane is a National Gallery and a Free Public Library, neither of which she possesses. The School of Art supplies the place of a subscription library, but the quarterly payment of five shillings is often considered outside the financial possibilities of the poorer classes, who would be the very ones greatly to benefit by free access to books. It is so much to a state's advantage that its citizens should grow up educated that with such a go-ahead colony as Queensland the free library can only be a question of short delay.

At present the colony has spent a large amount on public works—bridges, roads, railways, &c.—and as private enterprise is in large works so often replaced over in the colonies by a paternal government, the result is that it has its hands pretty full and its purse almost always empty. However, for Queensland there is no fear of bankruptcy if her administrators continue to show the same honesty and prudence as of old. Her resources are almost infinite, her capabilities immense, her territory seemingly elastic. Thousands of square miles of territory are still unsettled, and every inch a settler moves forward is another stone in the foundation of a monument of wealth and prosperity which will astonish the world for centuries to come.

Churches and cathedrals are here as at Melbourne, though on a smaller scale. All denominations are to be found in the colonies tolerably well represented, the Church of England having, according to the recent census, the larger amount of adherents, though in many colonies falling far short of aggregated dissenters of all sorts, both in the number of members and the accommodation provided for actual and active congregations.

Turning from grave to gay, at the Theatre Royal there is occasionally a good company from "down south" travelling from Europe or America. The city is not big enough to continuously support a first-rate company, but they take care to have "funny pieces," and the audience are just as pleased, and more so, than if they saw Mr. Irving in *Hamlet;* that is, the mass of the audience prefer farcical comedy to anything else. Small blame to them; their comic papers don't often make a joke, and when they do the editor has to be held in his chair by three men and a boy to prevent him doing any harm to himself by his convulsions.

The cosmopolitan element prevails here, so to speak. On Saturday the theatre is "used as sich," sometimes on Sunday as a mission hall. The lamentable feature, however, connected herewith was that on the Saturday night, when payment had to be made, the house was full; on Sunday the missionary and his supporters outnumbered the audience. Again, I know that the histrionic performance was crowded up to the end; my stay was too short at the second to see whether matters improved!

The fact is, that to have great sympathy for missionary work among the aborigines one must be content to see as through a glass darkly. Charity begins at home; why not commence on the "larrikins" of the towns, or go to the crowded manufacturing towns of the old country, where so many poor are so inadequately taught the great truth? But the matter does not rest on an argumentative basis such as this. Throughout the colonies over four-fifths of the people I have met tell me that the conversion of the blacks is a failure from beginning to end. It appears to be like the feeding of young babes on meat and strong drinks, and the whole matter requires reform.

As a rule, the "converted" black gives much more disturbance and is a worse member of society than his sinner-brother. The very fact that he has been converted gives him an *entrée* into the society of whites which he would otherwise fail to obtain, and he loses very little time to turn to his own advantage all that he can lay hold of irrespective of the rights of his white "brothers," and frequently to commit depredations and crimes which a white man's pen cannot write about. I have never seen the noble savage in his natural state, although I have come across so-called civilised blacks, whose civilisation seemed to begin and end in hanging around public-houses; but I have spoken with plenty of colonists who have seen, and that quite recently, the "noble savage" in his unadulterated state. Few give them a good character; even when kindly treated they are treacherous, and burst out in the indulgence of all their animal passions whenever an opportunity offers. The best I have heard of them, except in isolated individual cases, was something of this sort. "Oh, yes, I took a drove of cattle through 'black-country,' but never found them trouble me; the fact is, we were well armed, and they soon found it out."

An incident or two that follow, taken from the life of a notorious converted black chieftain, will give a better idea of the black nature than I could in half a dozen tomes. Somewhere about the year 1870 my informant, whom I will call Mr. Jones, was the manager of a large cattle run near the present town of Port Curtis, and on having the keys handed over to him by the retiring manager was told that the holes in the walls of the log-house or homestead were for ventilation—"that is," said the late manager with a smile, "to ventilate the blacks with these shooting-irons should they trouble the station." Very shortly after he was installed he found out the advantage of having these loopholes, as one evening the place was surrounded by blacks headed by "King Billy," as he was called, who demanded black mail before they would go away. After trying mild measures Jones was forced to show a firm front, and when they advanced with torches to set fire to the homestead, a well-directed volley sent over their heads so frightened them that they forgot their intentions and left hastily, having business appointments of a serious nature elsewhere.

This king, on the strength of a brass plate which he had received from a missionary with his name and date of "conversion" inscribed, ran about the country harassing and annoying settlers besides encouraging and aiding in theft of cattle and the like.

Coming home one night with a great mob of cattle numbering some thousands, Mr. Jones found to his dismay that the wretched "king" had camped right in front of the yard gates, and there with some scores of followers he stopped, resisting all entreaties to move a few hundred yards to the right or left. The consequence was that the manager had to take his charges by a detour so as to avoid bringing them into contact with their hated enemies the blacks, and was thereby delayed some two hours, which to a man after forty miles riding under an Australian sun without a bite or sup since breakfast, was no light matter. The next day the blacks were immovable, and consequently the operations of working the cattle through the yards, that is of drafting and separating them, had to be done under great inconveniences; and the second evening there were some hundreds of cattle in the yards who had to be let out. It was no use trying to drive them out through the blacks' camp during daylight, their mortal horror of black skins made them unmanageable. He and the stockman accordingly agreed on a line of action, as he said, for "frightening the blacks away," but before he did so he gave the contumacious "king" another chance of shifting peaceably off ground on which he was trespassing. Accordingly after dinner as Mr. Jones and his assistants were seated smoking, still indignant at the black's obstinacy, they heard a fearful yell from the stockman, "The cattle have burst the sliprails!" Running down, by the fitful light of the blacks' fires they see for a few seconds a great surging mob of horned heads rushing on the camp like a swollen river, hundreds of cattle stampeding over the camp through fires, and wigwams, over men, women, and children. What was meant for a scare turned out a punishment such as neither the manager nor his stockman ever anticipated. In the morning, after having collected the dead and wounded, the chief came humbly to the now-grieved manager (a man ordinarily of a most generous and warm-hearted nature) and asked him why he had not told him he had wild cattle there in the yard. The manager replied that there were none wilder than ordinarily, as the blacks knew, and he hoped the fearful scene of the night before would cause the king and his followers in future to respect the rights of the run-holders. The result was that these blacks decamped and never troubled squatters thereafter with a similar trick, which they had only practised in this instance with a view to levy black mail. Had any one been on the look-out a few minutes before the yell, tradition says he would have seen the old stockman pulling down the slip rails himself, but the old stockman never told any one so, and inferences only can be drawn. The course of this brutal chief in guilt was short and quick. His lesson seems to have been ill-learnt so far as regards other crimes, for after committing a series of robberies he turned his attention to more diabolical offences, and the whites far and near were provoked more than once to a combined rising on account of some hapless woman having suffered atrociously at their hands and then having been brained. At last and very tardily, for was he not a "converted king"? he was "outlawed;" any one might shoot him who wished, though such a course would have been murder before, and he died finally an ignominious death riddled by bullets while caught stealing a digger's clothes from camp.

This is only one out of many similar instances where the whites have been provoked to retaliation by these depraved savages; savages of the lowest type, incapable except in individual cases of being raised above the level of beasts. A black was recently taken as a young man, educated at Melbourne, and given first-rate facilities for self-improvement, of which he seemed at first to avail himself. He went to college and was treated as an equal by his fellows, he had the entrée of Melbourne society, and was made as comfortable as was possible. What was the result? He went on a visit to his tribe, and when I last heard of him was living the hand-to-mouth existence his fellows lived, a girdle round his loins, a mud thatch to his head, lost again to all civilisation.

It is said that in the early days the terror felt by squatters of the treacherous attacks made by blacks was so great, that if anything was observed moving in the grass and was undistinguishable, the answer to the question, "Is it a black or a kangaroo?" frequently was, "Never mind, shoot it down." The two, man and marsupial, were considered pests, but the man was an infinitely more dangerous foe than the kangaroo; the kangaroo only ate up the grass, the black speared the stock, killed their owners, and treated the womankind, if any, still more outrageously. What wonder, then, that the whites got callous to the feeling that they had to deal with beings who were men? What wonder that a father or a husband should wreak his vengeance upon the tribe or band whose diabolical crimes had reduced him to despair? If an Exeter Hall enthusiast had suffered as many of the colonists have, I cannot do him the injustice of thinking that he would not have requited the transgressors heavily, and for the reasons stated below lynching or summary procedure was necessary. Even now on the fringe of civilisation crimes of this sort take place, but the Government is stronger, and immediately despatches a body of armed constabulary who take the offenders dead or alive, preferably the latter; they then have the satisfaction of being tried in the usual fashion. Lynching is dying out in Australia, though it was a common thing in the old days when the hands of the Government were weak and required strengthening. Now it could rarely serve any good purpose and is seldom *heard of*, though in the outlying districts on the verge of civilisation the pioneer may still have to deal summary justice with his rifle or revolver.

View of Brisbane.

CHAPTER XVII.

The Railway Policy.—Election Cries.—German Colonists.—Queenslanders: their Children and Education.—Up and away to the North.—The A.S.N.Co.'s boats.—Maryborough and Gympie *en passant*.—Bundaberg Streets, Hotels, and Chemists.—Plantations.—Cleared Ground.—Roads and their effects on the Buggy.—The Plantation.—The Homestead.—Cooking.—Hot Work.—The lesser lights of a Plantation.—Tarantulas, Ants, and Fleas.—The Fourth Plague out of Egypt.—Plum-duff for Dinner.—Locusts.— Lady-birds.— Iguanas.— Centipedes and Scorpions.—Snakes.—Carpet-snake-catching Extraordinary.—Sugar-planting a Sticky Story.—Sugar-growing Lands.—Jungle-clearing.—Plantation Fireworks.—Yarns about Crosscut Sawing.—Crops.—Planting.—Rain and Sun.—Extremes of Heat.—Trashing.—Cutting.—Chinese Contracts.

"HOW tired I am of all this Railway Policy," said a friend one day to the writer in Brisbane. "Would to heaven that the Government would run some other show, we know this by heart."

Having been in Brisbane during this spring-tide of railway-projecting and discussing, I could not help sympathising with my friend whom recurring Ministries, with political frothing and squabbling upon this question, had reduced to a state bordering on imbecility. The cause of all the exuberance of verbosity that is forced upon one in the clubs, the papers, the hotels, to say nothing of the "cuisine" where all the stews are concocted, the Houses of Legislature themselves, rather lies in the hazy futurity than in the practical present.

For a time, even the latest novelty in murders by blacks, or the police reports themselves, sink into insignificance before the soul-absorbing topic, whether a line shall go here or there. Private enterprise could, of course, not be able to cope with the great difficulties and expenses, owing to the comparatively wild and unpopulated state of the country through which the lines are projected to pass, so the paternal Government decides the course and finds the ways and means. Not that because the learned Houses say it is to be, does it follow that it will be within a definable limit of years; that is where the rub comes in. The crack of doom will probably have long past before some of the railways now on paper are even commenced. The very authorities seem doubtful where some of these railways are intended to run. But other responsible bodies know where the lines are *not* projected to pass, and then woe betide the unlucky representative of that political division which does *not* happen to be about to be "tapped" in some sort or way. He will never hear the end of the anathemas hurled through his head on the idiotic and ridiculous Government which could not see that Camboon or Rolleston ought, in much greater fairness, to have had a railway than Gayndah, "which has not anything like such good country."

Queensland has already one mile for every 250 heads of population, while New South Wales has one for 630, Victoria one for 600, and the United States have one for 500. Many of the lines will not pay for years to come as commercial undertakings, though the Government appreciates fully that it increases the wealth and prosperity of a colony vastly to have a network of iron roads to expedite and facilitate transport.

"Advance Australia," says the motto. Sometimes she appears to go too quickly, particularly as when a locomotive the other day, near Oxley, advanced at full speed into another with a train behind it and shut it up.

The Railway Policy of each Government is a matter of vital importance to itself and the colony generally, and as party cry is at a discount, such matters as "Railway Policy," "Sugar labour" questions, and the like, decide the election.

The German element is a very strong one in Queensland and can often give the casting vote: a state of circumstances rather annoying to the English-speaking Queenslanders, one of whom informed me that he had an idea that things German were cheap and nasty—*e.g.*, German-silver, German measles, cousins German, and the like, and consequently was vastly disgusted that the German vote should have been able to decide the issue of the last election, and should have such influence in the colony. The matter is hardly one, however, requiring so much heat, as the Germans have the character here as elsewhere of making capital emigrants: quiet, steady, prosperous men who, in many respects, have adapted themselves and their belongings to their surroundings, and soon get turned into thoroughgoing Australians.

Their policy is the Conservative one, the slow and sure, and in acting as a drag it serves to prevent the coach from going too fast down the hill, and thus endangering itself and its occupants.

The Englishman in Queensland is, like the sheep, developing into a different species. American notions seize hold of him quickly, he is more often thin and nervous than stout and plethoric; but his great fault in the eyes of many well-wishers of the colony is the indifference which he as a rule pays to the religion of his mother country or any other, and the religious education of his children.

Brisbane does not contain such a "larrikin"[*] or socialistic element as Sydney, but the fact that the colony has no established church and displays so much indifferentism with regard to this portion of its children's education, is fast developing an under-current of these elements. "Bring a child up in the way it should go, and when it is old it will turn and rend thee,"

---

[*] The word larrikin is said to be the form in which Melbourne constables of Irish extraction used to denote the larking qualities of the young rowdies whom they had "run in." The article cannot be said to have an English equivalent as the colonial larrikin is often of respectable parentage and well dressed, and yet behaves like a common rough.

may be an improper but yet a peculiarly apt rendering of a familiar proverb so far as the colonies of New South Wales and Queensland may be concerned. They have spared the rod in more ways than one, and many a promising child has been bereft of half his utility to the State.

Precocity is more common among colonial children than those of English parents at home, and failing a wholesome fear and veneration for sacred things in their childhood, too many grow up godless and bereft of many good traits that our carefully trained youngsters at home possess. It was a colonial child of two years old that was said to have reproved its mother for speaking of a locomotive as a puff-puff, assuring its fond and admiring relative that the "term of classical derivation was the proper one." The worst of it is that the parents will not see the error of their own and their children's ways, and openly applaud or tacitly acquiesce with secret admiration in ways and manners which are sometimes pitiful to see in such tiny men and women.

To say that the absence of a State church or churches is entirely the cause of these childish misfeasances would not be true, but it is certainly the cause of an appreciable and ever-increasing proportion of them, directly and indirectly. Colonials urge the difficulty of establishing any one Church where the numbers of Church of England, Dissenting, and Roman Catholic adherents are so equal. This difficulty is hardly one of a serious character, as anyone may see who believes in liberalism in religion—a quality itself of some weight in the colonies.

The religious education of state-educated children is generally provided for by the Education Acts of a colony, but it is only so far provided in that each child has a certain hour or so per week during which a minister or teacher of his or her denomination may attend and give the religious education, a course which is not very widely adopted by the clergy who, in many cases, have their hands full in other directions, though scarcely in any so important as this.

After a week or so Brisbane may somewhat pall on the palate, and if one is not to get tired of its streets, river, and gum-lined suburbs one has to move on in some direction or other. If you ask whether it is worth while to go to Toowoomba, you are pretty certain to receive an answer in the affirmative and another in the negative. Settle it by going and seeing for yourself. It will remind you forcibly of the Blue Mountains; and you can sit under a vine and drink another man's wine to your heart's content, as vignerons flourish and prosper unheeded by phyloxera.

Down the Brisbane River is a sugar plantation connected with the convict establishment there, called St. Helena, but to see sugar growing to perfection the adventurous reader must come up with me farther north. Tumble your goods and chattels into a small portmanteau, jump in and squeeze them down; never let a sleeve or portion of garment hang outside your trunk; besides looking untidy and increasing the washing bill, it shows that you cannot subordinate matter to mind, a sign of approaching dissolution of the intellect.

We have the choice of two or three steamship lines by which we may reach Bundaberg, Gladstone, or any other sugar port along the coast right up into the tropics. The excellence of the A.S.N. boats is more conspicuous now than of old; competition has benefited the Australian traveller immensely since the time when he had to get about from one place to another by small, dirty, cramped boats belonging to a monopolising company. Some of these new craft are supplied with smoking and recreation saloons, electric light, suitable bathing-room accomodation, and many of those little conveniences and luxuries which reconcile one to life on board ship *for a time*. As it is, when these boats become crowded and get into rough weather, the amount of groaning and anathematizing sotto-voce confined within a few cubic feet of saloon and berthing accomodation is truly blood-curdling.

As far as Maryborough, some one hundred miles from the capital, sailing is smooth, for the Great Sandy Island protects the channel for some twenty miles along the coast. Of scenery in the strict sense, on the way thither there is little or none. The river Mary is lined with mangrove swamps and gums, and has not been much beautified by the town built some ten miles up its reaches. There is an astonishing amount of shipping lying at anchor in the river for such a comparatively one-horse place. There were twenty boats of all sizes, steam and sail, some of considerable tonnage, lying there when I passed through on two occasions. There is no explanation to be found in the streets, which though well lined with hotels and stores seem to grow more grass than the few passengers on foot or otherwise can keep down. A census I took of the town resulted in my concluding there were but three men and a little girl, whom I no sooner lost sight of at the end of one long vista of broad quiet road than they turned up at another. Clearly if Maryborough had to live on herself she would not fatten. Even a visit to the law courts, which were largely attended by half the available population, only resulted in the census being slightly increased and did not clear up the mystery of the river traffic. 'Tis not a mystery long, however, for Maryborough is but the half-way house to the goldfields of Gympie, whither runs a railway some sixty miles in length and a great quantity of stores, including " whiskey straight."

The gold mines, which are chiefly of the deep-working type, have turned out some two millions worth of gold since 1867 when they were first worked, and still in their percentages exceed an average mine in any other colony Matters here are brisker in one sense than at Ballarat, for shallow working is still going on and engages the attention of independent diggers, men who prefer to be their own masters.

The Botanical Gardens, intersected by the railway which runs to the quay, though stocked with tropical flowers and shrubs, cannot compare with those of the three capitals for size or care.

At the School of Arts, a species of library or reading-room, English and colonial papers and magazines may be read for the trouble of looking at them; and the permission to visitors to make use of the room, generally granted by the secretary on application, may be obtained *ex post facto*. *Experto crede!*

Coasting farther north to reach our *ultima thule*—the sugar plantations—after a quiet and uneventful voyage still protected for a greater part of the way by the Sandy Island, we reach the Burnett River, one of the most prosperous centres for the cultivation of this juicy reed.

The scenery and the township resemble those of Maryborough. The town of Bundaberg has a railway to the copper mines of Mt. Perry, but has reached its present importance chiefly on account of the sugar-growing population around it.

Parallelogramic in shape, with a matter of three thousand inhabitants, it boasts nothing remarkable except it be a sugar refinery and some gigantic stores which supply everything from a bride to a hairpin. Even with the knowledge one eventually gains of the number of plantations all around, one can hardly help wondering that so many and large shops are supported. Their stock in trade compared with the visible wants of the place is enormous.

The scrub and jungle which stretch up their arms close to the white one-floored buildings such as are usually found in colonial townships, show that the mushroom town was born but the day before yesterday. The broad streets of all Australian townships (this is no exception) have amongst their many advantages one or two disadvantages. In dry weather they are perfect deserts of Sahara, to cross which requires courage of the most advanced type; in wet weather, which does not happen so often as some would wish, the expression "ankle deep in mud" gives but a faint description of their condition. The number of hotels a colonial township supports is marvellous; every other house seems to be a hostelry of some sort or form, where liquids of all sorts may be imbibed. Chemists also flourish among the plantations. I should not like to have to calculate their profits on the sale of castor-oil and Epsom salts to planters and plantation managers, purchased not for their personal use so much as for their black employés.

THE "NEW CHUM" IN AUSTRALIA.

As we have come up to see sugar-planting, there is no use in kicking our heels about in an up-country hotel. If there is anything likely to make a man feel that life is a delusion and existence a curse it is such an avocation in such a place.

There are planters on all sides, and an introduction to one or another will speedily provide the lucky possessor with a

Grass Tree (Xanthorrhœa).

passport over his house and grounds, and probably with an invitation to stop, for a time at least.

Having accepted such an invitation we are driven by our new-found friend out past the galvanised iron roofs sweltering in the midday sun, past the glaring houses, through thick bush or forest land where the spiky grass-tree grows and the black snake thrives, over a road corduroyed with large logs of wood, where bad weather has broken it up; of a sudden we pass out of the gloomy gum forest and see a smiling vista of open country cleared of the jungle which here strides in on the forest, and bearing good crops of maize, cane, vines, and pumpkins, the tender tops of the maize and cane standing out in bold relief against the dark masses of jungle in the distance.

Here we drive past some scores of acres of jungle which appears to have been overthrown by some violent convulsion of nature. "Not a bit," says our planter friend; "simply by the axe." Great trees fifty and sixty feet long are lying in apparent confusion upon and under vast heaps of smaller bushwood and saplings, but the confusion is only apparent if the woodman knows his duty; he has cut them down so that they all lie in the fittest way for a "clean burn" when the opportunity comes. Within eight weeks we may see this very land cleared of all but the half-charred greater trees, sown with maize already some inches out of the ground.

A picturesque school-house by the wayside, better built than the ordinary planter's house, is a sufficient indication of the presence of a neighbouring population whom we cannot see, for the thick bush or forest or the still thicker jungle obscures cottage and bungalow alike.

The roads here as elsewhere forcibly remind one of the mutability of all things human, and especially of good temper, which too often changes to bad when a wheel comes in contact with a great rock in the way and bears one up towards the southern cross. Our friend says the stones are volcanic, and that if a man may ever aptly use a torrent of heated language he may to these rocks ahead. Geology is an interesting study, but my experience in colonial geology is that a knowledge of the anatomy of the human form should precede it, and render its students able to cure their bruises and wounds in the eager search after science.

At a turn in the road our nag bounds to one side, and brings the buggy wheel within half an inch of a great snake slinking away, and hissing like a Great Western locomotive. The turn and the bound combined bring us into such a pickle that it takes some time to sort ourselves, which having effected, we see the bright yellow-green canefields surrounding the corrugated-iron mill-shed and unpicturesque chimney where our friend's "fortune is being made."

Once fairly within the plantation gates, kept carefully closed to prevent ingress of kangaroos and wallabies, who have a partiality for cane, we rattle along the even roads, between high walls of cane, up to the mill, around which are congregated in picturesque confusion the kanakas' huts, the men's huts, the stables, and engineer's house, and that the scene is more artistic than tidy is one's first and last thought.

The homestead stands away some hundreds of yards from

A Queensland Sugar Plantation.

the mill in its own grass paddock, with the bush and jungle around it.

There are various ways of studying sugar-planting: either by strolling around during the morning and evening and reclining during the midday heat in a hammock under the verandah with a gentle breeze purring through the leafy vine or other creeper, or by taking an active part in the daily routine, or again by reading the matter up. All three have their votaries; I can recommend a mixture.

"Out here in the bush we get up early," says our friend as we go to bed, "and breakfast at six or half-past, so I'll give you a look in at 5.30." As he is living alone in the bliss of bachelorhood, next morning sees a motley group at the breakfast table in deshabille. Here we are in the land of beef. This is the *pièce de resistance;* bread, tea or coffee, and molasses afford us all alike a *varied* bill of fare. "Quantity without variety," says the planter; "but just you lay in enough of that molasses and you'll grow as fat as an agricultural show pig."

Our servant is a veritable specimen of an up-country domestic. Her resources are small, her cooking appliances few in number, her kitchen but a shed of galvanised iron, her *range* a couple of fire-bars over a wood fire, "but you have yet to see what she can turn out in the culinary way," says the planter. "We draw the line at fricasees, but I know not why, for I do believe the woman could make an ice-pudding out of the material for plum duff and a little cold water, so natty is she."

One does not know what difficulties a bush-servant copes with until, as happened once to me, a servant leaves unexpectedly, before another has time to supply her place.

The camp-oven, a species of baking saucepan on legs, is hardly the most satisfactory utensil wherein to cook one's first batch of bread or joint. At first one suffers the same vituperation at one's friend's hands as King Alfred did for the burnt cakes, or the plaguey thing gets into that obstinate state of being "half cooked" when it takes a poker to send a lump of the article down one's throat, and makes one wish rather to eschew than chew amateur cooking. Meat killed in the morning gets tainted or blown before dinner-time, and somehow it does not appear to add to one's relish to find a jumper or two on one's plate. Or, again, leaving some article, to run down the paddock and bring up the horses to water, may cause its being cooked in such an erratic fashion that, like a celebrated dish I still remember with grief, it may require being thrice-cooked, and then may not have arrived at that blissful maturity called "done." I wot of certain suet dumplings which, instead of having a consistency called firm and light, could have been safely thrown against a wall with the certainty that they would stick there. The planter on that occasion was suffering from dysenterical fever, and was cured effectually by eating one—not of his taste for dumplings, as a jealous friend asserts, but of his complaint. The process of cooking under a Queensland sun, with a blazing hot fire in front, a blazing hot sun above, and a hot walk of some yards to the homestead, has all the subtracting effect of the Turkish bath with none of its luxuries.

I think, though, of all hot situations, the hottest a man may be in, is on a galvanised-iron roof at midday of a Queensland summer, soldering up the cracks in the rain-spouting. Under such circumstances I have known that it did not seem much to matter whether the kanaka down below passed up the soldering-iron the wrong end first or otherwise. Once or twice he smiled feebly as a more than usually energetic expression or a bit of melted solder fell upon him, but he lightly brushed them both away, and seemed to regard the whole matter as a pious and devotional worship of the King of Fire.

I must say also that the minor carnivora on a plantation make it pretty "warm" for a man. The kanaka's companion *sans peur* is the flea, would that I could say *sans reproche*. He is by no means a faithful companion; he leaves him on the shortest notice for fresh pastures. One can always tell if a member of the homestead has been within appreciable distance of a kanaka, or more especially a kanaka's hut. They seem to find in their white friends a change of habitat pleasing to themselves—a pleasure, forsooth, entirely unilateral.

A favourite pastime among some colonial bushmen is to have flea races. At evening, when they draw near the fire with pipe in mouth, they resort to the intellectual recreation of sticking up little twigs in front of the fire, one before each man. The little parasite, drawn out by the genial heat, that first mounts the stick of its pristine accommodator, wins for him the pool, whatever it may be. The dizzy height of intellect one must aspire to, and the constant strain of brain-force required for excellence in this pastime, has prevented its attaining the popularity it otherwise should have, for when a lucky player has thus tempted his little friend forth from its retreat he may turn tail and leave his persecutor to its deserved fate.

Folks try to frighten new chums by fearful tales of tarantulas. A Melbourne friend of mine had a servant who was said to have been bitten on the ankle by a most ungallant tarantula, and was lamed for life. Tales I heard in plenty of like nature, but actual sufferers I never came across. My impression is that since the stigma of transportation has been taken off the Continent its tarantulas, in common with all its other inhabitants, have made great moral progress. As I have lain on my bed of an early morning watching these great hairy brown and grey spiders, some of whom could easily span three inches at a stride, running about on the sides, floor, and roof, I have come to the conclusion that they have been much maligned, and that they are peaceable citizens. I have caught them, but have never experimented with their appetites by thrusting my finger into their jaws; experience is a great thing, especially if bought at the price of other people's sufferings.

While defending the much-abused tarantula, whose size at least is a sufficient warning to the adventurous, it is but fair to add that there is a small red spider, no larger than a pea, which has got a most evil reputation in the interior. It is described as of a bright red colour, and though insignificant in size is most venomous and harmful in its effects should a man come into close contact with it. There was an authenticated story in 1884 of a child being found dead in its bed through its having inadvertently slept upon one of these little insects, and in another case I heard of an adult being laid up for many weeks through a bite received from a "small red spider," probably the same species.

In the scrub of Queensland it is well to guard by reasonable caution and occasional attention to the state of one's garments from the unpleasant adherence of the scrub-tick, a small insect which has an unpleasant way of introducing itself below the skin, and there remaining until expelled by an application of a hot needle. Bushmen assert that an attempt at excision is worse than useless, for the animal thereupon poisons the tissue around it, and is needless, as the remedy above mentioned is simple and efficacious. It may be added that comparatively few instances occur of whites being bitten by these ticks, as their clothes protect them, but horses and cattle are not infrequently attacked and irritated by them.

Ants form an article of diet in the colonies, not so much that they are voluntarily cooked and eaten, but that they immolate themselves "promiscuous-like" on the shrine of one's palate while one is eating. I have frequently seen these insects in the sugar-basins at Melbourne, Sydney, or Brisbane, in first-class hotels; and up-country the ant's sweet tooth is so much of a recognised fact that a few floating about in one's tea or coffee seem rather in than out of place. The winged kind of an evening when rain is looming up are somewhat too officious in their attentions; they seem hardly yet to have recognised the physiological fact that for inspiration one's nostrils should have an unblocked passage, for hearing one's tympanum should have a square millimetre uncovered, and that their bodies are scarcely so transparent as to make the presence of half a dozen in each eye desirable. Colonials think they circumvent these little busybodies by placing the legs of their sideboards or tables in saucers of water, but an observer would often be amused to see the festive little burglar chuckling with laughter as he and some thousand mates are removing the bread, sugar, or preserves of the enterprising colonial piecemeal.

Flies! When the fourth plague was removed from Egypt it was not exterminated, as commonly thought, but must have been bodily transported to the neighbourhood of the sugar plantations, to teach the planters and their workmen the utter uselessness of ornate phraseology. Kill one and a couple take his place (the men in buckram all over); call one bad names and two or even three approach to listen; use profanity and half a hundred come to render their shocked brother moral (and physical) support.

T

I write, as I have felt, acutely. The European race may die out of this terra Australis, but the European fly never; the future of this great nation may be in *its* hands!

Up at the workmen's hut I have seen flies so dense that you appeared to breathe insectile atmosphere. The workmen became tired after a time of having so much "game," and cried out for plum duff to counteract its effects. This request is of a most serious character. It bids fair to equal in excitement the revolution of a South American republic. As the planter rides up to the mill one morning, the whole gang of whites turns out in line and demands a parley. Their spokesman intimates that they hunger after the flesh-pots of Corinth and Muscatel, not those of Egypt, or, in his own language, "plums and currants instead of them derned flies." With due solemnity, to avert a catastrophe, the planter grants the request, first reflecting with good-humoured banter on their child-like affection for sweets. When that first duff "came off" some day or so later, a bystander could have seen that no ordinary event was happening. The rush of the white labourers, engine-driver and all, to their dinner partook of the energy, if not of the object, of the charge at Tel-el-Kebir. The solidity and size of this important dish was also apparent after dinner in the unusually slow movements and replete appearance of the partakers, who, however, under the effects of a Queensland sunny afternoon soon managed to regain their energy.

You are bound to have the whole category of insects if you go to Queensland. Even the little ladybird, rejoicing in a changed name, flourishes here. Its name has been filched by a great creeping gawky beast of the grasshopper tribe, legs three to four inches long, body ditto, and almost incapable of being seen edgewise. You grasp a leaf or branch and find it begin to crawl along. If you are of the feminine gender and new to the habits of the fauna you scream, otherwise you know you have come across a ladybird or something of the sort. Their wings, gauzy and light, glitter in the sun with the gloss of a dragon-fly, and as they hurt no one they are not destroyed.

The grasshopper tribe is strongly represented in Queensland. That beast with the bad name—the locust—finds its antecedents require it to act in accordance therewith, and many is the "Northern Farmer" or planter whose year's work has been almost completely destroyed in a few days by a cloud of this insignificant-looking insect. Other members of the cicada type perform their huge gymnastic feats as we walk through the grass, and somehow make one think that could a man jump as far in proportion to his size as those insects he would exceed the powers of him of the seven-league boots. Somewhere or another an author compares a flea and an elephant, and after careful calculation affirms that if the pachyderm were gifted with the proportionate jumping powers to those of this little parasite he could leap some three or four miles " every kick." It was the remembrance of this quasi-idiotic comparison that suggested my remark about the grasshopper and man.

Click-clack! click-clack! ".What are you playing at castanets for?" That is exactly the sound which a little-winged beetle makes all day long on a fine day, here and there, as he darts through the paddock.

Life? I should think there is life out here! See yon gum-tree trunk with its grey boles and knobs; I saw an iguana dart round the other side just now. He pops out his head to see if we're actually coming, and then commences a humorous game of hide and seek; the old dry-looking lizard dodges round and round the trunk until tired of the game, he clambers up and looks down with all the proud indifference of a superior in position. The iguana is said to grow five to six feet long. Our friend here, the biggest I have seen, is only about two feet six inches from snout to tip of tail. They are also said to resemble chicken when roasted. The whites commonly eat chicken and not iguana, the blacks *vice versâ ;* the similarity of the two foods must therefore be established on the veracious testimony of a half-breed (?).

Having cracked a bit off the bark of a gum-tree, you may often see regular tunnels and galleries where the great maggot-borer has been at work. Colonists cut out this *bonne-bouche* with a knife or tomahawk, at least some do, and eat him either cooked or otherwise. As he resembles a tremendous ringed white maggot as big as a man's thumb, new chums generally prefer to eat their share by deputy. 'Tis a question of association, the less impeachable when objected to by oyster-eaters, inasmuch as they are said to closely resemble this bivalve.

Centipedes and scorpions! What were these creatures sent for? The former, which grow to four and five inches in length, resemble the second in that they secrete themselves under logs and stones, whence on being dislodged their unfortunate aggressor may receive an unexpected bite as painful as having a dozen teeth out, and more lasting in its inflammatory effects. But the centipedes are honest, disporting grand brown and red colours; many of the scorpions are villainous and treacherous, rejoicing in a dirty black colour undistinguishable often from the log or the earth. They have ere now temporarily paralysed a man's limb with a bite, and consequently the handling of wood and stones on the ground requires, for perfect safety, almost a kid-glove delicacy, which however is not often to be witnessed.

In the jungle or scrub over there behind the plantation, a walk reveals a vast realm of fauna and flora such as delights the heart of the student of nature. But when rhapsodising on the exquisite scent and colour of yon hanging creeper, let him take care not to tread inadvertently on a black snake, a fact which he will probably remember for the next few minutes and then never again, unless he is lucky in the speedy application of cautery and the imbibing of vast quantities of alcohol. This is of all snakes the most common on the sea-coast of Queensland, and is a most desperate foe to have to tackle at close quarters, growing often from five to eight feet long. Its big brother the carpet or diamond snake,* which grows often to fourteen and twenty feet in length, is by no means so dangerous, being in fact according to most recent accounts non-poisonous, and befriending the planter and farmer by destroying kangaroo-rats, wallabies, and the like.

A short time since an old Queenslander offered to the kanakas or coolies on his plantation a reward of a few shillings for the skin of a carpet snake in good order.

Accordingly one Sunday (the nigger's holiday) a couple of coolies wandered through the jungle looking for "him big 'nake." Nor were they disappointed, for soon they came across a sleeping beauty some sixteen feet long. Making a noose with a green vine, one captured the prize by his head and dragged him off, the other seizing the tail and trotting after. Mr. Carpet Snake, however, seemed to have some difference of opinion with his captors, and releasing his head, turned back on his train-bearer, coiled round his arm and body, and violently attacked him. The plucky kanaka, however, held fast the tail while the other refastened the noose, and again dragged off their prize, but not before the train-bearer had had his face bitten and scratched after a manner dreadful to look upon. The brave fellow was quite right again in a week or so, although he had scars which he will bear on his face to his island home and to his grave under the waving banana or graceful palm.

The lozenge-marked skin of the carpet snake will indicate his character to an ignoramus, and perhaps save the life of a brother reptile more fortunate than a youngster some two to three feet long that I once found in a dining-room on a plantation. The most poisonous snake, the death, sometimes called deaf, adder, has a very bad character. Its ways are treacherous, and though its salmon-tinted belly should suffi-

* Natural historians distinguish the carpet from the diamond snake; but for all practical purposes colonists consider them one and the same, and use these names interchangably.

ciently indicate its presence, the viper generally keeps this to the ground until it makes its fatal dart.

Mr. G. Bennett, a naturalist, from whose works I have gained much valuable information, recommends a poultice of powdered ipecac. for the bites of scorpions and centipedes, but fears that without the auxiliary processes of excision, sucking, and ligatures above the wound, it could not avail the viper-bitten bushman. As a rule, the stupor arising from the poison is neutralised by constant motion, the imbibing of large quantities of alcohol or ammonia; and these and other remedies colonial governments instruct school teachers to explain to their charges at an early opportunity.

I have been all this time on the plantation without showing my indulgent readers over the mill and cultivation paddocks. I have had a reason. The very mention of the word sugar brings back to my recollection such suggestions of a universal stickiness that I have considerable diffidence in introducing the subject, fearing that I should have to ask you every other minute to go and rinse your hands.

There are mills where a high standard of cleanliness is enforced, but they are uncommon on ordinary plantations. As a rule, you may be walking on an earthy mixture of crystallised sugar and molasses, perhaps molasses trickling down from a pipe overhead, or sugar-syrup spurting out of the open pans, molasses or syrup on the stairways and ladders, on the feet and hands of the coolie workmen, in fact omnipresent.

The " modus sugerandi " is not of itself perhaps of exciting interest, but it has nevertheless its interesting features, so if any one finds no attraction in it let him skip the following pages and literally wash his hands of it now, a process necessary to the readers further on.

In Queensland the best sugar-growing lands are the jungle lands, which usually are of a red Devonian colour. The black soil of ordinary bush or grass land was until recently thought unfit for cane cultivation, but is now coming into favour.

The process of clearing bush-land is easier and cheaper than jungle, for the trees are much farther apart. There are no great fig-trees fifty feet in circumference at the root, no matted hanging vines growing and twisting round trees of all sizes, from a few inches to a few feet in diameter, no dense undergrowth in ordinary black soil. But the jungle soils give by some way the best returns, as they are richer and warmer.

After the woodman has made a clean cut of some acres of jungle, which he must do in a scientific fashion so as to make it lie well together and burn at one burning, it blisters and broils in the heat of the sun. Some recommend a little rain to quicken its arrival at a fit state, as this washes out the glutinous sap, but in Australia the recipe including rain is not always practicable, and so the coat must be cut according to the cloth.

It may lie for months—three or four, often longer—and then comes a fitting day for the bonfire. The whole mass is lighted in various places and burnt up—against the wind if a strong one—and for a few days and nights, if there is a good burn, there will be acres of cloud by day and a grand lurid glare at night, lighting up the clouds of smoke far and near. If the timber has been properly felled, only the largest charred trunks will be unconsumed, the rest are ashes and charcoal, a capital fertiliser if need be. The cross-cut saw is then brought to bear on the large logs; they are cut into lengths and rolled away.

History relates how the first coolies were instructed in the science of cross-cutting, a man being placed at each end of the steel blade. They soon were the centre of attraction of a laughing, yelling, chattering circle of their fellow-coolies, who laid odds as to which could pull the other over the log. It seemed so much of a joke that the two operators for a while enjoyed it *as such*, but, their strength failing, they suggested that two of the bystanders should take their places at the new game; for they had had enough of play for that day, they said, as their glossy skins shone doubly with the beads of perspiration, and they wanted some real hard work, such as looking on, hoeing cane, or the like. It was odd, so history relates, how soon each and every man in that motley crowd got tired of play and stood out for "hard work."

A story comes from Cooktown that an Irishman came across a couple of men thus engaged in cross-cutting. Ever ready to protect the weaker, Paddy steals behind the bigger of the two, pulls him back off his hold, and bids the other, "Now then, be jabers, little 'un, run away with it. I'll settle this omadhaun, the coward, trying to pull it away from yez."

If the burn is not a clean sweep the woodman probably *hears* of it from his employer, for the small stuff has burnt away from the larger, and the labour and cost of hauling and piling together the unburnt timber is not insignificant.

The next course is to plant the cane, or corn, or whatever is to go in the ground thus cleared. The stumps of the trees are still in, but it is of no use to lose time grubbing them out just at this juncture. The great object is to get a crop in, and make use of the clearing. The maize is sown, sweet potatoes and cane plants dibbed in, and so forth, in more or less irregular lines.

The inquisitive mind asks what is a cane plant. It is a small section of the bamboo-like matured canes, which has the undeveloped buds at every joint of its stem. The length of this section is not arbitrary, for the length of the nodes or rings from one to another is variable, close at the bottom, far apart high up. Three or four rings, that is three or four buds, is considered a tidy young plant.

The process of planting the section is easy, but there is one way where no results may be obtained, another the best. As a rule, folk prefer the latter, and plant the cane at an angle, the upper end right side up, with the buds on the sides and facing the upper end, so that no bud if possible is under the stock. The kanaka who has to dig straight holes generally considers himself at liberty to deviate a few feet or more to one side or another, the consequence of which is that in time two "parallel lines" do not satisfy Euclid's definition, but of course, if the ground is clear of stumps, the plough may be put in and the work done more accurately and quickly.

From ten to fourteen months the planter awaits the result; often anxious months they are, for though the sugar cane is only cultivated in Queensland on the sea-coast, even here droughts are not infrequent and crops ruined. Day after day he may see heavy clouds banking up without shedding a drop of the precious much-coveted moisture, a freak supposed to be peculiar to Australian meteorology, and ascribed by scientists to the fact, before mentioned, that the immense heated current of air poured forth from the vast sandy plains and deserts of the interior of this continent keep the clouds at a temperature above condensation.

If the plant thrives, in ten or eleven months, probably longer, it may be fit for cutting, but now it is hardly recognisable. The buds have sent up great stout canes, perhaps six or seven feet high, surmounted by another two or three feet of the delicate yellow-green coloured plume that makes a cane plantation one of the prettiest sights after a harvest-field. The canes, growing six to a dozen from each stool, interlace with their neighbours and fall over gracefully; the mazy avenues between the rows can be explored with difficulty, and assuredly with considerable perspiration. Of all warm spots in the globe, the interior of a standing cane-field will vie with almost any; the stifling atmosphere, unmoved by currents of wind, absorbing all the heat poured down by the tropical or semi-tropical sun, would run the temperature of San Francisco, before the Keyhole breeze sets in, close for first place. It is the heat of the cane-field which above all prevents white labour from replacing blacks in the cane-fields of the tropics.

During the process of growth the coolies pass throughout the plantation and "trash" the canes, that is, pull off the dead and dried blades and spathes from the lower portion of the canes. If this trash is not gathered away from the standing cane it may prove the ruin of the cane-field, as a lighted match dropped in amongst such rubbish will run through a hundred acres with the speed of a racehorse, causing irreparable damage to growing canes, but as a rule, planters in Australia take their chances of this danger, labour being dear.

When the crop has to be cut the coolie is told to cut the great stalks as near the stools as possible, which he does with a clean chop of his cane-knife, then he lops off the greener portion of the top with its blades and plume, and throws the bare stick behind him.

Some coolies never seem to learn how much to cut off from the top. They either cut off so much that they actually waste cane, which thus lies on the ground and gets burnt as rubbish, or they cut off too little, and send to the mill an article containing a considerable proportion of green watery fluid without *paying* saccharine qualities, thus rendering more boiling and condensation necessary, and moreover very productive of "ferment," the sugar-boiler's greatest enemy.

Chinamen often take contracts to cut so many acres of cane. I remember on one occasion a gang who were "bossed" by a couple of whites being so employed. Their day's work, however, showed the contractors that *they* would make a loss on the contract, so these got the planter to let them off. When the contractors had gone, a grave elderly Celestial informed the planter that, if he liked, they, the Chinamen, would take the work on the same terms for themselves, and that they would take care to work well. The proposal being accepted, proved that the Chinaman is an industrious servant when his own master, for at it they went, up early, to bed late, showering an *embarras de richesses* on the sugar-boiler, and clearing a handsome wage.

The proportions of Chinamen to whites in the colonies, and more especially Queensland and Northern Territory, is astonishing to any one who makes no study of the "dreary science" of statistics. In the latter colony, or portion of a colony, two-thirds of the inhabitants, exclusive of blacks, are Chinese. Despised openly by the whites, and secretly returning the contempt for those on whom he fattens, he continues to lead a peaceable, orderly, money-grubbing existence, until having made his "pile" Johnny takes it away, generally in the shape of gold, and goes home in the next steamer, probably with his treasure on his person.

Not long ago a vessel freighted with Chinamen, themselves thus freighted, was driven on the rocks on the Australian coast. The sardonic tragedy of the accident culminated in the death of a number of the Celestial passengers weighed down by their money-belts, who would otherwise have escaped with their lives and, as it eventually proved, their wealth.

A noteworthy event happened on one plantation while I was there on the death of a Chinaman. Dressed in his best, he lay in state for a short time, his body zealously watched by a brother up to interment, with meat and drink in his coffin to provide him with food for his journey, and to propitiate the authorities " beyond the gates."

a Kanaka's Hut

CHAPTER XVIII.

Mill Work.—Feeding the Rollers.—Small Talk and Big Talk.—Crushing.—Clarifying.—Evaporating.—Vacuum and Open Pans.—Drawing the Charge.—Coolers.—Drying.—Different Qualities.—Waste of Molasses.—Burning Trash.—The Kanaka discussed.—The Two Chief Objections.—Slavery?—State Supervision.—Before and After Service.—His Life in the Plantation.—Bright Colours.—Childlike Tastes.—The Second Objection discussed.—Revenge is sweet only when carried out.—Domestic Relations.—Washing.—Civilising the Kanaka.—Nomenclature.—Flirting.—Dusting the New Chum.—What he does with his Wages.—" This Fellow's sick."—The Reaper's Share.—A Corroborree.—Profits of Planters.—West Indian Negroes.—Singhalese.—Social Life on a Plantation.—Educating the Kanakas.—Missionary Work.—The Kanaka and the Copper.—Health on the Plantations.—Fever and Ague.—The Barcoo Rot.—Port Wine and Brandy a Specific.—Summary of Plantation Prospects.

WHILE chatting about the Chinese the cane-carts have come and gone, and have turned out their great loads of canes close by the massive fluted iron rollers where the juice is crushed out.

Nigger women in picturesque colours feed these three great rollers—one at the top above two below—which revolve at a slow rate with ponderous and steady motion. Down the wooden trough or feeder slides the cane, guided by the careless hands of the women, who think and talk too much of other and more frivolous subjects to judge by their merriment, for it would take Joseph Clements himself to get a joke out of a triplet of sugar-rollers, triplets, whether musical or human, as a rule not being such *sweet* things. Sometimes the dark-skinned Chloe or Cobar talks so volubly that she does not see that no cane is passing through the rollers. Of a sudden her attention is called to the fact by something or somebody, then jam goes a whole mass of canes down into the jaws, which, like a man with a big mouthful, strain and strive to swallow, then creak and stop. Then comes a shout from the engine-driver, for the machinery all stops, steam is escaping, and everybody in the mill gets excited and does— nothing to make things go right again. Then the engineer reverses the engine, makes the rollers disgorge, censures the guilty damsel or matron in chaste and select language, bids her pull out the abnormal stuffing, and everything goes right till next time.

The excitement lulls, so let us follow the juice in its further course. Expressed between these giant molars it runs into a tank below, whence it is pumped up to large tanks at a high level called clarifiers; but we have by no means saved all, for the fibrous portion of the cane passes out the other side of the rollers, apparently dry, but often containing as much as from 30 to 50 per cent. of its original quantum of juice.

The juice when pumped into the clarifiers has a greenish look, a viscid consistency, and a sweet sickly taste, and is mixed with lime and heated by steam-pipes. The lime combines with the vegetable matter, neutralises acids and other matters forming impurities in the juice, which impurities, called "defecated matter," rise to the top as a dark repulsive scum, which the grinning "boy" at the clarifier skims off with alacrity as he sees us approach. It is astonishing how deceptive the atmosphere is in a sugar-mill. The boys seem to be doing nothing until you get near them, when you find them working *like niggers !*

Now the juice becomes a clearer yellow, tastes much pleasanter, and is run out of the clarifier into a series of pans, whence the water is evaporated. The old style adopts a series of open pans, one above the level of the other, in all of which it is successively boiled and skimmed, flowing down slowly and thus out into another tank, whence it is pumped up for its final evaporation to the vacuum or other evaporating-pan. The clouds of sickly-smelling steam arising from these pans give the attendant niggers by no means a good time. This employment of skimmer is absolutely unhealthy, as the blanched faces of the white sugar-boilers and others thus engaged testify.

The more recent and improved French cylindrical boilers are in use on few plantations, their expense being heavy.

The last process of evaporation is done in various forms of pans, the vacuum being adopted for the best sugars, as thereby a lower degree of temperature produces an equal evaporation without the risk of burning the sugar, an accident *not* impossible when the syrup is finally boiled in an open pan. Its sugars are whiter and altogether more satisfactory, though the Wetzell and other pans, boiling under the ordinary pressure of the atmosphere, will give very good results in skilful hands.

The precise moment when the syrup is ready to be run out into the coolers calls for careful judgment by the sugar-boiler. If he lets it out too soon crystallization is imperfect, the crystals small, and a large amount of sugar goes away with the molasses; if he delays too long, the syrup may crystallise in the pan and refuse to "move on," thus necessitating much hand labour with a spade to dig it out, a process not always practicable. This "moment" he tells by feeling for the "grain" of the sugar. If, on dipping his finger and thumb into the hot syrup he withdraws his hands, and on separating the fingers against the light he can see specks of crystal in the transparent sheet of syrup, he must be looking alive with his wooden troughs, have his key ready, and see finally if his coolers are in due order to receive the syrup. The coolers which receive the charge are large wooden box-like vats, sometimes many feet across, whither the warm mass is directed along wooden troughs, and where it is allowed to cool and crystallise. This cooling takes place in two or three days or thereabouts, if it be open-pan sugar, while twenty-four hours is often enough for that boiled in vacuum-pans.

The next process, in which the sugar-crystals are separated from the molasses with which they are intimately mixed, is conducted in this wise: Johnny the Fijian, or Waitonga the New Ireland "boy," dig out the contents of the coolers into tubs, and when they near the bottom jump in with bare legs and shovel out the sticky contents. Others carry the tubs of this thick, stodgy, light-ochre mass to the centrifugals, where a large basket of wire gauze revolves within another cylinder at a high rate of speed. The contents of the tub are emptied into the inner cylinder, and straightway get tossed against the sides, through which the centrifugal force drives the molasses into the outer cylinder, whence it runs into the molasses tank. A little water materially assists to wash out the molasses.

The sugar crystals, unless very small, do not escape the gauze, and on stopping the machinery the sugar is scraped out with wooden scrapers in very much the same form as we see it in our sugar-basins. I may add that Johnny and Waitonga seem to be rather reckless of washing *before* they jump into the coolers. Much of this plantation sugar is bought by the large refineries in Australia, and refined down to the purest whites, such as our best loaf sugar is made of, in which state it, however, has lost much of the delicate aroma it possessed before. The process detailed in the preceding pages applies, *mutatis mutandis*, to all the sugars, "firsts," "seconds," and "thirds." The "firsts" are the sugars we have just seen carried away to the sugar-house from the centrifugals, where they are stored to dry, and then bagged in 70 lb. bags suitable for ready transport. The molasses from these "firsts" is slightly diluted with water, evaporated down again, and the brown sugars therefrom stored separately and called "seconds." The second molasses are treated in the same way, and form "thirds." In some very economical establishments the molasses from the third sugars is reboiled to make "fourths," and so on, until almost every crystal of cane-sugar crystallises out; but as a rule on plantations, this "third" molasses is run out into a hole in the plantation close by—a harbour of flies and ferment, and not altogether a sweet-scented spot.

To look at the large bins of sugars in the drying-room, one would never think that beneath its placid, colourless form lies such a depth of feeling as they find in it in Brisbane or Melbourne, where it is "firm" or "quiet," "promising" or "dull," "moving" or "stationary" by turns.

The inconsistency of many matters human appears in the fact that near many large townships in Queensland there are annually thousands of gallons of molasses wasted—run out on the soil—while in the townships themselves they are importing treacle and golden syrup from America.

As yet, in describing the culture of that article, which makes the hearts of our youngsters at home to leap like a young unicorn when seen in perspective through a confectioner's window, no mention has been made of the cane-field after the crop has been cut. Many folk seem to think that it has all to be planted over again. The contrary is the case.

After gathering together, digging in, and burning the trash and the severed "tops," the cane-stools are left to themselves for a bit. Within a day or two of cutting, so quick is growth if the season is at all propitious, up come the cane-shoots from the stools, and in their turn furnish the standing crop for the next season. The first year the stools are called "plants," the name being obvious; after the first cutting they undergo the indignity of being called rattoons, on the *lucus a non* principle; after the second cutting, second rattoons, and so on. I heard of cane cut without transplantation for twenty successive years, but there are other soils or methods of cultivation which only give it a five years' lease. The fact is that as long as it will furnish sufficient "paying" juice it is allowed to send up its fresh shoots every year. The burning of the trash and "tops" is often an exciting event, for should the wind spring up it may carry the great forking flames over into standing cane, which thus gets frequently damaged. To see a score or so of niggers silhouetted against the flames rushing with pails of water through the burning cane loses something of its weirdness and charm if the cane is yours.

The sugar-labour question was in a state of chaos while I was in Queensland in 1884, but recently matters seemed to have arranged themselves in a quasi-order. The kanaka or South Sea Islander, so often referred to in preceding pages, is paid £6 per annum in wages for three years, when his apprenticeship is over, and he can again leave for his home or re-engage himself. As a matter of fact, in articles of clothing, food, and these wages he costs a planter altogether about £25 per annum, and is the most suitable labourer at present for this purpose. This state of matters, however, does not suit either the advanced philanthropists or the white labourers. The former complain that the system is one of actual, though not nominal, slavery, and that under cover of hiring apprentices the recruiting boats often perpetrate cruelties on these children of nature. The white labourer objects that labour is so much cheapened by these means, for of course the least *he* would get for such work would be about £1 per week, with all food and housing found. I will deal with the objections in order.

That there have been great cruelties practised in past times on these unfortunate and confiding islanders by nefarious agents is admitted on all hands, but by the recent provisions for sending responsible Government agents with duly licensed recruiting-ships, Government has almost if not entirely prevented these grave offences.

That there is no such thing as an approximation to slavery in Queensland matters speak for themselves. As a matter of fact, from the time the kanaka leaves his home till he returns he is under state protection of an active character. The Government agent explains to the kanaka before engagement the terms, the nature and duration of his future employment, and the wages he or she (both men and women get the same) is to receive. When he is landed the islander is immediately taken in hand by a Government Inspector of kanaka labour, who is responsible for the good treatment of all the kanakas in his district, and who resents anything like cruelty with all the pains and penalties his office enables him to levy. As a matter of fact, the Queensland planter is not naturally a vicious, cruel, slave-driver, though in this, as in every trade or profession, unprincipled men do exist. For the cruel master the legal sanction is applicable and speedily vindicates the rights of his kanakas. I question whether now there is not more liberty to the kanaka than many a milliner's or manufacturer's employé gets at home.

A sight of a kanaka before, during, and after, his term of service would edify many folk who think his life is one of subtraction and reduction rather than addition. He comes, often a thin, meagre, undeveloped creature, almost naked, possessing bones but without muscle, without physique, possessing scarce any pride; he goes back with some money in his pocket, or its equivalent in value about him, with muscles well developed, frame stout, holding his head high, clad in civilised garments such as many a poor labourer at home might envy. Come and visit him during his term of service, and I think the veriest abolitionist amongst you will hesitate to talk about his slavish state.

Here he lives in a log or thatch hut, cosy and warm, with a fire if he needs it, bedding such as he cares about, generally the dried leaves of the cane, or a stretched hammock; perhaps blest with a wife, whom he keeps in "capital order," laughing and frolicking, with more than enough bread, meat, and potatoes to eat, and tea or water *ad libitum* for drink. Here he retires at mid-day for his dinner, and at 6 p.m. for his supper as regularly as clockwork.

As a rule they are a merry, smiling, childlike mob, except when ill, when they get sulky and seem to think their ills are not appreciated. Both men and women rejoice in glaring contrasts of colour in their dress, and in heavy feeding. For these two luxuries they often pay the larger portion of their wages, though they are decently clothed and amply fed by the planter. Except one or two old stagers, they are for the most part confiding and easily taken in, and the pedlars and storekeepers seem to have little scruple over taking a rise out of a kanaka by selling him an article for 150 per cent. above its value.

As a type of a pair of kanakas rigged out in Sunday clothes I will take these two—man and wife—haphazard. *She* walks along with a violet and yellow-striped skirt, a red and black bodice, a gorgeous last season's second-hand bonnet with all the ribbons of the rainbow, majestically holding above her head a crimson parasol trimmed with lace once white, but is without boots. In the week she has a stuff gown tied in round the middle like a bag of flour, a bandana or two, and *praeterea nihil*. Her companion affects a straw or light felt hat with puggaree of brilliant colour, a clean white shirt with collar and necktie, a pair of white moleskins, with a blue and white bandana sash, and a pair of stout lace boots. He, during the week, wears an old red shirt and a pair of inexpressibles cut to a pattern, but *not* fitting him like the paper on the wall. These pictures were drawn by the writer while lolling in the verandah of a Sunday morning.

The next objection to kanaka labour is that of the white labourer. He says it cheapens wages and degrades the country; the first is really his reason for objecting, and so far as he is concerned, it is a serious one, though political economists have yet to enunciate the statement that a country lives for its labouring class.

They also say that it introduces a class of labourers who take all their wages out of the country, and are enriching a set of masters who do the same. With respect to the first, it is a notorious fact that until recently a kanaka took little if any cash away with him, his wealth, what there was of it, being exchanged before he left for knicknacks. And in addition to this, he rarely has a year's wages over at the end of his term, the rest having been spent in the luxuries above-mentioned. The Chinamen are much more open to these counts than the South Sea Islander, according to an unprejudiced view of the question, for they do take all their wealth away with them and usually in specie.

With regard to the planters themselves the affair hardly admits of argument. Is it not a notorious fact that it is due to the introduction of men of capital from Europe that the sugar industry has succeeded as it has in Queensland as well as New South Wales, and that many a planter settles down and spends the rest of his days in this sunny land of the south? Even though he may take his wealth home again (a comparatively infrequent occurrence now, when a man may live as comfortably in the colonies as at home), he has enriched the colony by his improvements, his clearing of forests, and so forth. This sugar industry, which many pessimists have thought doomed, and have thereupon thrown up their plantations, has reached, as far as money value goes, the second place in the industries of the colony of Queensland, being in value next below wool and so far above the gold industry. Though the magnitude of this industry would not justify the most trivial cruelty, it remains an important factor for the consideration of those whose policy is directed directly against kanaka labour, and thereby indirectly against the sugar industry itself.

The childlike disposition of the kanakas has its disadvantages: they are quick at taking offence, and revengeful, though their anger cools down again rapidly; passionate with each other and their masters, and extremely jealous in domestic affairs. I knew of a case where a planter, irritated by the disobedience of a kanaka, boxed his ears in true schoolmaster fashion, whereby he unconsciously raised the man's ire, who in the evening came up as though with friendly intent, accompanied by a mate, to interview the planter on some pretext or other. While stepping out into the verandah, the planter saw a gleam and glitter of metal behind the kanaka's back, and with suspicions suddenly aroused jumped for him and knocked him and his would-be murderous knife over on to the ground some six feet below. The men ran away much scared, leaving the knife behind; but the would-be assassin proved afterwards the best worker on the plantation.

On one occasion I found a kanaka in a plantation workshop filing a species of knuckle-duster, a great jagged ring of iron, whose object was to spoil the *complexion* of a fellow labourer. My confiscation of the ring aroused the black's wrath to such a degree that I had to retire to the immediate vicinity of the forge, where a great glowing bar of iron lay between the tongs; when he saw I meant business too, he smiled, ran off, and soon recovered his usual equanimity.

There are so many women and so many men on a plantation, the women receiving the same wages, and often working as hard, as the men; and though some few—*i.e.* converted or missionary kanakas, as they are called—may adopt Christian rites of matrimony, the custom is for some one man and some one woman to resolve to become joined in the holy bond; nothing further is required. Childlike are they in their tastes! —Arcadian in their simplicity!

These informal marriages are, as a rule, lasting, and observed with constancy. Serious matrimonial squabbles are rare, though when occurring not confined to words of violence. If the lady gives her lord cause for jealousy woe betide her; he has a rod in pickle for her, and knows how to lay it on. I have known a scandal spread by one woman concerning another, during the absence of the husband of the latter, cause almost a mutiny— quite a feud—on the plantation, which has given the planter, or his manager, some trouble to put down, but has all subsided in a day or two, forgiven and apparently forgotten.

They are generally fairly quick at learning civilised pursuits, virtues, and vices, more especially the latter. They seem to swear in English before ever they can talk it.

Of all civilised virtues washing seems to come most amiss to them; an odd thing when one remembers the stories of Cook and other navigators about their love for sea-bathing. On Sundays they take a dip in the sea or river if they are near and have the energy to walk down to them, but their clothes and habitations are innocent generally of an *intentional* application of water. A rain shower can hardly be reckoned as such. If you set a kanaka "Mary" or woman to clean a floor you must expect it to be somewhat dirtier after than before; at least, it appears so, for she congregates the dirt in large sweeping circles and leaves it mingled with the soapsuds to ornament (?) the floor with its parquetry.

That kanakas can acquire certain skill may be appreciated from the fact that I have seen them ploughing a very tolerable furrow after tuition of a day or two, and with this advantage over their white brethren, that they were not too proud to be taught. This sight was too much for an "honest white labourer," who almost sickened at the meanness of giving a wretched nigger a job to do for about one-tenth of the wages the white man would have got.

The kanakas vary much in build, and physical as well as mental development. The "boys" from the Tonga Island are considered among the best workers, and one or two were as handsome as many a fine Italian, though a trifle darker in complexion. The New Ireland men are hard workers, big and courageous, but quarrelsome with other races, and very quick tempered. The New Guinea men again are about up to the average, but the Solomon Islanders are much lower in stature and courage.

The names of these "boys" form a regular hotchpotch: Jack, Cockroach (from his resemblance to that animal, with all due apologies to the late serjeant at arms and *Mr. Punch*), Ipi, Wakatoki, and the like. As for the native names, I neither guarantee their spelling nor correctness; the phonetic style was adopted to turn them out.

The women again were all "Mary" if you didn't know their proper name, the term Mary being the phonetic spelling of a generic term of "woman," but if one wished to treat them to the right article one had to carry in the storehouse of one's intellect such names as Sobar, Coba, varied with Alice, Ethel, and the like. Some of them have charming faces, and—oh ye

English belles, think of the horror of it—flirt most outrageously with their eyes. They used to prefer, if they had any message to give to the planter or his storekeeper, to give it direct and not through the intervention of that "old-white-fellow-Mary," as they contemptuously dubbed our worthy but aged domestic.

They are often big strapping women, who have a keen appreciation of their own dignity. I remember on one occa-occasion a planter put a new " colonial-experience "* man on to " boss" a gang of black ladies. He was a pale young man, and remonstrated with the action of some one or other in mildly exhortative fashion. His pupil's answer was prompt and forcible in the shape of a box on the ears, and the next thing seen on that plantation was the mad chase of the poor little "new chum" by a dozen laughing shrieking Amazons. He got rather sick of " bossing" women after that, according to latest advices.

I have said on a preceding page that the kanaka sometimes takes back to his island home a portion of his wages if he does not spend all in extraordinary dress and victuals. He used not to do so; his custom was to invest his balance in a gun and ammunition, a good sheath-knife, and other such playful trifles, and retire to his native country, a king amongst men. The Queensland Government, with paternal solicitude, has ordered that no such playthings should now be sold to him, and consequently he takes his cash away, and exchanges it for the coveted "shooting-irons" whenever a French, Dutch, or German trader drops down on his island. The Queensland storekeepers argue at the folly of this arrangement, whereby trade is driven into foreign hands and markets, but they may argue till they are blue in the face, for the majority in the Houses is against them.

One further argument against the reported common illusage of the islanders is afforded by the fact, that after a man is out of his apprenticeship and has returned to his island, he will

---

* "Colonial experience" is equivalent to apprenticeship of the new chum.

often come back for a second dose of good victuals, housing, and clothing, instead of the banana and a palm-tree *in puris naturalibus*.

These islanders during illness undergo an extraordinary change, as already referred to, to be attributed partly to their medicine, partly to their natures. A light-hearted, merry, laughter-loving man or maid will become as sullen and sulky as a naughty boy, apparently under the impression that their friends and acquaintances underrate their sick condition. There is some excuse for these *malades imaginaires* often, for who can feel jocular or agreeable if he or she has just taken more than two-thirds of a breakfast-cup of crude castor oil, *not* the cold-drawn article! *That* is a luxury (!) for the white, who does not always carry the man-and-a-brother-theory into practice. No; crude castor oil or Epsom salts are the two, often the only, components of the planter's pharmacopœia, and the moral effect of an impending dose of either is if anything more substantial than their completed physical effect.

The worst feature of coolie-labour is the mortality. Consumption claims its annual roll of victims, and rapidly does Death aid his pallid colleague with his all-destroying sickle. They are often careless of wet, but most especially do these children of the sunny isles contract their lung complaints by coddling in a stuffy hut and burning, as they delight to do, the inevitable fire which, perhaps *unfortunately* for them, by some miracle never burns the thatched-hut down. In a township hospital near sugar-fields there is always a heavy percentage of sick kanakas.

From observation I am of opinion that many of their complaints are attributable to over-plentiful feeding on richer and more concentrated food than was their wont at home—a cause not unknown amongst more civilised communities.

In one case a couple of coolies who had intended to return home were cut off by the Reaper and taken to a longer and larger home; they were to have been much fêted on the day of their departure, but as they had by departing this life so inconveniently deprived their friends of a glorious chance for a "kick up" and a "big feed," it was unanimously resolved that on the ensuing anniversary of the day when they should consistently have been at hand to start off, a *corroborree* should be held. This expression for a feast, or rather orgie, has been borrowed from the aboriginal Australian tongue to grace the occasion. For two or three weeks before the event, ducks, pigs, sheep, fowls, and goats were arriving by twos or threes, besides a cask or so of a liquor suspiciously like whiskey, and other such trifles. Wisely they chose a Saturday evening to celebrate the sad event, for well they knew that every man and woman's duty was to put himself or herself outside as much food as the tensile accommodation of their interiors allowed. I prefer the word corroborree to their own expression " sing-sing" for applying to the scene on that Saturday evening. The blazing fires with some scores of niggers from far and near around, all busily engaged at first in eating, secondly, in drinking, thirdly, in dancing and singing, fourthly, in attempting the same operations, and lastly, in assuming a placid recumbent posture under the clear moonlit Australian sky, assisted in weird effect the awful discordant sounds that for a long time issued from their throats. Anyone by chance stumbling on such a camp would have felt quite creepy and gone away quietly, fearing to be dished up as cold "long-pig" on the sideboard. The effect of their extraordinary feed on the Saturday night was visible in their lethargic movements on Sunday, and an unusually long sick list on the Monday.

It is impossible while writing on the subject of sugar to avoid recurring to the sugar question, so if anybody has had enough of the sticky subject let him or her wipe his or her hands of it, and start on a new chapter.

If cheap labour for sugar is entirely abolished the industry will never stand in Queensland as it does now, the second industry in the colony.

It is certain that the profits of the sugar planters in the early days have been tremendous, and common report holds even now that not so many years back three good seasons would net the whole of the capital expended, *i.e.* a return of 33⅓ per cent. could be yearly made. I knew personally of a planter near Mackay who bought a place for £120,000, and the first year cleared £50,000. It is but justice to say he cleared barely half of that sum the next year, and as the markets fell in 1882, 1883, and 1884, his profits steadily decreased. Such large profits must of course be ephemeral, for such a money-winning pursuit attracts hundreds far and wide to itself, the markets are glutted, and prices fall. This has happened in Queensland; but even now, supposing cheap labour to be employed, a very fair profit may be made on a well and economically managed plantation. In 1884, near Bundaberg, a planter cleared £2,000 off land then valued with all improvements, &c., at £10,000.

But take away cheap labour and there's the rub; give the planter Hobson's choice of labour costing three or four times as much as he pays altogether to the kanaka, and his profits will be so much reduced that in a country like this, where a man thinks ten per cent. means an approach to poverty, and the bank rate itself for advances is eight or nine per cent., you cannot be surprised if he throws up the pursuit in quest of some other of the many more favourable sources of wealth to be found in this or some other colony.

In '84 a panic set in and many a fine plantation was thrown up and turned into a horse-raising or lucerne-growing station, or utterly abandoned. The planters acted in this somewhat prematurely, for coolie labour, though subject to some considerable qualifications, was still permissible. As a matter of fact, the white labourer of Queensland has driven a large amount of capital to Fiji, Borneo, Northern Territory, and the other places where cane-growing is to be carried on without so many restrictions.

One old West Indian planter advocated the importation of negroes from the British West Indies. He spoke of them as hard-working and faithful, who would come over in hundreds for fair wages and franchise as against poor living, small wages and an absence of franchise which they at present enjoy (?). Here the Government could hardly interfere, for coming as British subjects they would be entitled to liberty of ingress and egress and of the person, even to the "have-his-carcass" of old Mr. Weller.

The white labourers will never, if they can help it, permit the Singhalese or coolies of India to come in any large numbers. A few are to be seen about the plantations now, but of course in the case of their cheapening labour they will receive as little encouragement from Queensland labouring men's Governments as the kanakas are now getting. Although the white labourers cry out against the employment of coolies and so forth, they themselves are utterly unfitted to work in the burning cane-fields of the tropics, and curiously enough seem determined on killing the goose which has lain the golden eggs.

On a plantation one has many more chances of seeing neighbours than on a station, as the plantations are comparatively small and necessarily near together, occupying the alluvial flats on the sea-coast at the mouths of the rivers. Accordingly it is not, as on a station, a Herculean task to pay a call on one's neighbour, or run into the adjoining township, perhaps some eight or ten miles off. Hospitality and neighbourly feeling are much cultivated, and as soon as matters get into working order a planter's life is by no means an unhappy one. He may and often does interest himself in the education of himself or his children, or again may qualify as an amateur schoolmaster and missionary among his kanakas.

Missionary work has not so far been of great promise among these islands, though many of the planters' wives have hopefully and earnestly assisted their husbands in this direction. One parson,* who owned a plantation on the Herbert River, tried his hand at this missionary work on his own men, but

* A Church of England clergyman. Clergymen are "parsons" throughout the colonies.

though far from unsuited for his self-imposed task was forced to give up his efforts in despair, and told a would-be missionary that his efforts were fruitless, and though not absolutely harmful, at any rate negative. The whiskey-bottle, and the conduct of ordinary white men as a rule act as strong factors in the simple minds of these converts, to distract them from following up a religion which seems to have so poor an effect on its professors around and about.

A humorous story of the adaptation of the child of nature to the ways of conventionality was given me by a planter. Being on one occasion in an itinerant missionary's tent, with an attendant kanaka, he was surprised near the end of the discourse to see his "boy" slinking rapidly away. Questioned afterwards as to the reason of his conduct, he replied, "Well, massa, spose this fellow see white jelyman pass um round hat for um money, this fellow only got browny (a copper), no lily white piece money same like massa put in (sixpence); spose this fellow shamed put in browny, browny no good."

Culture, science, and art abound on the plantations, as any-one may discover for himself: the culture of cane, coffee, tea, cinchona and the like; the science of agriculture, which often, however, adopts no method ; and the so-called art (somewhat spurious) of money-making (by no means spurious). Of course there are individual cases, and more often to be found among planters than squatters, where the "boss" may be a cultured man who reads intelligently or represents his district in one of the Houses of Legislature, where the homestead may boast many of the luxuries of an English country-house with none of the vexations arising from a close proximity to the hurry and scurry of town life.

The postman comes out probably two or three times a week and leaves all the letters for a certain district at one planter's house, so the others ride in and take their own and their friends' letters. Probably news comes from Brisbane as often, so that a man on a plantation may be linked with the world if he wishes it ; not like a squatter often is, "the world forgetting by the world forgot," a state of things which sometimes suggests the poet's parody, "Himself a careless and uncared-for sot."

During autumn, winter, and spring the life is healthy enough for anybody : the evenings are cool, not frosty (sugar-cane and other tropical plants should not be touched by Jack Frost) and warm bright days that make the blood tingle in one's veins, that make one glad that there is such a thing as existence and make every one, even *malgré lui*, bless his Creator for life.

But, as in all countries where there is jungle being opened up, the wet seasons of late spring and early summer bring unhealthiness. The malaria comes with its attendant sprites of fever, ague, and dysentery, and lays folks on their backs for awhile, until their blood, overcharged with the fibrine of an excessive meat diet, has cleared and purified itself. I don't mean to say that this clearing process is always carried on successfully; sometimes the effort is too much for the sufferer, and he goes beyond the gates, but the life is generally so healthy, and open air and hard work build up such a physique, that the doctors as a rule only have to assist nature to recuperate.

If the Queenslanders in particular accustomed themselves to look less on meat as the bulk of their solid diet, and would partake of more vegetable food of all sorts, farinaceous and green, they could undoubtedly view with but little alarm the approaching wet seasons. As a rule a vegetable garden is one of the last *luxuries* the colonist thinks of establishing, except that perhaps he may, if he is on the sea-coast, grow a few sweet potatoes.

The folly of this abstinence from suitable vegetable food on the sea-coast is accentuated by the fact that all fruits of a tropical or semi-tropical character grow most luxuriantly and abundantly. A planter may (and the sensible man does) sit under his vine-shaded verandah with luscious pines, juicy guavas, grapes, loquats, Cape gooseberries, mulberries, lemons, oranges, melons, and other such fruits, all growing in his own garden with comparatively little trouble. Tradition has it that when a man plants a tree or seed he should do it cautiously as he would fire a mine, for so speedy is it when once it commences to grow that he may find himself suspended some feet from the ground, sharing the topmost branches with the flying opossums, before he can say "Jack Robinson."

These same flying opossums and flying foxes do an immense deal of harm to fruit-trees, and colonists are always communicating to one another specifics for their destruction, which turn out of little avail. They fly in regular clouds, hanging from one another when they roost, till the stout branches of trees bend and crack. They seem to be most in their element about the Clarence and Hunter rivers in New South Wales and the Moreton Bay district of Queensland.

The effect of a diet of much meat, very little bread, and fat puddings for breakfast, dinner and tea, is naturally disastrous to the tissues in such a warm climate as Queensland boasts. One of the most extraordinary features attendant on such a state of the body is a skin complaint known as the "Barcoo rot." Commencing as a pimple, the inflammation, rarely painful, extends to the size of a shilling-piece, sometimes bigger, builds up a little excrescence like a scab, which hardens, dries, and falls away, leaving a scar behind it which probably will be faintly marked all through the patient's life. As a rule colonists attach but little importance thereto, though if the scab should come on the face as well as on the arms, trunk, and legs, probably they make more fuss. The inflammation is local and seldom indulges itself to more than one or two spots at one time, except in bad cases, and is generally viewed as a healthy sign that the new chum is getting seasoned, after which he will not be troubled. This forms part of that training called colonial experience!

A common custom amongst Queenslanders when attacked with dysenterical fever is to mix a bumper of port and brandy, half-and-half, and imbibe the potent fluid. Sometimes the remedy is effectual; if the case is severe it only complicates matters, and the medical men step in and prescribe absolute fasting, a course which, prolonged for a week, reduces a man to that enviable condition when he may cheat a dun or pretend to be a second Enoch by turning edgewise to his spectators.

Medical men differ here as elsewhere, but I have heard it confidently asserted by many doctors of skill and experience that the deaths from this complaint are, with but few exceptions, avoidable by the adoption of proper remedies.

With regard to the question of health, some of the pleasantest people I came across in Queensland—a bank manager and his wife at a coastal township—had a fair bevy of children, the images of perfect health and freedom, enjoying liberty without liberties, their parents having learnt the value of experience and living according to the dictates of the climate.

As an addendum to my new chum's description of plantation life, I may say that anyone with application will do well, brains and application better, and brains and application plus capital very well, on any plantation on which he may settle. I have known men—civil servants, retired clergymen, naval and military officers and the like—men who would have " at home " resented the idea that they knew the difference between a spade and a tomahawk—acquire by perseverance and adaptation to circumstances a very tidy competency, apart from conventionality and noise, when at home they would have swelled the ranks of the poor gentility that acts such a lie to satisfy the outward requirements of the world.

Sugar has been, according to market phraseology, "very quiet" lately in Australia, but the low prices are the effect of that great inrush into sugar-cultivation some five years ago itself caused by the fabulous fortunes said to have been won in its culture.

The beet-root is being slightly cultivated for the purpose of cutting its more legitimate brother out of the market both in Victoria, Tasmania, and New Zealand, but the competition is not keen, and the evidence of the knowing ones that cane-sugar has at least thirty per cent. more sweetening power, bulk for bulk, than beet sugar, will probably for years to come keep the inferior sugar in the background.

At present the demand in Australia for sugar is by no means satisfied by the colonial supply, which has to be supplemented by Mauritius and West Indian importations, but the time must come when it will pay buyers better to get their sugar from Northern Australia than from the far-off islands of the Indian Ocean, over three thousand miles away from the most western point. With cheap labour the Queenslanders could drive any other sugars out of the Australian markets, for they are frugal and not so grasping as folk wish us to believe; without it they will turn their attention to other and better paying industries, the colonials will pay a higher price for their sugar, and a great industry will decay.

Screw Pine

CHAPTER XIX.

Alligators.—A taste for Eggs and its consequences.—The Cassowary.—Paradise-birds.—Leave-taking.—Trip southwards.—The free and easy Squatter.—Sydney Harbour by moonlight.—Railway to Melbourne.—The Murray.—A few inches of gauge-difference.—Intercolonial rivalry.—Federation.—Albury Wines.—Doctors advocate their use.—Glenrowan.—Bushrangers.—Melbourne and Civilisation with a vengeance.—Queer Hotel Customs prevalent in the World.—Diet.—Leaving Melbourne for Tasmania.

IN the preceding pages I have attempted to describe the ordinary work and life on a plantation within a degree of the tropics. The farther north one goes the more tropical the fauna and flora. The scenery near the Bellender Ker Peaks is said to be most impressive, and the bottle-tree grows within a few miles of the Burnett River, raising its curious gourd-like trunks with their magnificent heads of foliage—a startling invention of nature only reproduced in Africa.

Along the coast grows the screw pine,* which has made itself so much at home that it takes a naturalist to assure one that it is an import. Its great nuts take rank next to the Dead Sea apple as a vegetable fraud, so mellow yet so hard, so rich-looking, but as tasteless as woody fibre. Here also the bunya bunya, or *Araucaria Bidwelli*, which is acclimatised in Sydney and Melbourne, thrusts heavenwards its curious tufted spreading branches in great serried forests. The fruit or nut is edible, and is greatly in bequest among the natives, for

---

* See sketch at end of last chapter.

whose sake Government some time since enacted a law forbidding the destruction of the tree.

Long before one gets to Townsville one comes to suggestive names like Alligator Creek, Cayman Point, and so forth, indicating the inhabitants of the neighbourhood. One does not want a geography to tell one of the existence of these four-legged amphibious monsters however, for the Queensland papers not infrequently report the disappearance of a lad or a kanaka while bathing, or of some sheep or beast while drinking, pulled down by the cruel jaws of this terrific water lizard, which I have seen over twenty feet in length. Courage is a great thing in the right place, and the fearless way in which folks walked up almost within touching distance of that monster still lives in my recollection as an instance of bravery misapplied. Familiarity breeds contempt we are told in the copy-books; perhaps the contempt visible in this courageous behaviour was bred by the fact that the animal's eyes were glass, its vitals sawdust and arsenical soap, and its jaws stationary.

I proceed to narrate a story as it was told to me by an old Scotch planter, who was as veracious as the hero of the tale—the alligator—was voracious. *Verb. Sap.* On one occasion—I grieve to say a Sunday—my friend being desirous of getting some alligator's eggs for an omelette, set out in company with a friend on horseback to a notorious sandy creek near Townsville. Tying their horses up to a tree, they began their search along the beach, and in time came across fresh tracks of the cayman, with other signs showing a disturbance of the ground. They had scarcely commenced to scoop away the warm sand with their hands before they heard a great gape in the river behind them, and turning round were horrified to see the putative mother or father making towards them. No time for calculation; flight their only chance; so off they set in the direction of their horses, where one of them had a revolver. The younger called out in terror to the other, "Climb a tree or you're a dead man, the crocodile's too quick for us." The statement that an alligator is too quick for a man in good condition on a sandy beach has been questioned by some as being too *thin*, but the sooner the fact is accepted that the alligator can race with a horse and prove a worthy competitor, the better for my friend's reputation as a story-teller and the confirmation of natural history truths. At any rate they both climbed trees and were thus watched by the alligator, who like the conventional bull having treed his victim, seemed to have no business appointments to call him away. He got tired out soon, however, or perhaps Mrs. Alligator was waiting for dinner and the bell had rung; at any rate off he went, fortunately without seeing the tethered horses, who only a few yards off stood shivering and almost paralysed with terror. After giving the irate old pachyderm a few minutes' grace, the planter and his friend descended, but (and here is a strange physiological fact for physicians to study) without any further desire for alligator's eggs—a curious instance of two men simultaneously losing their appetites by climbing trees.

Besides the alligator, another remarkable creature is the cassowary, more properly though less commonly known as the "mooruk." Fortunately for the spread of science, zoological gardens familiarise every one with the sight of this handsome black and crested bird, which far outrivals its humbler brother the emu in general appearance. Besides its glossy black plumage and its neck iridescent with a hundred hues, it rejoices in having a poem dedicated to itself, in which a poor missionary is made to rhyme with it, with a view to taking "an inside seat." Presumably it is the knowledge of its poetic reputation that gives this bird its haughty air of indifference and contempt for all things not cassowary.

In the secluded forests of Northern Queensland the paradise-bird roams more at its ease than in Brisbane Botanical Gardens, but is distinctly more of a *rara avis* than in New Guinea, where it is as common as a pheasant in a preserve.

My last memory of Brisbane is that of a city in tears; a few of its fifty inches of rain were coming down that last day, and a lachrymose town even with Brisbane's clean streets is not the pleasantest feature in a campaign. Conceit, in the shape of one of our passengers, would have that the rain fell on account of *his* being on the point of leaving, whereon a practical Brisbaner gravely began to demonstrate that the meteorological office (they have them all over the colonies) had signalled a great depression, &c., &c. The man wise in his own conceit muttered something about "insensibility to poetry" and "practical humbug," but the demonstration of a well-developed biceps appertaining to the practical one speedily soothed him—a most desirable event, as it required a Mark Tapley to enjoy the trip to Sydney.

The Christmas holidays were approaching and folks were thinking of Tasmania and New Zealand, and the consequence was that our stewards told us before starting we should have to lead a Box and Cox existence so far as bunks and food were concerned, a prophecy destined to prove partially true. Fortunately for the selfishness of the seasoned ones, the weather prevented most passengers from keeping their dinner engagements on the three days' trip, for these waters, usually so quiet, were, except where protected by islands, greatly disturbed.

The free and easy manner which one of my cabin-mates, a squatter going south, displayed in using the various toilet implements of us, his fellows, was worthy of a better purpose, and was only equalled by the ingenuity displayed by ourselves in secreting any article not meant for "public circulation."

Sydney Harbour is always beautiful, and at night, under the gentle influence of chaste Luna, it presented its sweet quiet face with such a calm soothing expression that even the prosaic became poetical, the poetical qualified for the state asylums. "Queen of Australian waters," Sydney folk say of their harbour, and gaze at it when you may, unless a fog have enveloped it, its bights and bays and its heights and headlands sparkle with varied loveliness.

Unfortunately, Sydney rates cannot as yet afford to pay for a full moon all the year round, consequently the presence of a new moon may interfere with artistic expectancies. The express speed at which the colonies are going indicates that if the lunar lamp-trimmer, the old man in the moon, persists in being economical with his oil, the men of Sydney will find a substitute. Already the blazing electric light on the south head of the harbour signals out its brilliant white rays twenty and thirty miles; the matter is merely one of evolution.

The rail journey from Sydney to Melbourne is productive of little enthusiasm in the breast of the lover of scenery. Except over the range, where the usual mountain views of Australia open up, the gum-tree forest, either alive, or ring-barked and ghostly to allow the grass to grow beneath it, seems almost interminable. Houses or homesteads are, like Mr. Pecksniff's acts of charity, few and far between.

The townships that we pass through seem to be so reproductive of one another, that one cannot help thinking the rail just circles around and is passing over the same ground again. About half-way a change comes; the far-famed wine district of Albury presents itself before our eyes, and contrasts with much advantage its vine-covered slopes to the long tawny grass-plains gone before.

A meal of quite a *recherché* description is served at the station on the frontier, with accompaniments of plate, glass, &c., a pointed rebuke to many of our refreshment rooms at home. The visible border of Victoria and New South Wales here is the river Murray, about fifty feet wide and very shallow, the very infant of the great ocean river which is navigable for several hundred miles from its mouth at Lake Victoria, South Australia.

At Wodonga, the first station within the Victorian frontier, an episode takes place. We are searched for contraband and are transferred to another train. "Why the transfer?" we ask. The intelligent officials inform us that the gauge of the New South Welsh is forty-four inches wide, that of Victoria fifty-one. Was ever such inconsistency, when presumably these railways were meant to meet each other? Not so quick, my good friend. They didn't care about meeting each other so much as preventing one from stealing a march on the other by having a right of *entrée* into his neighbour's colony, and carrying off the other's produce to his capital. Victorian enterprise at first shot its lines northwards so quickly, that before Sydney knew what was going on, they had begun to tap the rich district of New South Wales called the Riverina, the trade of which, having gone so long to Melbourne, is only by degrees returning to its own metropolis.

For many years this lamentable intercolonial jealousy was further evidenced by an absence of all railway line between Albury on the New South Welsh side of the frontier and this little township of Wodonga, so that within the last few years horse conveyances had to be used to convey passengers from one terminus to the other. The raking up of bygones may appear to be unnecessary and undesirable, but *not*, it is submitted, if by so doing the still-existing jealousies may be even in some slight degree diminished, as colonials on both sides of the frontier see the petty folly of this act of jealousy, and will the more readily bring about their own approaching reform.

A Victorian minister told the writer that the primary cause of this jealousy, which is comparatively of recent existence between the mother and her bairn, lies in the fact that the bairn has made more progress and got a higher tone than her parent, having in half her mother's term of life reached a step some distance ahead of her in commerce, enterprise, prosperity, culture, and sociability. It is quite natural when the mother is always calling her bairn hard names through her press that she should receive some sharp answers; but although Victorians now may talk with amused magnanimity of this unnecessarily bitter rivalry, the New South Welsh would not, I verily believe, reciprocate the same feeling under reversed circumstances to a similar extent.

It is this feeling, that Victoria is showing her a kindness, that makes the cup of a New South Welsh press-man still more bitter. What is the way to embitter an acquaintance? says the philosopher. Why, lend him an umbrella! Their feelings have got into that hyper-sensitive state when they imagine offence where no offence is, and so make themselves and offshoot colonies unhappy.

The federation scheme has been much delayed through the cold water thrown on it by New South Wales, who declines to form a unit of the "Happy Family" because, so the other colonies assert, she did not originate the notion. Reader, pause here awhile, and note how a difference of seven inches in the gauges of two railways may bring about a learned disquisition on intercolonial rivalry.

Albury, which we have just passed through, has a vinous sound in colonial parlance. Albury wines have the best reputation, though the vignerons of Toowomba in Queensland, and Oakbank in South Australia, turn out very fair "vintages." Albury vineyards have been established longer by far than the others, and in this lies the secret of their good name, according to a Melbourne medico, who had made this a special study in its relation to his patients. He contended that no more suitable or more wholesome drink of a fermented character could be consumed by Australians than these wines, if only they were at least ten years old. As a rule, they have been in wood such a short time, and fermentation has been so partial, that they are not at all unlikely to turn sour, and partially ferment after being imbibed. I have known an abstemious man who could barely take a glass of sherry without being much put out of condition, drink a whole bottle of Hermitage, Sauvignon, and the like, with no apparent deleterious effect.

The ageing of these wines will be for a time-to-come a stumbling block in the grower's way. In Australia capital and labour are expected to make immediate returns, and to have to wait ten or twelve years for such a *præmium laboris* is almost too much for any vigneron's patience. In the chief cities one can have a small bottle for a shilling and a glass for a few pence, but even at this price it is astonishing how those unsuitable fiery spirits and heavy beers maintain their claim on the confidence of the population. Colonial beer is more often spoken of than drunk; why I know not, for they have the best opportunities for brewing light tonic ales similar to those German beers of which Herr Nasekopf can drink a score of "bocks" of an evening without feeling any the worse.

Beyond Wodonga pastoral country again asserts itself. The iron road passes over mile after mile of waving grassy plains, where the bush or forest stands in its original condition or has been thinned. To the east lie the intensely blue hills which form the spur of the Australian vertebra, the Dividing Range. Homesteads when seen are made a note of; life is evidenced by sheep and little else. Comparatively few beasts graze on these pastures; sheep pay better down here, and who would have his broad acres encumbered with the common or garden cow when he may himself "boss" some tens of thousands of tweed-producing quadrupeds?

At Glenrowan, which we pass on our way, old chums riding in the carriage become enthusiastic on the bushranging gang who were hunted down here.

"There!" says one as we glide along; "see yon verandahed house standing in its garden; that house stands on the site of the shanty where the Kelly gang were caught."

It was a festive time, according to all accounts, for the citizens of the township. Surprised in the midst of their revelry by a posse of constabulary, the bushrangers barricaded the house and fought desperately for dear life. Finding finally that things were becoming too hot for them, the leader, Ned Kelly, on the homœopathic principle, is said to have fired the wooden house, and in the confusion tried unsuccessfully to escape, leaving behind him his living and dead companions, the former to be hung, the latter to be involuntarily cremated. One feels quite an additional respect for a colony that can boast such a romance, particularly in that it occurred so recently as in June, 1880. This gang is officially announced to have cost the colony £50,000 from beginning to end.

Queensland, too, has had its bushrangers, one, a Scotchman, having within the last few years disturbed quiet respectable folk with the usual order of "Bail up!" But he was quite a respectable, almost a virtuous robber, for he never once took a human life, and seems to have retired from the profession when he had made enough to settle quietly down in the tavern up-country of which he is now the guiding star.

Let those who boast about the good old times remember the brave "broths of boys" who would suddenly "bail up" the travelling coach or "stick up" a station, running off with whatever they thought fit as portable booty; for my part the pleasures of a life in Australia appear by no means diminished because the chances of dying in your own bed are more even, and because there is no fear of becoming a target for the well-aimed bullets of the rowdies of those early days.

Jack Sheppard the highwayman is a very romantic and picturesque creature when seen through the leaves of a yellow-back or a penny dreadful; but "Old Mike," with his unerring deringer aimed at your wife while his comrades bind you and carry off your portable goods and chattels, when seen through a normal atmosphere at the distance of three feet, is by no means so picturesque. The old aphorism of theory and practice makes all the difference in such matters. All honour then to the colonies that have thus, at any rate for the present, stamped out a pest from their midst which, on account of the breadth of the country, the connivance of their confederates, and the thinness of the population, was, and may be again, so difficult to cope with. Every respectable squatter, selector, or planter, who now lands in the colonies adds an additional nail to the many already in the coffin of this scourge, not soon to be forgotten, and, it is fervently to be hoped, never again to raise its cruel head.

After passing Glenrowan the country again becomes uninteresting to the artist, though attractive to the selector. Vast plains of the waving tawny grasses, shaded by gaunt gum-trees and bordered by the intense blue hills—plains which at the present time are wholly used for growing wool—stretch down to the vicinity of Melbourne.

At Melbourne the usual famine of porters—a seventy-seven years famine apparently—prevails, so if one is lucky enough to be met by friends their kindly services as amateur porters should be enlisted.

The flood-tide of civilisation after our journey southwards sets in when, seated around the classic board where once the Speaker of the House of Assembly gave his well-remembered dinners, a member of the household, species homo, genus mas, ætat 4, exclaims in a hoarse whisper after sad contemplation of the empty egg-stand and the wreck on the visitor's plate, "I say, Mar!" "Well, my dear." "Why, Mar, Mr. Clarke has eaten up all the eggs." Denouement! another child sacrificed on the altar of conventionality.

I purpose now personally guiding the patient footsteps of my readers to the adjacent island of Tasmania, separated from the mainland by Bass's Straits, dangerous for navigation, wide though they be; but before doing so I wish to enter a protest against a practice widely indulged in throughout the colonies at the hotels. That the same course is adopted in the old country in many first-class hotels is no defence, for there as elsewhere the hotel proprietors have their own interests to look after, which are not *always* identical with those of their lay brethren.

I refer to the principle of paying at an hotel so much per diem whether a visitor be a fixture or a movable. The custom to a member of the general public appears not only unjust but ridiculous. Why Jones should help to pay for Smith's or Robinson's dinner or lunch when Jones is perhaps dining or lunching away from the hotel, simply because he lodges under the same roof as Smith or Robinson, is a matter which Jones cannot see the sense of, and which does not affect Robinson or Smith so much as the host's annual income.

The coffee palaces, which in most parts of the colonies rear their massive stone fronts and point a finger of scorn at their bibulous licensed brethren, do not adopt this custom; but there every man gets his quid pro quo, or pays his "*quid* pro quo habeat." But then, except in fashionable Melbourne, the residential portion of a coffee palace is not of the most luxurious type—a matter of importance to many folk when travelling around.

Another curious subject to notice in the hotel management of the colonies is, that owing to various causes often to be traced to the host's pocket, you may find the sum of half-a-crown will both supply you with a banquet that does the cook and her patrons credit, with the accompaniments of plate, glass, flowers, &c., around you, and will also be charged you for any meal you may have at a "bush" tavern with stockmen, coach-drivers, and shepherds around, all intent on putting themselves outside some tough mutton or salt beef, which not improbably each man has to cut with his own knife, followed mayhap with a pasty (very much so) containing those apple chips whose presence tides over many a difficulty in the bush menu.

I have known meat up-country so tough that the diners found a relief in the occasional mastication of a skewer, and as for bread you may likewise have it of all sorts. There are some loaves which to this day rise up in judgment against me and sit heavy on my conscience whenever I think of the golden opinions and large consumption their lightness and good flavour won for them; but, on the other hand, there are some which never will rise anywhere not with half a pound of dynamite under them, and as for sitting heavily they were content to leave one's conscience alone and locate themselves on a more material portion of the human organisation.

My purpose in discussing diet is deep-laid, so that our sensitive nostrils as the good ship swings away from the docks at Williamstown and stirs up the deep-laid mud of the Yarra may not affect our equilibrium. 'Tis a flat and unlovely river down below here, as bad as the Thames at its most uninteresting points below bridge, without its width or depth. The town with its chief buildings fades back into the gathering gloaming, the lights on the river shine up, and merrily we steer across Port Philip by its deep-water channel. The pilot says that it's blowing a stiff breeze outside, so discretion being the better part of valour, and sea-legs after a long course of horse-legs being articles more sought after than attained, the chapter closes on the usual preparations for a sleep.

A fallen Giant.

CHAPTER XX.

Bass's Straits.—A Double Signification.—The Tamar.—The Boat walks ashore.—The Cabman and his Wiles.—The Sweetbriar, its Poetry and Prose.—Launceston.—Its Appearance.—The Devil's Punch Bowl.—The Falls of the Esk.—The Band.—The Wild Beasts of the Bush.—The Convict Curse.—The Railway.—Jericho and Jerusalem.—Consequences of Joking.—Nomenclature again.—New Norfolk.—Hell Gates.—Salmon.—Ladies to the Fore.—Hobart Lasses.—Hobart Town.—The great Gums on the Huon Road.—Mt. Wellington.—Jam-making.—Fruit-growing.—The Cow in the Streets.—Government House.—Houses of Legislature a Barrack.—Tasmanian Progress: does it exist?—Immigration.—Mining Industries.—Wheat.—Agriculture.—The Prisoner at the Australian Bar pleads Not Guilty.—The Australian "Case."—Climate.—Great Expectations.

"THE voyage from Melbourne to Tasmania should be a terror to teetotallers," said a white-haired wag referring to the Bass's liquor that flows through these straits, but as a matter of fact those who do quaff the flowing bowl enjoy no special immunity from disturbance while crossing to this Switzerland of the South as it is often, but erroneously, called, what with the eddying current that washes through Port Philip Heads, and the varying breezes that blow, now with antarctic chill or ocean strength, through this channel of a hundred and fifty miles in width. However, everything comes to him who waits, even that much over-worked and abused creature the steward, and what with his sympathy and the enterprise of the Tasmanian Steamship Company, with their well-appointed and swift steamboats, the twenty hours from Melbourne to Launceston somehow take wings to themselves.

Four hours before reaching this charming township we "make" the mouth of the river Tamar on which it is built, in the county of Devonshire, Tasmania. The consistency with which the old country nomenclature has been adopted cannot blind one's eyes to the fact that it is an Australian river that sparkles in the early morning sun, broad with frequent shoals where our steamer sometimes touches; its banks, at first thickly wooded to the water's edge, receding in low hills on either side; in the extreme distance, a higher range of mountains sombre and blue against the clear sky. Before the forty miles of river are navigated, however, the woods and forest give place before cultivated corn-fields and grassy paddocks hedged in with gorse, sweetbriar, or hawthorn—a thoroughly English bit of scenery is this immediately around Launceston.

A sharp curve in the winding stream, skilfully negotiated, opens up the red-roofed town before us, picturesquely clambering up the hills around, looking with its timbered gardens rather like a straggling Torquay. Our entrée into the town is by no means dignified; first the boat has to turn such a sharp curve that its bows are run aground on the mud and grassy bank, while its stern is towed round and backed into its berth; secondly, an enterprising jarvey, with more cuteness than honesty, seduces a friend and myself to commit ourselves and baggage to his waggonette, which we find, on preparing to carry out the contract, already laden with three passengers and about twenty packages of assorted sizes and weights.

'Tis not an uncommon custom in the colonies, where the demand for vehicular accommodation exceeds the supply, for a cabman to adopt this *multum in parvo* principle. Let not the new chum object, rather let him admire the pertinacity with which the driver loads up his charges and parcels, the patience he displays when, as they often will do, they fall off again on the *near* side while he is engaged on the *off*, and the skill he eventually displays in himself mounting his triumphal car, and from that lofty eminence guiding the career of his steeds. The Jehu generally has the worst of it; the waggonette is built to stand these trials, and one's fellow-passengers generally prove worth knowing.

The town itself appears quiet after Melbourne, *a fortiori* after Sydney, nevertheless the tramcars and omnibuses, the shops and stores, betoken activity and enterprise.

Within easy reach of the town are many remarkably fine pieces of scenery; their wild grandeur serves as a foil to the quiet pastoral appearance of the sloping fields and hawthorns and flowering sweetbriars around. The sweetbriar grows so rapidly and thickly that its blossoms give a bright warm tinge to the landscape, but the prosaic graziers and farmers, find it becoming a nuisance, as when once established it encroaches year by year on the fields and paddocks. Climbing one of the hills which shelter this Torquay of the South nestling in the valley below, passing mansions built for retired squatters and others, in the solid Jacobean, Elizabethan, or the revived Queen Anne style, themselves embosomed in gardens of English flowers and trees, our way takes us through a wild patch of fern and scrub to a weird chasm of water-worn rocks where a purling stream leaps innocently away from the stern boulders and many-coloured cliffs to vanish in fine rainbow-hued spray amongst the tree-tops far below.

Here one notices a remarkable difference in the climatic influences of the country from those of Australia generally. The rocks are beautifully clothed in lichens and mosses of a thousand tints and hues. The extraordinary beauty, after a few years in this country, of a piece of old rock or post-and-rail fence, taxes the resources of an artist's colour-box to its limits.

All over the world the "old gentleman" is supposed to be fond of punch, milk or otherwise; so here, this rocky chasm, with its forest-covered arena opening up far away to the distant hills, is called the Devil's Punch-Bowl.

At the other end of the town, the North Esk,* a tributary of the Tamar, rushes with the roar of the waterfall of Lodore over

* The North Esk and South Esk combine just below the town to form the Tamar.

a rocky ledge, and runs through a precipitous gorge whose only defect in an artistic sense is the fact that it is bridged, though the bridge itself is not, as such erections often are, inconsistently ugly. The slowly grinding water-mill with its wooden shutes conveying a stream from the falls above, the brewery hard-by, and the cottages with their cottage-gardens, are remarkable reproductions of English scenery such as one hardly expects to find in such altered circumstances.

The falls of the river at Cora Lynn are fine, though not rejoicing in any remarkably distinctive Australian features.

The thirteen thousand men, women, and children who form the population of Launceston are justly proud of their pleasantly situated town and the surrounding scenery; and I should advise anyone who desires adversely to criticise colonial scenery or institutions to do so at a safe distance on paper, and not to act like an Englishman I met while travelling in Tasmania, who, in and out of occasion, gave colonials (whether muscular or not) sharp raps over the knuckles, often undeserved and sometimes of questionable taste. How he ever reached home alive will ever remain a mystery. But the fact, if anything, proves the tolerance of his audience.

"Gay Lutherians" in Launceston urge a "new chum" to visit the illuminated public gardens at night, where the band is said to discourse sweet music. Experience teaches that three or four coloured lamps may make an illumination, and that a discourse of sweet music may often resemble a discord so closely that to an unrefined ear it may appear a synonym.

Mount Barrow, 4,644 feet high, one of the loftiest mountains in Tasmania, stands thickly wooded, but rarely visited, some twelve miles distant from the town. On all sides one can get into the primeval bush within a few miles, though it contains to a globe-trotter little of interest except snakes, of which perhaps the most venomous in Australia are denizens of this little island.

The tiger-wolf and the "native devil" are to be seen by penetrating still farther into the long mountainous ranges of the interior, but the stride of civilisation is making them both look foolish. The first, an omnivorous and therefore carnivorous marsupial, is about the size of a wolf, but higher on its legs, and handsomely marked with tiger-like stripes on its back and hind quarters. It shares the bad character of the stage policeman of liking mutton, but for reasons best known to itself, samples a good many sheep before it settles on a good joint for dinner. Its smaller *confrère* has developed a taste for poultry which rather annoys the confiding settler, who, knowing himself out of the land of Reynard, hugs himself in fancied security.

Here, in the river bights and bays, one may and does suddenly come across that duck-billed *platypus* or *ornithorhyncus*, whose heavily sounding name has crushed what little rotundity its body ever possessed and made it the laughing-stock of all other animals, birds, and fishes. Amphibious, with four feet, and a flattened badger-shaped body, however the poor animal, fish, or bird has managed to prove the exception to the rule of the survival of the fittest and preserved its duck's bill, will remain a mystery to ordinary mortals until the millenium. This curious little animal is found in Australia especially around the Murrumbidgee, according to Mr. Bennett the naturalist, but I could find no record of its having been seen lately, so conclude that it does not affect the habits of civilisation. The new chum may be contemptuous of this little animal's power of defence or offence, but on high Tasmanian authority I learnt that in its fore paws it carries claws perforated with poison-ducts, and that more than one colonist has been severely injured by its venom. This is the only animal in Tasmania which has no pouch wherein to place its young, all the other animals being marsupials.

Launceston began to weep a few of its thirty inches of rain on the day of our departure, which so conciliated our caustic critic that he made great haste to run away before a recurring day of sunshine should give his eyes and tongue free scope. If Launceston on a fine day resembles Torquay, it appears but as a first cousin once removed on a drizzling day.

Y

It is connected with Hobart by road and rail, the first of pathetic interest, the second likewise. This high-road across the island, itself somewhat over a hundred miles in extent, was built, old settlers say, every hundred yards at the cost of a man's life. The stories of convict labour still told by gray-headed sires are of the most harrowing description.

One cannot help feeling some pity when hearing of hardened villains either dying under the lash or heat of the sun, or risking the still more fearful deaths of starvation or cannibalism by attempted escape; but when, as we now know to be the case, many of these wretched convicts were transported innocent of offence, or guilty of such offences as now would merit a fine or a few days in gaol, one's blood begins to curdle. Although abolished as far back as 1853, the curse still hangs over the country, and its slow progress in comparison with its younger sister, Victoria, is notorious.

The railway has its pathetic interest too. After leaving behind the meads and cornfields of Launceston, the line pierces first, flat uninteresting bush and scrub, then hills covered with the interminable gum-tree to the summit, with, at rare intervals, cleared and cultivated patches in the valleys which look like mere dots in the vast receding sombre gorges. We speed along, now round spur and crag, now laboriously climbing an incline, now running down the other side, through a land where nature appears so much to have resented the puny efforts of man to change her face, that she has already planted her flowers all along the line, and covered the fences with exquisite hanging lichens. We pass through Cornwall, thence into Somerset, where, to our astonishment, we find another landmark of early youth ruthlessly destroyed. Jericho, a township of two or three wooden buildings, a saw-mill or two, and the inevitable hotel, hardly does justice to the city which required to be encompassed seven times. Its men of war, its turrets, its flags, all were absent, and as we left the station and stationmaster perplexed with our questions, which proved his blissful ignorance of the old story, we shed a tear on this new and authorised version that had to replace the romantic tale of earlier years. A traveller, whose identity was lost in the excitement of the moment, suggested that perhaps the Hebrews *meant a lot* by going round the *allotment* so many times, but there is no record that any one present in the Pullman car received any consolation thereby.

After finding that Jericho was in Somerset, my readers can more easily imagine than this pen describe our dissatisfaction on finding Jerusalem a small mining town famous for coal in the county of Monmouth.

Seriously speaking, if indeed one can speak seriously on such a ludicrous subject, in Australian nomenclature there is a vast deal of inappropriate and confusing naming of the places in particular, and all things in general. Some dismiss the matter by saying "We are in the land of topsy-turvydom." What think you? Many towns are called after Australian governors, explorers, hotel-keepers, and other such *grandees*. So far so good; again, no great confusion is caused by borrowing once in a way the names of the old country intact. But when every colony has its Salisbury, Richmond, or Brighton, where there are two Gregory rivers in one colony, and so forth, the traveller is being continually deceived and imagines himself anywhere but where he really is, and confusion in postal arrangements is more than confounded. It is but a poor compliment to the inventive genius of the Anglo-Saxon race that this is so; and not only is this repetition of old-country terms conspicuous in local nomenclature, but also in that of the fauna and flora of Australia, especially the latter. Colonial indigenous, "cherry-trees," "plum-trees," "apple-trees," "daisies," &c., to the unimaginative mind, unfortified by spirits of the vasty deep, or any other sort, bear but little resemblance to their old-world prototypes, and the impartial critic has often to remark that both the native plants and their so-called prototypes lose by their nominal resemblance.

About twenty miles before reaching the delightfully picturesque town of Hobart, the railroad and roadway together strike the Derwent River. Within ten miles there is a place called New Norfolk, where hop-gardens and sweet-briars vie with the native flora in the broad meads and wooded hills through which the river meanders. A view up the valley discloses a charming vista of blue ranges, softening off into the distance. Down below the pent-up waters of the river boil and roar, choked up by massive beetling grey cliffs, called somewhat appropriately "Hell-Gates." The ten-mile drive from the railway station by the flowing stream, between sweet-briar and hawthorn hedges, past the odorific gum or the sweetly-smelling acacia (the wattle of colonists) which overhang the road, without any other allurements, is a sufficient advertisement of "what to expect."

Close by are the salmon-ponds, where the finny pupil is cared for and brought up by an efficient staff of nurses, but only as a rule to disappear and never turn up again when placed in the waters of the Derwent. He keeps his reasons for his unsociability to himself, but so far they have found so little echoing sentiment in the breasts of the Government that a premium of £5 has been offered to the first man who actually catches a salmon. On the other hand, trout are rapidly making themselves at home in all Tasmanian waters, and will soon prove worthy rivals of the native fish.

Hobart itself earned an enviable notoriety in the early days for the number of pretty girls it contained, who, common rumour used to say, were to the male sex in the proportion of three to one.* If a stranger of gender male, *ætat* over ten or out of long clothes, were seen in the streets, rumour used to assert that half a dozen windows would be thrown open, and the cry be passed on: "A man! a man!" This golden age has given place to a decidedly bronze one, wherein the males exceed the females, as they do throughout Australasia, though here the disproportion is not so great as in the other colonies. In consequence of this degenerate state of things, visitors

* The gold-fields of the continent attracted 46,000 persons, almost if not entirely all males, during the three years succeeding 1854.

cannot expect a triumphant entry on a car drawn by Hobart girls, as the fancy of up-country bushmen used to anticipate.

Truths are stubborn things, and you may, notwithstanding the reputed beauty of Hobart belles, see as many in Melbourne or the old country. The climate is more gracious to the complexion than that of Melbourne, however, and of pretty, fresh-looking plump mammas and their daughters Hobart can boast a greater proportion than her larger sister. I remember a student of sexes saying that even after he had acquired his degree in old chumism, the nicest-looking colonial girls he knew turned out to have arrived but a short twelve months before from England.

At Hobart, fortunately for the mental development of both sexes, there is less incentive for a lady to "do the block" (equivalent to Regent Street parade). They possess a sufficiently high tone and healthy common sense to spurn the low ambition of being milliners' models or circulating library supporters, the final end and aim of many a Melbourne and Sydney lass. Hobart does not really possess a "block" to be "done." Though its shops are many and good, they are not of that pretentious style affected by Melbourne or Sydney "emporia," nor do their frequenters parade up and down in front, but act in business-like manner and walk inside. The climate being less enervating gives a healthier tone, and a taste for the exercise of mind and body.

Hobart, indeed, prides herself on being the home of Australian society, "culchah," music, and art. What are her pretensions to the latter virtues man knoweth not, as she has no public picture galleries, and has not such a fine organ or concert-room as Melbourne. Australian society has, indeed, begun to move and have its being in this sanatorium of the south, where the enervated mind and body of the Melbourne merchant may be braced up and turned out as good as new. With her public free library well furnished with an olla podrida of literature, Hobart certainly has made a move in the direction of education and culture which her utilitarian sister the capital of Queensland may do well to copy.

Tasmanians consider the influx of wealthy residents settling down to spend their lives and money among placid scenes and in an equable climate as one of the greatest blessings in store for the country. The fickle goddess has not sent her satellite—Prosperity—too often to Tasmanian shores, until within the last few years, so that the settlement amongst them of substantial men, with money to spend and not to make, has come as a species of godsend to the gentle Hobartians.

Mt Wellington (from Hobart)

The town stretches back far from the docks and piers on the Derwent along the gently sloping grounds that culminate in Mount Wellington—its big guardian to the West, whose gum-covered slopes and clear-cut precipitous "organ-pipes" help the hills on the north and east, over the river, to shelter it. The Derwent is here a broad tidal piece of water rather than a river, of a Mediterranean blue under congenial circumstances, and the gum-tree retrieves its much-abused name as an ornamental plant by growing on these slopes to a tremendous size. One reads about these great trees on the Huon Road, but there are astonishingly few people in Hobart itself who know where two of the largest giants are; but even though one were never to happen across these Goliaths, the road thither—this same Huon Road—affords a unique feast for the eyes. Cut through the dense bush, it now plunges in amid a wealth of fern-trees and gums, now emerges again and shows, framed between massive gums two and three hundred feet high, vistas of the blue Pacific rolling twenty miles to the southward, a sea of gum-

Gums: View from the Huon Road.

trees in between; round sharp curves, where our horses cut at right angles to the coach; over deep gullies full of ferns of all sorts, from the stately tree of thirty feet in height to the diminutive lomaria; with the ofttimes snow-covered crest of Mount Wellington on our right.

In winter the scene is even more beautiful, for snow sometimes lies on the road up at this elevation, to some depth, and the fern-trees and gums get clothed for a short time with thin fairy-like prisms of ice, which sparkle in the light. After a drive of about four miles the coach passes a gully, called *par excellence* the Fern-tree Gully, though, except that the torrent which supplies Hobart with the raw material gurgles down, this glen has less to call for attention than many another wilder gully less frequented by the Hobart Harry and Harriet.

Six miles beyond this gully, after passing a small accomodation-house, a scramble up the hillside for a few yards brings one to the trunks of some of the tallest trees that ever crushed the soil with their massive weight. The largest, called the Lady Franklin Tree, is not "all there." Her ladyship fell down in one of the violent storms to which these hills are no strangers many years ago, and was so damaged by her *lapsus arboris* that all the Queen's horses and men could but make patchwork of her if they tried to restore her. The whole of the head of this tree has been burnt at some past date, but from the portion remaining her length is estimated at four hundred and eighty feet; nor is the estimation *over* the mark, for there are younger brothers and sisters of hers all around who bid fair when they have filled out their trunks to the same diametrical proportions to be as high, if not higher, than this their fallen relative. When one gazes at the tremendous thickness of the two portions snapped off like matchwood by her fall down the hill, one shudders at the idea of the fearful crash as she levelled all other trees within her reach, and, like Samson, wrought destruction in her death. Tree-ferns grow around and cover up some of those unsightly scars which the frequent bush fires have left in her sides; and close by, fallen amid a wreath of similar foliage, is another huge giant, a fitting colleague for his lady friend below. There is a ricketty seat on a projecting root, some twenty or thirty feet from the ground, which gives to the adventurer mounted on this unsteady pinnacle some idea of the size of this giant.*

Like the sequoia of the Mariposa Grove in America, the tufts

---

* The root-end of this tree is sketched at end of Chapter XIX.

of foliage at the summit of these giant, cold-grey trunks look very disproportionate, and, so far as these trees are concerned, the gums, although they exceed them in height, have to take second place on the score of diameter. In Gippsland there is said to be one tree over five hundred and twenty feet in height, according to surveyor's measurement, which in common with these giants in Tasmania, cleaves the higher reaches of the atmosphere with a trunk as straight as a die. The diameter of "Lady Franklin's" waist is about twenty to twenty-five feet—pretty considerable for her time of life, growing as she has been for centuries; but were a tape taken right round the boles and bumps, lumps and gnarls, where the tree joins the ground, or rather used to when she occupied a perpendicular position, the reel would probably run out the hundred feet which she is said to measure in circumference.

The ascent of Mount Wellington is not unattended by danger, for mists are as common on the top as "misses" at the base—a parallel not exactly perfect, as the embrace of the mists is a most unpleasant one, particularly if one be near the organ-pipes, a series of precipitous rocks, shown in the plate, which form a perpendicular face some hundreds of feet in depth on the north-east side of the mountain top. Another striking feature in the ascent of this mountain is a plain of boulders and rocks, as though Jason's giants had been heaving stones at one another, but the latitude and comparatively low elevation (very little over four thousand feet) of the summit rarely gives the mountain, except in winter, the Alpine look that some writers claim for it.

To call Tasmania the Switzerland of the South Pole would appear to be an error of speech. Where are the snow-peaks, the glaciers, and the glacial valleys which are such distinguishing mark of the Alps? where the mountain-pastures and the smiling valleys? In the vicinity of towns, it is true, the hand of man is opening up the bush and gradually reducing the heavy burden of interminable forest, but these patches of cultivation are as small islands in the ocean of gums. It is true that in the centre of the island there is a large plateau of grazing country, but this does not of itself constitute a Switzerland; rather should I say that Tasmania resembles the Austrian Tyrol.

In the vicinity of Hobart fruit-growing is carried on to a very large extent. All English fruits thrive well and ripen splendidly in a climate whose mean temperature is 54° Fahrenheit, the winter mean being 47°, with a minimum on rare occasions of three degrees of frost. A man need not go outside Hobart to learn these facts concerning fruit; his nose and palate will tell him all the year round that he is near large fruit-growing areas. Some say Tasmanian fruits surpass their English brethren; the average, however, does not, as already the codlin-moth and other blights have proved the fruit-farmer's bane and lessened his profits and quality. As at home, too little care is taken to prevent these pests until they have taken a tight hold of a district, and consequently the codlin-moth has become such a pest that New Zealand at one time forbade the importation from Tasmania of any apples, and the Tasmanian Government has had to take the matter up.

During the season when Hobart is turning out those jams for which she is so deservedly famous in the colonies, even the visitor becomes an expert in detecting what particular "brew" is being manufactured at the factories. An all-pervading scent of raspberry jam throughout Hobart is an additional attraction to this quiet retreat. The fruit grows sometimes so thickly on the trees that much is allowed to drop unpicked—a state of matters rather encouraged than otherwise by the dear state of the labour market and the protective tariffs of other colonies, which levy duty on Tasmanian imported fruits and fruit-pulp. While Tasmania is thus glutted with the choicest apples, pears, plums, strawberries, cherries, and the other English fruits she grows, residents on the adjoining continent, tired of the routine of peaches, oranges, grapes, mulberries, passion fruit, melons, and so on, hunger and thirst after this overflow.

To add to the misfortunes of Tasmanian fruit-growers, a ring of fruit-brokers surrounds the export market of Hobart, which greedily decreases by a large percentage the fruit-growers' profits. The remedy is obviously for the fruit-growers to associate and to deal without middlemen, a proceeding which though oft discussed seems as far from actual application as ever. Even under these circumstances, men, although unskilled in farming, can make a fair income out of a few acres of orchard, as Tasmanian apples and pears, more especially the former, find ready consumers from Melbourne to York Peninsula, from Sydney to Perth.

A friend in Hobart—an ex-business man from the Hub-of-the-Universe—managed, with the assistance of his younger children as fruit-pickers, to lead a varied and healthful life, to see his wife and young ones happy ornaments of his household, and to save every year an income which, though not in Australian eyes large, must appear to an English farmer who rather expects a loss than a gain, a very fortune.

Only the other day news came from the colonies that Tasmania and Victoria were coming to an understanding whereby mutual free-trade with regard to fruits should be adopted, so that this industry is now looking up. It is an important one for Tasmania, as she is eminently suited, from climate and character, to be the orchard and garden of the other Australian colonies, in whose uncertain seasons and enervating summers English fruits languish, and though often grown, do not come to perfection except in isolated localities.

That Hobart is quiet and rural although it possesses over twenty-one thousand inhabitants, anyone may guess when, as I have frequently seen, he meets milch kine wandering at free will down the High Street, undisturbed by the occasional van, bus, or cab. But for all that, few could choose a pleasanter spot to which to retire, there to spend their fortunes in peace and quietness; for the repose of the surrounding scenery, the heathiness of the climate, and the well known hospitality and kindliness of the inhabitants combine to render life as near a paradise as Australasia can afford.

Then again, the Domain with its cricket-grounds touches the end of the principal street on the one side, and the Botanical Gardens and Government House in their midst on the other. As a residence of an Australian governor, this is perhaps the most comfortable as it certainly is the most picturesque, embosomed as it is in the flowers and foliage all around, with the blue Derwent at the bottom of the grounds and the distant background of Mount Direction and Mount Dromedary. The Governor, although ruling the smallest of these colonies, gets an income of £3,500, being in this respect seventh in the list of the eight Australasian Governors. While the Government House is thus noteworthy, the houses of Legislature on the

Government House Hobart

other hand are no credit to the colony; they form portions of a building eminently suited by its architecture and position to be a custom-house, but not a place where the weighty matters of State are discussed. The Lower House, a large room, as for a debating society, with even scant accommodation for the thirty-two members it seats, and with no decoration, artistic or otherwise, is perhaps a trifle plainer than the Upper House, which happens to have carved wooden seats and some decorations in the way of cornice and wainscot, and although only requiring accommodation for sixteen members, is yet double the size of the other. One is astonished in a democratic country to find the Lower House, which as a rule bears the heat and burden of the day, so poorly housed, an astonishment not altogether, though somewhat, reduced by the information that Parliament only sits two or three months in the year.

The Legislative Council is chosen for six years by the aristocracy, landed and professional, while the Lower House, being elected by £7 householders or feeholders, sits for five years. Latterly Tasmanian legislators have been agitating their minds on the payment-for-services question, but so far as experience goes the matter is a very ticklish one, as payment of members offers an aim to penniless adventurers not altogether conducive to the public good.

Tasmanian progress has been more than once adverted to in the preceding pages; it is a subject fraught with interest to all Englishmen. The other colonies go ahead, thrive, increase, and multiply exceedingly, whereas Tasmania seems to an Australian, if not retrogressive, at any rate stationary. The convict curse has been referred to, but does not altogether account for the extraordinary fact that so few Englishmen come to this island (although bribed with free grants of land), which has the climate and conditions most similar to those of the old country.

One of the many reasons for this apparent want of progress undoubtedly is that Tasmania has hitherto had a bad name. Her mining industries, tin and gold, have been reported as not very flourishing; and although there is a considerable tract, of country grazed by sheep and cattle, there are vast tracts on the other hand, in the interior, where the cockatoo and the wallaby can thrive, but the sheep or bullock must starve. For many years, too, until recently, she received no fresh infusion of blood, and her sons left her for the more prosperous mines and wider plains of the adjoining continent.

Assisted immigration has done something to remedy this evil, but even on this point Tasmanians pull long faces, for say they, "We import at some expense farm-labourers and their families, who eventually leave the lonely country and take up some town industry, so we are no nearer the solution of the agricultural difficulty than before."

In 1884 a serious feeling prevailed in the colony that immigration should no longer be assisted, as colonials were confident that the matter would right itself. One would certainly have imagined that the authorities, by taking proper precautions on the other side of the globe, could have secured the proper men for their identical wants. Hitherto, however, Crown grants of land gratis to every would-be settler are promised and given, but when a man sees the heavy bush he often has first to clear, although far from desirous of looking a gift-horse in the mouth, he may well hesitate at spending so much time and labour before even he can fence in his paddocks and grow his first crops.

The tin mines of Mount Bischoff have a large area, and are certainly in a flourishing condition, if one may judge by the fact that the five-pound shares of the company, of which only a quarter has been paid up, have fetched quite recently ten times their nominal value in Launceston, where the ore is smelted in a somewhat *al fresco* style, much simpler than any-one who has heard of the Tasmanian tin mines would imagine. The gold-fields of this colony have an astonishingly small repute in the colonies, and the two or three millions sterling that these have in the aggregate produced pale in insignificance before the two hundred millions that Victoria has exported since '51.

As a wheat-growing country Tasmania stands second of all the colonies (being next after New Zealand), in the proportion, that is, of the number of bushels to the acre, and is considerably above United States average. According to statistics the acreage of all wheat-growing colonies—and these include New Zealand, Victoria, Queensland, New South Wales, and South Australia, as well as Tasmania—has been rapidly diminishing, a fact most surely due, as in all new countries, to the exhaustion of the soil by improvident settlers, who wring it of all its resources in one direction, trusting to their being able when the land is too poor to throw it up and seek fresh country. The mysteries of artificial manures and "rotation of crops" are too deep for a layman's understanding, but it is obvious that you cannot be continually withdrawing and never replacing without finally finding your land of as little use as the Irishman's stocking, "a footless thing without a leg."

Some portions of New Zealand are said to grow sixty to seventy bushels to the acre, and even more, and the *average* has been placed as high as forty, but recent statistics (that dreary science!) show that the average yield should be rather taken at thirty, whilst Tasmania is not even of age with her twenty, and South Australia hardly out of long clothes and pinafores with eight, but in quantity this latter colony grows by far the most wheat grown in Australia.*

We are so accustomed in the old country to associate rural work with agriculture, that the two terms have become fairly synonymous and interchangeable in such phrases as "agricultural outlook," "agricultural interests," &c. ; but in Australia, where vast acreages are held entirely for grazing, the terms pastoral and agricultural are strictly opposed, with defined and distinct meanings in ordinary, not merely technical, conversation. A "new chum" cannot at first get out of the way of speaking of *rural* interests as *agricultural*, a term which has a very limited meaning in rural Victoria and her mother and sister colonies, where there is comparatively little agriculture, but so much of the pastoral interest.

Talking of rural matters reminds me that colonial friends at home and in the colonies object that Englishmen do not sufficiently praise Tasmanian or Australian scenery, especially Tasmanian, which many writers seem to lose their heads over; and where the scenery is praised it is because of some real or fancied resemblance to that of the old country. In common with other Englishmen, I would stoutly deny the truth of the accusation. When one has taken a series of sketches of places, that is (as the writer has often done), when one has been

---

* Authorities differ. Some place New Zealand at 26, Tasmania at 16, New South Wales at 15, Victoria at 14, South Australia at 8, Queensland at 4.

stationary for hours together, watching and noting down to the best of an amateur's ability, the features of a place, preferably those that were fine, one may without much presumption affect to know more about that scene than the person who comes, has a look round, and then either hurries along somewhere else, or, as is not unusual, commences to picnic or take a doze. I have no doubt but that this latter method, so far as one's material tastes are concerned, is the most preferable of the lot, but it can hardly be said to have many advantages over the *method*, strictly so called, pursued by the man who comes with intent to "do" a series of scenes, and "does" them with all that conscientious gravity which the Anglo-Saxon race possesses.

Is not nature *herself* all the world over? Can a man be so prejudiced as to allow his narrow mind, with the bias of nationality or birth, to jaundice his eyes, and his microcosmic views to affect the far-reaching macrocosmic beauties of Nature?

In Tasmania the bush scenery, more especially in the gullies, is wonderful in its colouring—chiefly dark greens—wonderful in its formation of the fern type, and extraordinary in chaotic conglomeration; but after a while the eye vainly seeks relief from tree-ferns, particularly if the summer growth is aged, from the Australian scrub, even though the young shoots are tinted with yellows and "lakes," and from the lofty bare gum-tree trunks with their melancholy flapping bark disturbing the dull echoes of the forest, which alternatively resounds to the erie screeches of the parrot or the sharp cries of jays and other small birds; and if accustomed to the more delicate hues of our home scenery, with its graceful forest trees and coppices, its meads and singing birds, its spring tones, its summer richness, its autumn warmth, and its winter tracery, one finds it difficult truthfully to write, "I could never tire looking at *this*." You *could*, and that perhaps too quickly for your own safety, if a sensitive Australian with a bowie-knife stood ready to resent your versatility.

Nature seems in these vast tracts of bush over which one looks from hill and mountain side, in these intensely blue-green undergrowths of confused foliage, and in these cold, bare gum-trees, to be too melancholy, too sombre; she depresses, she oppresses. One's feelings, to be able to speak lightly and joyfully always under such conditions, must either be those of a mind " hanging on the balance of the lightest joke " or of one

" Sighing his very soul into his lady's eyes,"

in which condition a London square in winter might appear a very Eden.

Again, old colonials say, "Ah, you're a new chum, you can't appreciate colonial scenery; all you new chums have yet to be educated up to it for a considerable time." "What is a considerable time? " Oh, twenty years or so." Supposing for the sake of argument that new chumism affects one's powers of judgment, how is it that the average Australian in so few cases appreciates this same scenery himself to this great extent, but when he goes to New Zealand and sees the Alpine or English scenery there, talks but little on his return about his Australian gorges, but more often discourses on the more appreciable beauties of those very Alpine and English scenes? It is because the Australian is, even more than the ordinary Englishman, an admirer of the mirthful and living rather than the melancholy and dead-like in nature; and one of the chief reasons that the Australians are not affected to the detriment of their good spirits by these wild and melancholy scenes is that they very seldom bestir themselves to go and look at them. Few Australians I came across, have ever seen the grander sights of their own country, partly because they lacked the opportunity, partly because sight-seeing is not a very lucrative operation, and partly because they live next door to them—like the man who lived all his life in St. Paul's Churchyard without ever going within the cathedral.

A final word about the climate of Australia generally. Where a continent covers so many parallels of latitude of course generalisation must be of a somewhat elastic character. All the information one receives, and experience one enjoys, point to the conclusion that the Australian climate has not, from a globe-trotter's point of view, been too much praised. Queen's weather is the rule. Rainy days of course occur, fortunately for the colonies, though the fifty to one hundred inches of the southern, eastern, and northern coasts compare rather oddly with the fifteen, ten, eight, or even less of the interior. Tasmania is much more regular in this respect, but even here Jupiter Pluvius gives twenty inches to Hobart and the east coast, and about five times as many to Macquarie on the west.

When the rain comes down in Australia, generally it means business and has it all over, and then for weeks one has a succession of glorious mornings, noons, evenings, and nights. Cool are the nights as a rule, except in the height of summer; brisk often are the mornings; warm, not to say hot, the noons. The much talked-of dryness of the climate allows, except in the very hottest weather, when the vacation is in force, exertion without excessive fatigue, though this remark must be qualified when speaking of the summer weather of the coastal towns of New South Wales, Queensland, and the tropical portions of the colonies.

With such a climate, such agricultural, pastoral, mineral, and manufacturing resources, what may not this vast continent become! What position can there be too high for her to take in the ranks of future nations! To what grandeur may she not by co-operation and unity attain! And, on the other hand, how slow her progress if Disunion, Dissension, and Unhealthy Rivalry, rear their Gorgon heads to petrify the glowing sympathies of men who have a common bond of ancestry and language. It does not behove me to be a prophet after the scandalous way that "past futurity" has treated Mother Shipton; but it is obvious to anyone who wanders through this bright and sunshiny *terra Australis*, no longer *terra incog-*

nita, as in old Tasman's time, that if but the reins be in the right hands her resources are practically limitless, her prosperity as incapable of definition as of calculation; and it is also obvious to any right-minded person that all these platitudes and truisms merit for their author at the least canonisation in the Australian calendar of the future.

THE END.

Printed in the USA
CPSIA information can be obtained
at www.ICGtesting.com
LVHW011736111223
765930LV00070B/22